Changing the Tune

The Kansas City Women's Jazz Festival, 1978–1985

Carolyn Glenn Brewer

UNT Press
University of North Texas Press
Denton, Texas

Printed in the United States of America.

10 9 8 7 6 5 4 3 2 1

Permissions:
University of North Texas Press
1155 Union Circle #311336
Denton, TX 76203-5017

The paper used in this book meets the minimum requirements of the American National Standard for Permanence of Paper for Printed Library Materials, z39.48.1984. Binding materials have been chosen for durability.

Library of Congress Cataloging-in-Publication Data

Names: Brewer, Carolyn Glenn, author.
Title: Changing the tune : the Kansas City Women's Jazz Festival, 1978–1985 / Carolyn Glenn Brewer.
Description: Denton, Texas : University of North Texas Press, [2017] | Includes bibliographical references and index.
Identifiers: LCCN 2016041686 | ISBN 9781574416664 (cloth : alk. paper)
Subjects: LCSH: Kansas City Women's Jazz Festival—History. | Jazz festivals—Missouri—Kansas City—History. | Women jazz musicians—United States—History.
Classification: LCC ML38.K18 K364 2017 | DDC 781.65078/778411—dc23
LC record available at https://lccn.loc.gov/2016041686

The electronic edition of this book was made possible by the support of the Vick Family Foundation.

Cover and text design by Rose Design

Contents

List of Illustrations

Begins after page 150

Acknowledgments

IN 2010 WHILE I WAS INTERVIEWING Carol Comer for a local jazz magazine about another Kansas City jazz festival, the Women's Jazz Festival inevitably came up. Carol's enthusiasm for the subject hadn't dimmed. She suggested I write an article about WJF, so I did. But I could no more contain this vast subject in a few pages than reduce Mahler's Seventh to a few measures. Work on the book began even before I had finished the article.

Carol and Dianne Gregg couldn't have been more generous. They gave me access to the "world headquarters" archive where through tapes, photos, festival programs, and news clippings the individual festivals spoke for themselves. But always it was during conversations with Carol and Dianne that WJF came to life. Over shared meals and relaxed evenings in their magical backyard their stories became the heart of this story. These two remarkable women not only created an event that changed the course of jazz, but their persistence in promoting jazz connects those events of nearly forty years ago to today's jazz world. They also have proven to be exceptional dog sitters.

Social historians dream about sources like Mike Ning. Not only was he instrumental in the success of WJF as a piano player, artist, and board member, he kept all papers pertaining to the festival. When he handed me a large box full of board meeting minutes and reviews, I knew I had hit the jackpot.

At the top of the list of friends who encouraged me to write this book, Paul Smith takes first chair. His lists of musician emails, photos, and recordings gave me the boost I needed at times when the project seemed overwhelming. He never lost patience when I'd ask him *again* to tell me about the time he played with Anita O'Day or Dianne Reeves. At gigs, parties, even funerals, he always asked how the book was coming, and if there was anything he could do to help.

My brother—and I'm happy to say my oldest friend—David Glenn, provided insight, valuable editing input, contacts, personal stories, and reminders of the importance of this story.

The staff of The State Historical Society of Missouri Research Center-Kansas City couldn't have been more helpful. Always friendly, even when I handed them yet another stack of photocopy requests from the three cartons of WJF memorabilia, they encouraged me to take as much room as I needed and to not feel rushed.

To all those I interviewed I give special thanks, first because they all furthered the advancement of women in jazz and secondly for sharing their memories and candidly setting the tone of the time.

I'd also like to add a nod of appreciation and respect for authors Linda Dahl and Sally Placksin whose groundbreaking books on women in jazz were invaluable resources, and to Judy Chaikin for her outstanding movie, *Girls in the Band*. Seeing these brave women on screen personalized their experience and underlined the importance of their stories.

I confess to not paying attention in high school typing class. I thought as a professional orchestral clarinetist typing would not be necessary, so I viewed the class as another opportunity to improve my finger technique. Unfortunately, I dismissed the importance of punctuation as well. But life takes us to places we never expected. Lucky for me, it also gives us angels. Collene Sulzer is my editing angel. This book truly would not have come to life without her cool and practiced eye, and the hours we spent at my dining room table analyzing chapters and talking over edits. I can't thank Collene enough.

Beyond my dining room table, the editorial staff of the University of North Texas Press made the daunting task of turning these pages into a polished work painless. Thanks to Karen DeVinney, Ron Chrisman, Bonnie Stufflebeam, Bess Whitby, and all who helped. A special thanks also goes to Peter Brigaitis and Marie Nuchols of IndexingPros.

This aging baby-boomer is eternally grateful for her technically savvy millennial children. So many times they pulled me out of computer-glitched corners. On our most recent family vacation they gaggled around me—Laura, Elizabeth, Peter, John, and daughters-in-laws Kylie and Bonnie—to collectively explain the mysteries of formatting. Together with sons-in-laws Craig and Evan, I couldn't have a more supportive family.

And finally, to Tim, my sounding board, my jazz advisor, my first reader, my best friend, my true north, my husband, abundant thanks.

Chapter 1

Crazy Little Women

THE IDEA CAME TO THEM while driving home from the 1977 Wichita Jazz Festival. It was a boring, flat, dark drive with plenty of time for conversation. They rehashed what they had seen and heard that day, but kept coming back to the same point. After twelve hours of jazz, they had heard only one woman performer.

"Sarah Vaughan was terrific," singer/pianist/songwriter Carol Comer remembers, "but she wasn't enough. Dianne and I lamented the fact that women players were mostly passed over, not just in Wichita, but everywhere."[1]

Dianne Gregg hosted a radio show called *Women in Jazz*, as well as two other jazz shows on the Kansas City National Public Radio station, KCUR. Every week she talked to women jazz musicians who were deserving of more exposure. Both women were well aware of the fact that all jazz musicians struggled to be heard, as they were aware that, even in this era of debate over the Equal Rights Amendment, women musicians continued to have more to prove.

Dianne and Carol had gone to the Wichita Jazz Festival as members of the press. Carol was covering the festival for *Down Beat* and Dianne for KCUR. As much as they enjoyed the bands, they were there to work, and that creative thought process was still flowing when Carol said, "I have a really radical idea—why don't *we* have a women's jazz festival?"[2]

They both had a good laugh over the improbability of that happening, but by the time they paid their Kansas Turnpike toll, the idea had taken hold. Why not? There was no shortage of talent, and how hard could it be to organize a concert? Between them they had plenty of contacts and gumption enough to pursue those they didn't know. They hadn't heard of anyone putting together a jazz festival that focused on women, but that wasn't a good enough reason not to do it. Kansas City was the perfect location: right in the middle of the country and known for its jazz heritage.

By the time Carol dropped Dianne off at her apartment in mid-town Kansas City, they were laughing about the fact that an hour before they had thought the idea was radical. "It isn't a radical idea. It's a great idea," Dianne remembers saying. "So we said, 'Let's do it.'" They'd sleep on it and check in with each other the next day. The two women had plenty to think about.[3]

Everything's Up to Date in Kansas City

Miles Davis had pronounced jazz dead. 1977 K.C. Show-Me-State jazz fans still scoffed at that statement. According to the song, everything is supposed to be up to date in Kansas City, and local jazz roots ran deep. In truth, theoretical pride in a historical musical heritage wasn't enough to keep the city's jazz clubs full and, undeniably, tastes were changing. Live music fans were seduced by rock and all its glitz, as they were elsewhere, and pop singer lounge acts were more popular than ever. True jazz gigs were as scarce as benevolent club owners, yet baby boomer jazz musicians, who had been brought up on both school jazz programs and exposure to the masters of Kansas City Swing, were tenaciously staking a claim to the scene alongside their mentors. Swing era hometown favorites pianists Jay McShann and Willie Rice, jazz violinist Claude "Fiddler" Williams, and iconic drummer Sam "Baby" Lovett could also be heard around town. The paradox was there were a lot of clubs, and not just in the traditional downtown area, but on the Country Club Plaza—an upscale shopping district south of downtown—in the suburbs, and beyond in the far reaches of the city limits, and in Kansas. The Kansas City metropolitan area also supported nine country clubs and at least half a dozen hotel ballrooms, all with dinner and dancing, some six nights a week. Bandleaders Steve Miller, Vince Bilardo, Warren Durrett, and Tony DiPardo not only had big bands that played regularly but combos for the dinner crowd. Jazz musicians were working all the time. They just weren't playing much pure jazz.

"Pop music has always been more popular than jazz," says first-call Kansas City jazz drummer, Tommy Ruskin. "The name 'pop' says it all. I played with the Pete Eye Trio for years. We had lots of regulars who came to hear us wherever we were. But in the late seventies, we got fired so the club could put in a disco disc jockey."[4]

"The Playboy Club had two rooms where jazz was played," remembers Paul Smith, a pianist who frequently worked with Carol Comer in the seventies. "The audience was a little more sophisticated, and they were hipper to what was going on in New York and L.A. Before the singer came out for each set, we played two or three tunes of our choosing and maybe again at the end of the set. The singer sang a mix of standards and pop tunes, but in a jazz style."[5] But by 1977 the Kansas City Playboy Club was closed.

Singer Julie Turner had similar experiences. "I was singing with the Steve Miller band during those years, and we played lots and lots of country club and hotel ballroom jobs. We played what the people wanted to dance to, and more and more that was rock. But even though we stuck pretty close to the records, we'd add some of our own slant."[6] Frequently that slant involved swing.

Kansas City Swing had been passed down in the city's cultural DNA. Almost from its beginning, jazz found a home in Kansas City. As it left New Orleans in the early twentieth century and moved up the Mississippi River, it spread to towns hospitable to the new sound and lifestyle. Nowhere were jazz musicians more welcomed than in Kansas City. A crossroads for commerce and transportation, Kansas City attracted musicians from all over the southwest and east. The wide-open, vice-friendly atmosphere of political boss Tom Pendergast's town generated permissiveness unheard of in other places. It was a twenty-four-hour scene. Bars never closed. The music never stopped. As many as fifty clubs along the streets of 18th and Vine and beyond gave work to hundreds of musicians, and those musicians turned Kansas City into a testing ground, a musical incubator. At a time when jazz was quickly becoming the popular music of the day, the wild exchange of musical ideas born in jam sessions created Kansas City Swing.

This hybrid sound exploded onto the jazz scene in the mid-1930s as an antidote to the formulistic arrangements of well-established, white swing bands such as Benny Goodman and Tommy Dorsey. In early K.C. Swing, there were no written arrangements, only what the band members made up, called head charts. These players combined elements of gospel call and response and blues with swing beats and developed a sound that was infectious. It was partially based on a twelve-bar blues, something territory musicians from Oklahoma and Texas understood. That set up the possibility of forty-five-minute tunes that would be different every time.

Kansas City Swing claimed the spotlight and the right to change the jazz vocabulary. Coleman Hawkins and Lester Young transformed the tenor saxophone from a marching band instrument to the sound of the human soul. The spontaneity and freedom displayed by Mary Lou Williams, Julia Lee, and Jay McShann redefined a piano style that was emulated all over the world. Although Charlie Parker would later help give birth to bebop, his early years in Kansas City playing with McShann taught him the foundations of swing and formed his musical imagination. Count Basie's band was said to have the best rhythm section in jazz: Basie on piano, Jo Jones on drums, Walter Page on bass, and Freddie Green on guitar. For a time Billie Holiday was their singer. Kansas City had changed the tune.

Ever since then, that easy-going, happy, hyper-syncopated feel had colored the playing of many Kansas City musicians like a family trait. It's the sound that former *Kansas City Star* entertainment editor Shifra Stein wrote, "put the city on the musical map and gave our town an international reputation."[7] In the late seventies, Kansas City native Claude "Fiddler" Williams explained to Stein that European crowds recognized Kansas City as a jazz capital. By mentioning he was from Kansas City he was automatically in. Guitarist Rod Fleeman, born and raised in Kansas City and playing in New York City about this time, remembers musicians who didn't know him pegging him as a Kansas City player. "They'd say they could hear a bluesy element to my playing. I didn't even have to talk."[8]

While Kansas City jazz fans marked time to a swing beat, and European fans held it in the same regard they would works by Beethoven or Brahms, local players incorporated the essence of swing into their own styles. Many had the opportunity to play gigs or jam sessions with some of the old masters from the golden era of swing. Others attended the Kansas City Jazz Incorporated Festivals held in the sixties where swing was the patriarch to all other styles. "Swing was in our drinking water,"[9] recounts Fleeman. Whether by personal contact or osmosis, the baby boom generation embraced swing's best but then moved on.

The late seventies were a time of transition in all jazz. Straight-ahead, progressive, avant-garde, post-bop, cool, and fusion all competed with as many different styles of rock for the audiences' attention. With so many styles and schools of jazz readily heard on records and in concerts, movies, and clubs, the cacophony made for either nostalgia or experimentation. Kansas City boasted two avant-garde groups in 1977: drummer Arny Young's Advertisement for a Dream and The Ron Roberts Concert Ensemble led by bassist Ron Roberts. Both groups played mostly original material and intellectually pushed harmonic limits and their audiences' ears. These groups introduced an important new element to the local scene, and reminded discerning listeners that audiences of the past had been open to innovation. But Kansas City, with its slower-paced, salt-of-the-earth, got-to-get-up-early atmosphere tended toward nostalgia rather than innovation. That's why the swing arrangements of pop tunes and standards that dancing audiences clamored for in clubs and ballrooms alike remained so popular.

The irony was original Kansas City Swing was meant to be improvised. It pushed beyond stock arrangements and eight-bar solos and wanted nothing to do with restrictions. Kansas City dance bands and combos had come full circle. Because club owners only thought of bodies in chairs buying drinks, and country club and ballroom managers didn't want things to be uncontrolled, jazz musicians were back to playing commercial swing along with their record-copy pop tunes.

Joanne Brackeen, Stan Getz's piano player in 1977, once said, "Standards are tunes that somebody else wrote . . . and sometimes you don't want to stop where someone else left off."[10] That's where jam sessions came in.

Kansas City bassist Greg Whitfield recalls, "Many of us had six-night a week gigs with a singer, but we only got to play jazz on Saturday afternoons at jam sessions."[11]

"Jam sessions were wildly popular," says drummer Helen Marquette. "Not only were they a great way to hear lots of players you couldn't possibly see in one night, jam sessions were classrooms. You had better not show up without having done your homework, because you just had to get up there and play."[12]

Besides private sessions held all over town all the time, the weekly jam sessions on Sunday nights at the Boardwalk and Saturday afternoons at Putsch's 210, both on the Plaza, and Monday nights at the Signboard at the Crown Center Hotel downtown gave jazz musicians a chance to sharpen their skills and try out new ideas.

Drummer Brooks Wright, who had worked with Carol Comer earlier in the decade, fronted the house band at the Putsch's jam in the late seventies. He recalls, "At our club gigs night after night, we'd have to play sets of tunes like 'Proud Mary' and 'The Shadow of Your Smile.' That would go on for months; same tunes played the same way. Then we'd get a call to do a true jazz gig somewhere, and I'd feel like I couldn't do justice to what was a much more demanding music. Jam sessions helped keep me from becoming stagnant, but if you don't play jazz often enough, you lose your jazz chops."[13]

The spirit of Kansas City Swing in its purest, unrestricted form blessed those sessions. They were parties. They were celebrations of that intangible communication among musicians that knows neither race nor gender nor age but is simply joyous sound. And then the party was over.

Greg Whitfield summed it up. "If you wanted to play jazz six nights a week, you had to move."[14] If a jazz festival featuring women became the new act on the scene, where would the audience come from?

Now's the Time

The morning after the Wichita Festival, Dianne called Marian McPartland. The two had met when Dianne interviewed Marian over the phone for her *Women in Jazz* radio show.

"I wanted to get Marian's take on the idea of creating a women's jazz festival," Dianne recalls. "It still seemed like a good idea to me in the morning, but I knew Marian would give me her honest opinion about the feasibility of putting something together."

Dianne was well aware that the jazz scene was in flux and of how fickle jazz fans could be. Just the year before, the thirteen-year run of the Kansas City Jazz Incorporated Festival had ended, largely due to changing trends and a drop in attendance and revenue. Several very talented young players had recently left Kansas City—Bobby Watson, Rob Whitsitt, Danny Embrey, Rod Fleeman, Pat Metheny—following the tradition set by Charlie Parker, Count Basie, and countless others. It wasn't just the idea of women musicians that Dianne wanted to ask Marian about. She wanted the perspective of someone from out of town. She wanted to just put it out there: How successful could another big festival in Kansas City be?

That phone call gave the idea its first breath. It was kismet.

"Oh my God, what a wonderful idea!" Dianne remembers Marian's instant enthusiasm for the idea. "I wish I'd thought of it myself. I'll do anything to help."[15]

Well into her fourth decade as an internationally known jazz pianist, Marian had the excellent reputation, the contacts, and the gregarious personality to make that offer invaluable. The first thing she did was put Carol and Dianne in touch with Leonard Feather, a long-time champion of women jazz musicians. Although years before Feather had written in an article for *Down Beat* that as a jazz musician McPartland had three strikes against her—namely she was white, British, and female[16]—their mutual respect for one another and common support of egalitarian jazz had developed into a trusted friendship. Besides, Marian had proved Leonard wrong.

Long known as a jazz critic and record producer, Feather had put the spotlight on scores of female musicians with his *Down Beat* column, "Girls in Jazz." He had a sixth sense about new talent and, as jazz critic for the *Los Angeles Times* and the British magazine *Melody Maker*, plenty of opportunity to exercise that skill.

"Marian said she'd take care of finding people on the east coast," Dianne says, "and Leonard could take the west coast." Carol adds, "Dianne and I already had people in mind, but with this kind of input right from the beginning, we were ecstatic."[17]

Marian was not a vocal feminist. Her work spoke for her. Always impeccably dressed in a classy, no-nonsense style, she embraced her femininity without exploiting it. She didn't think the adjective "woman" was necessary when describing herself as a musician. When people told her, "You play like a man," she first took it as a compliment, but she got to the point where she couldn't help but quip that she'd known plenty of men who played like girls. She had played with female jazz musicians throughout her career without making gender an issue. But in the mid-seventies, with all jazz in transition, she didn't like any exclusionary attitudes.

The timing of Dianne's call was serendipitous. Just the month before, to prove a point to Newport Jazz Festival promoter George Wein, Marian had formed an all-female quintet. She had asked Wein about scheduling a women's night at the festival, and he answered back that they wouldn't be able to find a night's worth of female talent. Shortly after this, *Today* show film critic Gene Shalit came to a set at Marian's Carlyle Hotel gig. As the two visited during the break, Marian told Shalit about George Wein's comment. Shalit assured her that if she put together a female combo, he'd see to it that the group got a spot on the *Today* show. Not only were they broadcast on the nationally televised morning show on March 31, 1977, they closed out the season for the PBS show, *At the Top*. When Dianne called Marian, the quintet was preparing for a three-night gig in Rochester, New York, and a live recording.[18]

Marian had picked an eclectic bouquet of players. Veteran guitarist Mary Osborne, whom many called the best guitarist of her generation, was already well known to New York audiences.

Dottie Dodgion on drums had made her reputation playing and singing in Chicago, Washington, D.C., and San Francisco with Charles Mingus and Al Cohn, among others. Vi Redd's soulfully fearless alto saxophone sound had complimented the groups of both Max Roach and Dizzy Gillespie. Marian picked bassist Lynn Milano, the youngest of the group by a generation and a graduate of Eastman, because her sound contradicted her petite size.

None of the women had played together as a group before.

There was nothing new about a group of women playing jazz. Since baby jazz wailed its first double high C, women's groups have played in ballrooms, in vaudeville venues, at movie premiers, and on every imaginable road gig—right alongside the men. As early as the 1920s, bands such as Babe Egan's Hollywood Red Heads and The Bricktops contributed to the popularity of the new sound. Peggy Gilbert's All Girl Band and Ina Ray Hutton and her Melodears attracted the attention of promoters Florenz Ziegfeld and William Morris, and both bands participated in early, short subject sound films for Fox, Movietone, and Vitaphone.

That women could hold all the chairs in a performing jazz band was unique only in the sense that, in the early-twentieth century, female musical education was predominately gender specific. Girls were encouraged to play piano or sing, perhaps play the violin, but blowing was considered unfeminine. Females were not thought strong enough to hold and play, much less carry, large instruments such as the baritone saxophone or string bass.

By the 1920s much of that changed. High school concert bands either integrated both genders into their programs or formed all-female bands. With the availability of jazz recordings, female and male musicians had access to the same music to listen to. Female ears absorbed the complexities of what they were hearing as well as those of their male counterparts. They may have grown up playing Chopin or Gilbert and Sullivan or Sousa, but their musical souls were open to the fresh possibilities jazz offered. As jazz spread into the popular culture and became accessible in a variety of venues, everyone absorbed these new sounds into their musical vocabularies. This was visceral music that you felt as much as understood. It defined the tempo of the times and was everywhere in popular entertainment. While dancing to Count Basie or Benny Goodman, girls learned to swing as strongly as their dance partners.

But firmly established cultural stereotypes kept denying that this was so. In a February 1938 *Down Beat* opinion piece, an anonymous writer stated, "Women as a whole are emotionally unstable, which prevents their being consistent performers on musical instruments."[19]

Bandleader and saxophonist Peggy Gilbert lost no time writing a rebuttal. "The manager is constantly reminding the girls not to take the music so seriously, but to relax, to smile," Gilbert wrote in *Down Beat* in April of 1938. "How can you smile with a horn in your mouth? How can you relax when a girdle is throttling you and the left brassiere strap holds your arm in a vice?"[20]

The undeniable truth was that a female jazz artist's popularity was based on visual attributes rather than musical expertise. Long, flowing, tight-waisted gowns, with billowing sleeves, in cotton candy colors, defined the dress code. Saxophonist Roz Cron remembers a particularly humiliating outfit. "I was playing at the Oriental Theater in Chicago with Ada Leonard's band," Cron recalls. "The manager brought out this god-awful, pink thing and said that was what I was to wear. It had all these flounces and flares and ruffles. I was mortified. I'm a professional, not a dress up doll. I hated that costume with a passion."[21] Another member of the band stated, "A man could have white hair and glasses and weigh 300 pounds, but if he could play, great. The girls had to look like starlets. And the things they put on us were unbelievable."[22] Vocalists and a few instrumental soloists, such as pianists Hazel Scott and Mary Lou Williams, managed to break the gender barrier, but they too were expected to present themselves as sex symbols in provocative clothing. Women jazz musicians put up with this because they wanted to play and their opportunities were limited, but the bitter reality was their performances were seen all too often as highly sexualized spectacles.

Peggy Gilbert lamented in her *Down Beat* piece, "Men's orchestras are usually hired because of their ability as musicians. Their good looks, their presentability other than neatness, will rarely enter the question."[23]

Not only men criticized female jazzers. In a 1951 *Down Beat* interview, Lorraine Cugat, then wife of Xavier Cugat, stated that she would use all men in her new Latin band. "We might as well be honest about this. A girl, no matter what she's got, just can't be a glamorous creature with the mouthpiece of a saxophone between her pretty red lips or while blowing her lovely face all out of shape playing a trumpet or trombone."

Waggish gossip columnists of the day speculated that Mrs. Cugat's interest in glamour and an all-male band was motivated by revenge against her philandering, estranged husband more than by a lack of faith in female players, but she went on. "Girls who want to be musicians should stick to any instrument . . . the playing of which doesn't detract from their feminine appeal."[24]

Some all-girl bands had drummers who played in high heels. Brass and reed "fem cats" were told to paint their lips with Mercurochrome rather than wear lipstick. In some bands eyeglasses were forbidden. Contact lenses were very primitive, not to mention painful and expensive in those days, so near-sighted players had to memorize the music.

Even the highly successful and popular all-female group Hour of Charm, led by Phil Spitalny, one of the few men to front a girl band, was founded in musical compromise. Spitalny publicly made it clear that he wasn't looking for a powerful, hard-swinging sound. In a band that employed more violins than brass, two pianos, and a harp, it's not surprising their repertoire consisted of mostly mellow, sweet tunes. That also pleased the sponsors of the Sunday night radio show of the same name. The listening public deemed Hour of Charm the ideal all-female band.

It wasn't only the jazz world that discriminated against female players. Girl harpists and violinists might be acceptable on a stage clouded with taffeta and sequined dresses. Anonymous female trombonists and bassists could be heard on radio broadcasts without public outcry. But in the male dominated world of symphony orchestras, the subject of female members wasn't even open for discussion. It would be 1982 before the Berlin Philharmonic hired a woman. In Vienna it was 1997.

A Beautiful Friendship

When Dianne updated Carol about her conversation with Marian McPartland, neither woman thought about Kansas City's place in jazz history or what ridiculous outfits women had worn to gigs decades earlier. They were thinking about the "Now." Both women were in tune with the Kansas City jazz scene and very involved.

Dianne's three jazz shows, including *Women in Jazz*, gave her listeners the benefit of her keen ears and encyclopedic grasp of the subject. Co-host Mike Metheny, who worked with her on their Wednesday night *Jazz Magazine*, remembers that Dianne was "the consummate professional, always prepared and knowledgeable."[25] She set tunes up as if she were taking her own jazz solo, with impeccable timing and phrasing, in a velvety, tenor sax-like radio voice.

Music had always been in her life. Born near Bedford, Iowa, Dianne's family moved to Sikeston, Missouri, and then to the Kansas City suburb, Overland Park, Kansas, when she was in the fifth grade. Dianne's mother, a church organist who also played cello and sax, taught piano lessons in their home. "Growing up I heard a lot of John Thompson," Dianne says. Her younger sister played trombone and Dianne played clarinet, both B flat and alto, through high school. The first record she bought with her own money was one of Benny Goodman's. It was the mid-sixties, music was everywhere, and Dianne listened to it all, favoring the Beatles and Barbra Streisand. The piano at home was like another family member. "I grew up around the piano and have always been partial to piano music. We also had a pretty good collection of big band records at home, and I remember my brother, who played piano, had a book of Dave Brubeck tunes and a Mary Lou Williams Boogie Woogie book. So I didn't have exposure to a lot of different jazz growing up, but it was a consistent presence."

Then in college at Memphis State, a sorority sister introduced her to a wider jazz repertoire. Dianne still remembers the thrill of hearing Aretha Franklin live while in Memphis, but she was excited about lots of music. "I started hearing Stan Getz, Wes Montgomery, Ramsey Lewis, and most of all, Coltrane. I was used to a background of music, so I soaked everything up."

While still at Memphis State, Dianne got a job as a disc jockey on the campus radio station. The broadcast range didn't go beyond the campus, and the format ran more toward Strawberry Alarm Clock than Stan Getz, but Dianne had great fun playing and talking about records on the air. "Remember in the late sixties and early seventies," Dianne says, "tunes like Ramsey Lewis's 'Wade in the Water' and 'In Crowd' were still popular. On regular mainstream radio you could hear Wes Montgomery play 'Goin' Out of My Head' and everybody played Herbie Hancock's 'Watermelon Man.' It wasn't all rock & roll." When she came to Kansas City to finish her degree in Communications, her previous radio experience led easily to a job at KCUR.

One of the best parts of her job as a jazz show host was listening to as much live jazz as she could. At clubs and concerts and jam sessions, she was always listening and absorbing, always processing what she heard to see what she could use on her shows. It was at one of those gigs that she first met Carol.[26]

Carol doesn't remember a time when she wasn't singing. Even as a child, she and her brother and sister sang as a gospel trio at the church where their dad was a minister. Carol too grew up around a piano. "There was always a baby grand in the house. My sister played classical piano and I played by ear. There might have been weeks we didn't have meat, but we always had a piano."

Carol came to Kansas City from Wichita in 1957. She remembers that one of her favorite pastimes in the city was to go to the record store at 40th and Main. "It was one of those places where they had listening booths. I could listen to Peggy Lee and Jo Stafford, Ella, anyone I wanted to for as long as I wanted. And of course, I couldn't help but sing along."The storeowner got to know her voice and asked her if she had ever heard Chris Conner. "He was the one who introduced me to Chris Connor, who became one of my favorite singers. He said I sounded like her, so I was terribly flattered." Before long Johnny, the storeowner, told her he had a friend who had a club called the Interlude, and if Carol ever wanted to sing and play, he was sure he could get her a gig. "I had sung and accompanied myself a little at sorority parties in college, but nothing professionally." Carol didn't know quite what to make of Johnny's offer and filed it in the back of her mind.

Then she fell in love—with a 1958, red Porsche convertible. Her job typing papers for a radiology group at Research Hospital didn't pay nearly enough to afford the car payments, so she told Johnny to go ahead and get her that gig at the Interlude as a single. "I was listening to singers like Rosemary Clooney and Patti Page on the radio, learning tunes and writing them down. I bought records by Chris Connor and June Christy. I really wanted that car, but I fell in love with the music, too." She happily drove the Porsche to the Interlude gig and many to follow.

Johnny continued to get her work. Her first job singing with a band, where she wasn't accompanying herself, was at an Elk's Club. Standing out in front of a band instead of hiding behind the piano made her self-conscious anyway, but the first thing she encountered was a wall-mounted elk head with red, blinking eyes. "I found myself keeping tempo with the blinking. 'Blue --- Moon,' like that. In order to avoid being distracted by the head, I shut my eyes. When I did that, I also found I could really get inside my soul and sing better. That's why I shut my eyes when I sing."

By 1960 Carol had steady work as a singer not only in clubs but also for advertising jingles. "One of my good friends in those days was Marilyn Maye, and she told Warren Durrett about me. He booked all the jingle work in town, so we were always busy." Carol broadened her musical knowledge and reading in those studio sessions while going back to the trio singing she had done as a child. "I sang lots of jingles standing between Marilyn and Patty Tucker, who just happened to be Marilyn's husband Sammy's first wife. That was pretty interesting, but it was also great fun."[27]

Throughout the sixties and early seventies, Carol's musicianship made her a favorite among players. Her impeccable pitch and musical honesty fostered the essential trust needed among band members and, at the same time, her smoky voice invited the audience to join her inside the tune. "I loved playing with Carol," Paul Smith says. "She had such a cool aura that carried over into her singing. She would scat a little, but it was mostly her treatment of the lyrics and her ability to play around with the melody that made gigs with her so fun. She also wrote some great tunes." Paul spoke for all of Carol's friends. "Plus she was always a hoot to be around."[28]

Quickly, before the enormity of their decision sank in and changed their minds, Carol and Dianne started making calls. The first order of business was to incorporate and form a board of directors. It didn't take long. Some agreed to join the board because Marian McPartland and Leonard Feather supported the idea. Some felt Kansas City needed another big jazz festival. Others just loved the music and wanted to do anything that would promote its continuation. All trusted Dianne Gregg's and Carol Comer's instincts. They saw in the two friends the perfect combination of organizational skills, persistence, daring, and gregarious good humor. It was a visionary idea. The new board members knew that no matter what wild road these two crazy little Kansas City women took them on, it would lead to something special.

Chapter 2

The First Year

March 17–19, 1978

"Only God can make a tree, and only men can play good jazz."
—George Simon, jazz critic

THE FIRST BOARD MEETING, Sunday, June 12, was in an apartment complex clubhouse room, the same room used for the bi-monthly meetings of the North American UFO Organization. "Somehow that seems appropriate,"[1] Carol remembers board member Julie Turner saying. Although at that first meeting a successful festival may have seemed as elusive as life on other planets, Carol and Dianne wasted no time getting organized.

"We'd never been on a board, much less tried to run one. We were the first to admit that we knew nothing about bylaws and articles of incorporation."[2] Carol remembers, "I knew a little something about grant writing, but otherwise we didn't have a clue."[3]

Dianne adds, "We picked people who we thought would be interested and energetic, and turns out we were right. Most boards like to have someone who can bring in the money. We didn't have that."[4]

"About half of the original board members were musicians, and God knows jazz musicians don't have money," Carol says. "The ones who weren't musicians were big jazz lovers, and they loved the idea. We had their enthusiasm. We had their support. And we didn't have any stuffy old men, or old women, who were going to try to tell us what to do—although we should have, because we didn't know our ass from a hole in the ground."[5]

Carol and Dianne had assembled an ensemble of people with a unique group of skills. Outstanding tenor saxophonist and lawyer Mike White also happened to be County Executive. His insight into city politics was invaluable. Mike Ning, well known as an artist for Hallmark Cards as well as a very fine jazz pianist, took care of any graphic art issues and had T-shirt designs to choose from at the first meeting. The venerable disc jockey and jazz educator Dick Wright had connections and friends all over the Midwest, as did jazz educator John Leisenring, head of the jazz department at the University of Missouri at Kansas City. Other musicians, who could spread the word at gigs and sessions, were Frank Smith, Julie Turner, Nancy Van Fleet, Milt Abel, and Sylvia Bell.[6]

"At that first meeting, we formed committees," recalls Dianne. "Everyone picked what they felt they would be best at, and it worked out that way."[7]

It was an ambitious first meeting. It had been an ambitious six weeks. Dianne and Carol reported on all the preparations that had taken place, which included this definition of purpose: "A non-political, not-for-profit group to educate the public in aspects of jazz, especially women's contributions; to promote workshops, clinics and concerts, to offer scholarships for students of jazz." They also reported on the selection of name, their choice of concert venue, and whom they had contacted to perform. They discussed a tentative budget. They mentioned their meeting with lawyer Sally Wells to draft Articles of Incorporation, bylaws, and IRS tax-exempt status. They reported on their meeting with the chairman of the jazz section of the National Endowment for the Arts and the $10,000 grant they were applying for.

The board voted on officers, talked about advertising, chose the T-shirt logo, and discussed student scholarship logistics, possible clinicians, and a pay schedule for the artists. The longest discussion of the day was over main concert ticket prices. The decision: $6.50 and $7.50.[8]

After an amazingly efficient two-hour meeting, they adjourned so that everyone could make it to the Charles Mingus outdoor concert in Swope Park.

Summertime

Kansas City was blessed, in that summer of 1977, with a jazz-loving Parks and Recreation Department. Charles Mingus's group was the third jazz headliner to perform an outdoor concert in one of the city's many spectacular parks. Already that summer Joe Pass at Penn Valley Park and Art Farmer at Parade Park had performed for Sunday evening audiences. Later, on a hot, muggy night in July, an estimated 6,000 jazz fans sat blanket to blanket along the banks of Brush Creek to hear Duke Ellington's band under the direction of his son Mercer. Band and audience alike swung to old Kansas City favorites such as "Satin Doll," "Sophisticated Lady," and "Take the A Train." Three weeks later the Glenn Miller Orchestra took over the same spot. Before the summer ended with a finale concert by the Kansas City Philharmonic, Jimmy Rowles and Louis Hayes played in Penn Valley Park, and Joe Williams took over the grounds of Parade Park.[9] In a city known for its fountains and parks—one city official called it a city within a park—outdoor concerts had been a part of the city's culture since the 1880s. In those days, community bands brought out picnic crowds who were happy to sit on blankets and listen to Sousa marches and selections from light operettas. In later years, members of the Kansas City Philharmonic performed a summer series.

By the early 1970s, the focus shifted to bringing in "big name" groups under the auspices of the Parks and Recreation Department's Music in the Park Series. Sunday evenings from Memorial Day to Labor Day, music fans flocked to free concerts at a variety of showcased parks where they enjoyed bluegrass, pop, and rock mixed in with the jazz.

The most popular concert location, Brush Creek, wasn't a park at all, but a (then) cement-bedded dry creek that formed a border to the Country Club Plaza. Brush Creek had been the pet project of Tom Pendergast, the infamous Kansas City political boss from the 1920s and '30s. Pendergast also happened to be the owner of a cement company. With only a trickle of water nicely contained in the middle of a wide concrete space, the Creek offered a perfect setting for as many drums and amplifiers as any jazz group needed. Grassy banks along the Creek accommodated thousands of fans and gave all a perfect, unobstructed view. A bridge spanning Brush Creek offered an overhead view. As long as rain didn't swell the ankle-deep stream of water, the amplification and acoustics in this urban canyon were exceptional.

During previous years, both Woody Herman's band and Stan Kenton's played concerts in the Creek. When an ambulance screamed along a street flanking Brush Creek during one of Stan Kenton's introductions, Kenton couldn't resist poking a good-natured jab at Herman's tempos and volume. "There goes Woody," he joked to the audience.[10]

The Sunday evening concerts also became the ideal setting for early Women's Jazz Festival PR. "We wanted to go anyway," says Mike Ning. "We'd wear our Women's Jazz Festival T-shirts and bring a stack to sell. People would ask us about them, so we'd get a chance to talk about the festival and sell a shirt at the same time. It was beautiful."[11]

The light-blue T-shirts with a black-lettered WJF logo proved to be the group's best ambassador. Their serious intent about putting this festival on was now tangible and, as fans, musicians, and festival organizers wore the shirts around town, also highly visible.

"We had a very good relationship with the Music in the Park people," says Dianne. "They bought T-shirts, too. They encouraged us to use their concerts to spread the word about the festival, and Joyce Stuermer, who was in charge, came to our concerts to find performers for their next season. With her help, the Kansas City Parks and Recreation eventually sponsored our jam sessions."[12]

All that summer and fall, the board met on a regular basis. After applying for non-profit status, filing letters of incorporation, and writing bylaws, they turned their focus to raising funds and securing artists. The newly formed committees—advertising, logistics, performance space, and public relations—made lists of everything they could think of that might come up regarding a festival.

The selection of a concert venue was quickly made. Memorial Hall in Kansas City, Kansas, had 3,580 seats split between a main floor and a balcony. Just as importantly, there were seven dressing rooms backstage and two backstage bathrooms.[13] Although there were other concert hall options in downtown Kansas City, Missouri, the fact that Kansas had passed the Equal Rights Amendment and Missouri had not made Memorial Hall far more attractive. Dianne explains, "We wanted to make a statement about the importance of ERA. Not to be exclusionary in any way, but to support the meaning of equal."[14] It was also a bargain with a rental fee of $700.[15]

Memorial Hall took care of the main Sunday night concert, scheduled for March 19, 1978, but a space was needed for the other festival events added to the schedule during those first few board meetings. "Every time we mentioned to someone that we were organizing a Women's Jazz Festival, they would bring up another activity," Carol remembers. "They'd say, 'Oh, are you going to have clinics? What about jam sessions?'"[16] Saturday, March 18, was added to the schedule. "'And school bands, aren't you going to have school bands?'" So a Friday night high school/college Big Band Invitational to be held at KU Medical Center's Battenfeld Auditorium rounded out what became a three-day festival.

Dianne explains: "We heard from people all over the country, and we knew that, if fans and other musicians were going to travel to Kansas City for this festival, they didn't want one evening concert and then go home. We wanted to give them as much jazz in as many venues as we could. We wanted everyone to be happy."[17]

When approached, Crown Center, a downtown shopping and hotel complex affiliated with Hallmark Cards, offered free performance space for clinics and jam sessions. They also threw in hotel rooms for the guest artists at a greatly reduced rate.

Tenor saxophonist John Lyman, who had a steady gig in Crown Center's Signboard Bar, got his bosses to further sweeten the deal. They agreed to have female jazz artists perform at the Signboard during the month of March 1978. They would also include, free of charge, a ballroom for a kick-off party the night before the festival and a hotel suite as an acting headquarters the weekend of the festival, plus help with overall publicity.

With the issue of performance space settled, obtaining a National Endowment for the Arts grant became top priority. In order to qualify for the $10,000 grant they applied for, the WJF board had to line up matching funds. Initial solicitations were not promising. Hudson Oil, owned by a woman, flatly refused to make a contribution. Marion Labs, along with the Kauffman Foundation, showed interest when first approached, but ultimately denied all monetary requests, saying their charitable commitment went to medically related organizations. H&R Block didn't return the call.

"We truly felt a festival of this importance would be a huge boost to the city," Carol explains. "We knew WJF would draw people in from all over the country who would need a place to stay and places to eat. They'd want to see other sights. It would give the city national, even international, attention and all of it would be positive. We were going to have top jazz talent, and this was the first festival of its kind."[18] But as an organization, in the eyes of the city's philanthropic leaders, they were as yet unproven.

Dianne and Carol hadn't expected it to be easy. They refined their prospectus and kept knocking on doors. Board members were asked to compile lists of possible donors, and Carol applied for a non-profit mailing permit so all of those letters could be mailed with two-cent stamps. In the meantime, they had 1,000 T-shirts to sell.

There's No Business Like Show Business

Floating above the necessary but tedious organizational tasks, a Christmas-catalog list of potential stars held out the Festival's promise. The music was the point. Music emphasizing equality was the larger point. The lineup was a work in progress, but from the beginning Marian McPartland committed her trio, and Marian agreed to put together the All-Star band. Most of the members of Now's the Time, the New York female quintet she was working with, signed on, with the possibility of vibes player Terry Pollard joining them. A short list of potential horn players to round out the group included Janice Robinson on trombone, Nadine Jansen on trumpet, and Bobbi Humphrey on flute. Hometown girl Marilyn Maye, now a national singing star, came on board along with her trio.

Everything was possible during those first few months, and the board thought big. It was decided at the first meeting to ask Ella Fitzgerald, Mary Lou Williams, and Sarah Vaughan. Carmen McRae was at the top of most board members' lists, with Betty Carter as a back up. Someone suggested finding local businesses to "sponsor a star" to help defray costs. Pianist Patrice Rushen's new twelve-piece, all-female group was on the docket, pending negotiations with a new manager. [19]

This schedule allowed for a mix of straight-ahead jazz and newer sounds. Not just singers and pianists, but guitarists, drummers, and bass players along with horn players would offer a selection of women players never seen before. The intent was never to exclude men, and there would be male sidemen, but women would be running the show in all musical aspects. Dianne told *Kansas City Star* reporter Steve Paul in July 1977, after two board meetings, that "We don't want to be misunderstood, though I'd like to stress that it's not a feminist organization. Because it is a nonprofit group, we can't be political. We don't want to be."[20] It was stated in the first line of the WJF's purpose that the organization was meant to be nonpolitical. They were trying to break up decades of prejudice by not doing to men musicians what had been done to women musicians.

Sweet Georgia Brown

"We wanted our fundraisers to be fun,"[21] Carol says. The first was literally a ball—a basketball.

"I don't remember whose idea it was," says board member Mike Ning, "but Milt Abel and I kept the bench warm. I'd never played basketball in my life. I told Carol and Dianne from the start that I couldn't dribble, but they had me out there."[22]

This was the first and only basketball game played where there was no listing of positions on the program, but instead, what instruments the players played. All proceeds went toward the WJF scholarship fund.

Not only did this all-male team of jazz musicians substitute a November Sunday evening on an unfamiliar-to-most basketball court for their comfy club gigs, they were pitted against the

Varsity Sports, an all-female team of Parks and Recreation A.A.U. District champions. For only two dollars, the public was invited to see their favorite, local jazzers perform in a very unique and, as it turned out, hilarious way.

The rhythm section was well represented. Pianists Pete Eye and Mike Ning suited up, with Greg Richter and Frank Smith on standby. Bassists Andy DeWitt, Bruce Holm, Milt Abel, and drummers Tommy Ruskin, Sam Johnson, and the eleven-year-old wunderkind Scotty Robinson rounded out the section, along with guitarist Steve Cardenas. Reedmen Horace Washington, Bill Hemmans, and John Lyman, joined by Mike Metheny and Mike Eaton—billed as flugelhorn players—filled out the home team.

Dianne took on the position of coach, but with no practice time, the players were on their own. "Mike Ning and Frank Smith have taken up jogging," Carol told *Kansas City Star* Entertainment Editor Shifra Stein, "and Tommy Ruskin, I hear, has been playing 'Take Five' with his feet." Dianne assured her team that she had three plays, although she was pretty sure they were all illegal. Publicly she described one: "We call time out and when the whistle blows, we rush five guys onto the court. I think 10 of our players against five of theirs will stand a good chance of getting a basket."[23]

At the last minute Coach Dianne added her secret weapon. Two Kansas City Philharmonic musicians, French horn player Dale Weddle and assistant-principal trumpet Chris Gekker joined the roster. "Unlike most jazz musicians we have to sit still when we play," Weddle remarked at the time. "We're always happy to have a chance to play physically on a team."[24]

Wearing the blue Women's Jazz Festival T-shirts with contact paper numbers on their backs, the Jazzers took an early lead only to be trounced in the end. Even with the enthusiastic encouragement of the half-time entertainment—a seventeen-piece big band led by Jim Booth and Mike Young—they kept the ball on the ground more than in the air. Too many successful dribbles became double dribbles. Their numbers, cut out by board members, kept falling off. *Kansas City Times* reporter Jeanne A. Fox remarked that as the women worked "quietly and efficiently," the men "bumbled along." In the end, the Philharmonic players scored most of the points.[25] "It was a massacre,"[26] Dianne remembers.

"But what a bargain," Carol jokes. "For only two dollars we got to see jazz musicians become basket cases."[27]

This Could Be the Start of Something Big

As 1978 began, all the pending questions about performers and funding needed resolution. There were some rocky moments during the last couple of months before the festival. Although everyone who was approached to play thought the festival was a good idea, it was an unproven one without the clout to force anyone's hand. Potential financial backers had the same caution.

Patrice Rushen's group originally made a verbal commitment to attend then mentioned they were in the middle of a management change. Whether is was Patrice's decision not to come, or management's, or they were one and the same was never made clear. Toshiko Akiyoshi and Lew Tabackin stepped in just weeks before the festival, and their big band was added as the last performance of the Main Concert.[28]

Marilyn Maye, a Kansas City favorite and long-time, close friend of Carol's, was one of the first to accept the invitation to perform in the Main Concert. Although her contract was signed and sidemen hired, she had a last minute conflict—after the programs were printed—and was unable to attend.[29]

At $25,000, hiring Ella Fitzgerald was out of the question.

After months of negotiations between the board and Carmen McRae's manager over a fee less than her usual $7,500, her manager sent the festival board a letter saying, "Even if she was in the Kansas City area on tour, her fee would be over WJF's budget." He wished them luck. Betty Carter was hired for the spot. The board was pleased with that decision and the opportunity to give the lesser-known but excellent singer more exposure. Then, after the program was set and national publicity was taking off, McRae's manager had a change of heart and said Carmen would do it for half her normal fee. The board stuck with Carter.[30]

Even performers who had every intention of coming wanted to make sure everything about the Women's Jazz Festival organization was legitimate. Carol and Dianne still laugh about revered pianist and Conservatory professor George Salisbury telling them that he had received a phone call from Mary Lou Williams asking him if everything was on the up and up with these two women trying to put on a jazz festival.[31]

Those involved with organizing the first festival understood the leap of faith they were asking for. But they also knew nothing would stop them from making the festival a success, even the burned reputation of another Kansas City jazz promoter. Trumpeter and big band leader Eddie Baker had been on the Kansas City jazz scene for decades and had successfully petitioned the city to support a Charlie Parker Foundation Center for concerts and private lesson studios to serve the inner city. He also personally knew all the swing and bop-era players and produced many of their local concerts. Unfortunately, Baker had the unhappy inability to keep track of money, even when it wasn't his. The stories are legendary. One of the most extreme involved Count Basie. Every time Basie came to town, he'd park the band bus outside the city before the gig until Baker showed up with the money. WJF board member Mike White remembers standing backstage with Mayor Richard Berkley before a Woody Herman concert at the Parker Foundation. "As his band was setting up, Woody went to Eddie and said he needed the money up front. I heard Eddie say, 'Leonard has the check and he's not here.' Woody turned to the band and said, 'Pack up boys.' All of a sudden Leonard showed up."[32]

"Eddie was a lovable guy and his intentions were good. He just had trouble with the follow through," Dianne remembers. "But even though we weren't associated with him, some out-of-town musicians automatically thought of Eddie Baker when they thought of booking a concert in Kansas City. It didn't take us long to disassociate that impression, but I do think that's why Mary Lou Williams called George Salisbury."[33] Eddie had also tainted the civic money pool. Mike White remembers that Baker was always trying to get money from city and business leaders, and that made it difficult for other cultural organizations.[34]

When it came to selling the festival to civic leaders with money to invest, Carol and Dianne's knowledge and professionalism trumped any fears of making a bad investment. "We could have just sent letters," Dianne recalls. "We did send letters, but we felt it was important for our potential donors to meet us and for us to give them a sincere presentation."[35] Getting the early endorsement and support from Hallmark went a long way toward attracting the attention of other business leaders.

One of the first local businesses they approached after Hallmark was Kansas City Southern Industries and president Bill Deramus. They tried not to let his gruff manner intimidate them. They knew the worst he could do was say no, so they each took a deep breath and smiled.

"We went through our whole talk," Carol recalls. "We showed him Leonard Feather's letter of support and told him about Marian McPartland's involvement. We outlined our bid for an NEA grant. We told him that Crown Center had come on board and laid out copies of all our press, both local and national. Through it all he didn't say a word, and none of his expressions encouraged us either. When we were finished, we sat back and waited. Finally he said, 'What will you do if I say no?' We said, 'Well sir, we'll just go somewhere else.' He pulled out his checkbook and wrote us a very generous check. Kansas City Southern became one of our best underwriters."[36]

Yellow Freight became an early contributor through the Powell Family Foundation. Dianne and Carol's first meeting with Foundation president Marjorie Powell Allen at the Yellow Freight offices proved memorable. "We got off the elevator," Dianne remembers, "and stepped right into Marge's office, which was more like an apartment than an office. She offered us tea from an English tea set while we gave our presentation. She was very attentive and interested. We sensed she saw right away that our festival was good not only for the city but would make a difference in jazz history."[37] The Powell Family Foundation made a contribution to WJF every year.

The National Endowment for the Arts grant was contingent on raising matching funds. That meant donations had to be in the bank well before the festival dates. That first year the *Kansas City Star*, Mr. Guy's Inc., Western Union, and Whitaker Cable Corporation added major funds to those already raised. In addition scores of individuals and businesses contributed smaller amounts that added up to top the $10,000 mark and assure the grant.[38]

Before a note was played, much of the money was earmarked. Out-of-town artists required half their money up front, per their standard contracts, and deposits had to be made to Memorial Hall and Sound Dynamics. Ads would underwrite most of the cost of printing the thirty-two-page festival booklet and program, but that meant collecting and depositing money for those ads or fronting printing costs. Transportation arrangements for the headlining artists, paid for by WJF, were settled as soon as schedules were finalized. Everything from the plaque for the scholarship winner to commemorative medallions for all the artists to a complimentary bottle of liquor in each artist's room had to be paid for in advance. At the last pre-festival board meeting on February 26, 1978, the treasurer reported an account balance of $124.06.[39]

Spring Can Really Hang You Up the Most

And then it was March. With all the anticipation of a first pregnancy, festival organizers—board members and volunteers alike—finished up their nine months of details. And when this baby was born, one board member quipped, it was born running. "We had no choice but to chase after it," Dianne says.[40]

Friday, March 17, St. Patrick's Day, marked the opening of the festival with the High School/College Big Band Invitational. This evening concert, held in Battenfeld Auditorium on the University of Kansas Medical Center campus, featured the Raytown High School Big Band under the direction of Barry Hartman and the Raytown South High School Big Band led by Carroll C. Lewis. The UMKC Jazz Ensemble, WJF board member Dr. John Leisenring's top band, and the University of Tulsa Jazz Ensemble with director Clifford Whitelegg rounded out the concert.

Dr. Leisenring organized and produced this evening of school jazz to serve dual purposes. Besides launching the Women's Jazz Festival, it acted as the opening activity of the Mid-America Jazz Festival sponsored by the University of Missouri at Kansas City. This collegiate festival included adjudicated sessions and workshops conducted by Jamey Aebersold.[41] What better way to stir up excitement for a weekend of top-notch music than to have the enthusiasm of young, jazz-charged, student musicians filling the eight-hundred-seat auditorium? Any baby leprechauns that night were nailing high Cs and wailing out arpeggiated solos.

WJF volunteers manned the ticket booth, with tickets going for two dollars. The ubiquitous blue WJF T-shirts, still only three dollars, made a timely and fashionable memento for any attendee. Friday night, with so many jazz fans in town for both the Mid-America Collegiate Festival and the Women's Jazz Festival, Crown Center's Signboard Bar was overflowing. Most WJF performers were staying at the Crown Center Hotel, and as they checked in, they couldn't help but be drawn in to the Signboard and its open jam on the other side of the lobby. As leader of the resident quartet, tenor player John Lyman, joined by bassist Milt Abel and drummer Tommy Ruskin and a rotating guest pianist, welcomed everyone who wanted to play. Although the air in the packed club was stifling, the creativity was anything but.

Many out-of-town attendees came to Kansas City that weekend with the promise of jam sessions in mind. That night, one of the most impressive was Bostonian soprano saxophonist Jane Ira Bloom. A recent graduate of Yale and before that the Berklee School of Music, she mesmerized the crowd with her unique style. "I read about the festival in a jazz magazine, maybe *Down Beat*," Jane remembers. "I didn't know anyone else there. I just loved having an opportunity to play. I wasn't aware of the historical significance of the jam sessions at the time."[42]

Leonard Feather, whom Carol had picked up at the airport earlier that day, was delighted to find that most of the weekend's events were scheduled at the hotel. As he settled into a choice spot in the Signboard, he was most impressed with drummer Scotty Robinson from the Kansas City suburb of Lee's Summit who, Feather wrote, "is an astonishingly prodigious drummer who barely looks his age, which is eleven."[43]

If Friday served as the intro, Saturday started the head off with a swingin', up tempo beat that kept its groove until well after midnight. Beginning with Carol's workshop on jazz singing at 9:30, Crown Center's Shawnee Mission Room hosted a rotation of top-notch clinicians that lasted all day.

Carol's background as a composer and pianist as well as a singer all came into play as she reminded clinic attendees that "the blues is to jazz what air is to your lungs." Leonard Feather, who along with John Wilson of the *New York Times*, attended all of the clinics, later told *Melody Maker* readers that Carol's "effusive enthusiasm was the dominant note throughout the weekend."[44]

Taking over after Carol, Joe Morello, Ludwig Drum Company clinician and long-time drummer for both Marian McPartland and Dave Brubeck, demonstrated techniques outlined in his drum set method books. His seeing-eye dog aided Morello, by this time almost blind, as he demonstrated in a humorous way how to tune a drum.

Lynn Milano, a 1968 Eastman School of Music graduate and formerly of the New Orleans Philharmonic bass section, took the 12:30 slot. Milano, who had also worked with Jack DeJohnette and the Jazz Sisters, was the bass player in Marian's Now's the Time band from the previous summer and the scheduled bassist in the festival's All-Star Band. She spent her allotted hour-and-a-half explaining avant-garde rhythms to her mixed audience of aspiring and professional bass players. After the rigorous workout these rhythms demanded, her comments about building up endurance seemed especially appropriate.

Sponsored by Selmer, Bunky Green took on reeds at 2:00. His audience of around two hundred benefited from his years of playing with Charles Mingus, Freddie Hubbard, Yusef Lateef, Cannonball Adderley, Roland Kirk, and Sonny Stitt. With what Leonard Feather referred to as "ear-boggling displays of virtuosity on the alto," Green left little doubt as to why he was a sought-after sideman and a frequent Vanguard recording artist.[45]

Then wrapping up a day of incredible, shared musical knowledge, Marian McPartland took the ballroom stage. A consummate teacher with a style of communicating that would stand her in good stead as the host of *Piano Jazz* starting the next year, Marian charmed all in attendance. She opened her clinic with one of her impromptu portraits, this one of fellow pianist and Kansas City favorite Bettye Miller who had died the year before. When Marian called bassist Milt Abel, Bettye's husband and musical collaborator, up to the stage to join her, she set the tone for this loving tribute and the rest of her allotted time. Her demonstration of how to improvise on a tune managed to astound and inspire at the same time. The *Kansas City Star* reported that fellow pianist Ramsey Lewis, who had played an unrelated concert the night before at the Jewish Community Center, was in attendance—incognito. Elizabeth York, a young pianist in the audience, remembers, "I was thrilled when she asked me to come on stage and play with her. She empowered and inspired me, and I carry her spirit as I empower my women students to improvise and find their own creative voices."[46] Many new shoots of creativity sprouted that weekend.

And if anyone still doubted that women were deeply entrenched in jazz, there were tables set up outside the clinics stacked with records for sale. Some of the female artists represented were well known, some obscure, many on record labels owned or produced by women.

A total of over five hundred women, and men, attended the clinics. They came from thirty-six states. A semester's worth of information and insight was presented that Saturday in March, all for two dollars a session.

With the atmosphere super-charged and crackling with information about metric modulations and tri-tone substitutions, the post-clinic crowd moved to the Signboard once again for a special VIP jam with the John Lyman Quintet. But there was still more. An open, free jam session on the lower level of the Crown Center shops began at 9:30 and wrapped up about 1:00 Sunday morning.

"God smiled on us," Carol remembers thinking. "She gave us good weather for the festival."[47] After a typical Kansas City March week of cold dreariness and fussy skies, Sunday, Palm Sunday, shone clear and calm.

As a special gift to the city that had been so important in her musical development, Mary Lou Williams presented a free performance of her mass to the people of Kansas City. This was the second Kansas City performance of this third and best known of Mary Lou's masses. Controversy had blemished the first performance, held at St. Francis Xavier Catholic Church, when protesters picketed outside with signs that read, "NO JAZZ."[48] Those inside far outnumbered those outside. Hundreds of appreciative fans found a spiritual affinity with Mary Lou's music.

Conceived as a papal commission called *Music for Peace*, this Vietnam War-era piece, which focused on peace, joy, and hope, was first performed on July 15, 1969, at the Holy Family Church in New York City as a tribute to assassinated Kenyan leader Tom Mboya. In 1971 choreographer Alvin Ailey approached Mary Lou about collaborating on something for his American Dance Theater with *Music for Peace* at the center. New mass parts and songs were added, resulting in the thirteen-movement composition forever after known as *Mary Lou's Mass*. This spiritual jazz testimony immediately found a home not only in dance performance but also in concert form and as liturgy at St. Patrick's Cathedral in New York City. *New York Times* jazz critic John Wilson called it "joyous," and Walter Terry of the *Saturday Review* told readers, "It is a beautiful work, filled with reverence and jubilation, confession and great humor."[49]

For the Kansas City 2:00 Sunday afternoon performance at the Cathedral of the Immaculate Conception, the Hallmark Crown Singers—an amateur group made up of Hallmark Cards employees—joined Mary Lou along with Carline Ray on bass and local drummer Everett Brown. Mike Ning arranged for the singers, and Father Ambrose Karels, musical liturgist at the Cathedral, rehearsed the group.[50]

In a letter dated February 1, 1978, Father Peter O'Brien, Mary Lou's manager and spiritual confidant, suggested to Father Karels that he not give the volunteer singers copies of the music, but only the words. The vocal ensemble parts from a simplified, traveling version of the mass were in unison. Father O'Brien wrote, "The rehearsals before we arrive should be merely to get a familiarity with the actual notes of the songs that will be sung." With jazz rhythms and tempo changes throughout, Ms. Williams preferred the choir learned the music with their ears and their hearts. Father O'Brien assured Father Karels, "Mary Lou will change keys, eliminate or add notes to everything very flexibly to make the singers sound good." He then stated rehearsal preferences for the day before the concert and, with a practiced confidence, added, "It always works out well."[51]

The critics weren't so sure. Gerald Jordon of the *Kansas City Times* felt that the choir seemed unsure of what to do. Leonard Feather told his *L.A. Times* readers that, despite moments of reverence and jubilation, the choir didn't swing enough.[52]

These, however, were minor criticisms overshadowed by the brilliance of the piano trio. Mary Lou conducted from the piano and was solidly supported by Carline and Brown. Clearly impressed when Carline doubled as the contralto soloist, Jordan reported, "her interpretations were too melodic to be called merely a chant and too penetrating to be compared with ballads."[53] At the center of it all was Mary Lou's command of the work and consummate professionalism in working with new people.

This music was meant to open the soul, and there was no doubt that the 950 in attendance were musically and spiritually touched by the power of Mary Lou's message of brotherhood. In a tune called "One," the simple lyrics "If we all could love one another all the world would be one" summed up the point of the day.

Spring Is Here

Memorial Hall, sometimes called Soldiers and Sailors Hall, in Kansas City, Kansas, is an imposing, Federal-style stone building originally built in 1925 as a veteran's hall. Despite its somber appearance it became a popular venue for rock concerts and professional wrestling matches. On the evening of Sunday, March 19, 1978, it housed a very exuberant jazz crowd. Two thousand-plus, many with their ears already full of the weekend's music, eagerly took their seats in the shabby old building.

As she had with her clinic, Marian kicked off the concert with mention of Bettye Miller. Carol and Dianne presented a small sculpture of a grand piano and bass to Milt Abel, as they told the audience that the concert was dedicated to Bettye. Then, as Leonard Feather told his English readers in *Melody Maker*, "Marian . . . opened with a gracious tribute to the promoters."[54]

Getting down to the business of music, Marian and her trio, consisting of drummer Rusty Jones, formerly of the George Shearing trio, and bassist Brian Torff, played a series of tunes written by women. Besides two of her own compositions, "Ambiance" and "Afterglow," they played Ann Ronell's "Willow Weep for Me" and Bernice Petkere's "Close Your Eyes." Rounding out the set with "Sweet and Lovely," "There Is No Greater Love," and "All the Things You Are," the trio "spun webs of shimmering linear strands,"[55] as *Down Beat* critic Chuck Berg reported. The critic for the Warsaw, Poland-based *Magazine of the International Jazz Federation*, on the front row of this historic concert, informed his readers that Marian "played sprightly, meticulously and even semi-classically" and that Torff and Jones provided "a manicured rhythm line."[56] In his *Los Angeles Times* review, Feather said that Marian had "grown consistently in harmonic sophistication and melodic creativity."[57] The performance spanned swing, bop, and contemporary and left the audience eager for more.

Although he had been visible all weekend at clinics and jam sessions, Leonard Feather's official capacity as volunteer emcee didn't begin until the Sunday night concert. He introduced himself as the master of ceremonies and then quickly corrected himself—person of ceremonies. From the time of his first letter to Carol announcing his support of the Women's Jazz Festival, Feather had pledged to help in any way he could. Standing on the Memorial Hall stage, talking to the audience, his resonant baritone voice betraying a hint of an English accent, there was no doubt he was the ideal person for the job. Carol jokingly referred to him as Learned Father.

Feather had moved to the United States from his native London in 1939 and set about building his reputation as a composer and arranger. He had studied piano and clarinet as a child. But his best talents lay elsewhere. As a promoter and producer, Feather had helped debut Dinah Washington and Sarah Vaughan. His all-women recordings broke civil rights barriers decades before others. Through his writings, both as a critic and in his ground-breaking *Encyclopedia of Jazz* and its many subsequent editions, Feather advanced the careers of countless women, including Mary Osborne, Vi Redd, and Vivian Garry. His syndicated columns on jazz appeared in 350 newspapers. Feather invented the "blindfold test" that he used in various forms for *Metronome* and then *Down Beat*, and finally, *JazzTimes*. The genesis of this revealing, popular feature stemmed from his live-audience radio show called *Platterbrains*. Besides being an entertaining look into the musical brains of famous musicians, the feature became a subtle way to promote women players by underlining the fact that gender is not audible.

It was Feather's sophisticated professionalism that kept an even tempo all evening. Although he had columns to write afterward, the man on stage was Leonard Feather the promoter. He had told Shifra Stein earlier in the week that, after the festival, "people will, perhaps, begin to realize that women definitely have an important place in jazz."[58]

Even Leonard Feather's introduction couldn't do justice to Betty Carter's unique and very personalized way of presenting a tune. "I have no idea what my mouth is doing when I sing a song," Betty told Cace International T.V. "I don't see my face the way the audience does. I try to deliver the mood of a song. I'm inside the music."[59] Betty was a horn player's singer, with an elastic smile that was as much a part of her developed sound as any embouchure. She felt jazz and spontaneity were synonymous. Her musical interpretations couldn't be contained in a single melodic line any more than a horn player could stop at playing the head. Considered theatrical, quirky, and highly stylized by some, she moved among the musicians (Leonard Feather called it "constantly stalking the stage"),[60] weaving that mood into a cohesive sound. She thought of herself as an instrument, and she didn't want anyone on stage holding back for the girl singer. The sound came from the energy of the combined players. Her unconventional scat solos, with harmonic liberties and unexpected rhythms, could be off-putting to those who expected a traditional, pretty performance. Feather called her "an acquired taste."[61] John Wilson wrote that the essence of her style was "controlled tension."[62] Perhaps these male critics, enlightened though there were, were uncomfortable with a woman who rejected the expectation of a sweet, pretty tune. Her creativity owed more to her bop roots and Thelonious Monk and Dizzy Gillespie than to Rosemary Clooney.

For the Memorial Hall concert she was backed by the John Hicks Trio. Besides Hicks on piano, Jerome Hunter was on bass, and Cliff Barbaro played drums. After the trio opened with an up-tempo tune that Feather said contained "McCoy Tynerish ferocity,"[63] Betty joined them. Their set proved to be the longest of the evening. Her choice of tunes ran the gamut from "Zing Went the Strings of My Heart" to a swinging jazz-waltz, semi-comic version of Cole Porter's "Most Gentlemen Don't Like Love (They Just Like to Kick It Around)" to a satirical turn of "Music, Maestro, Please." Her version of "Trolley Song" started off fast, then dropped suddenly to a relaxed swing, giving Betty plenty of room to bounce the melody and trolley sounds around with onomatopoeic accents. Her soulful version of "Can't We Talk It Over" proved her versatility, and a medley of Charlie Parker tunes gave new insight into the familiar. Through it all, the audience was entranced. She added the perfect spice to Marian's more ethereal opening set. Yet, Leonard Feather told his readers that he found her long set of stylized arrangements "wearing."[64] The crowd, in the mood for something different, contradicted that with a standing ovation.

For those who found Betty Carter's interpretations too adventurous, The Women's Jazz Festival All-Stars were the comfort group. The multi-generational combo, put together specifically for the festival, had as its nucleus the Now's the Time road band that Marian had formed for the Today Show the previous summer. Led by Marian McPartland, the sextet included veterans Mary Osborne on guitar, Lynn Milano on bass, Dottie Dodgion on drums, and newcomers Janice Robinson on trombone and Mary Fettig Park[65] on alto saxophone. Their musical sorbet consisted of "Blue Bossa," "Things Ain't What They Used to Be," "Now's the Time," "Autumn Leaves," and "Straight No Chaser," all tried and true tunes that required little rehearsal time, which is what they had. "We only had time for a quick let's-figure-out-what-to-play-and-talk-it-through,"[66] Mary Fettig remembers. "Marian had a pretty good idea of what would work. There was a wonderful vibe, and I couldn't stop thinking, 'There are no guys up here.'"

Drummer Dottie Dodgion adds that festival gigs rarely have rehearsals. "There are no run downs, no time to second guess anyone's playing. Everything is a first take."[67]

Leonard Feather voiced disappointment that each player wasn't given ample opportunity to shine individually.[68] *Down Beat* reviewer Chuck Berg wrote of impressive solo work by Fettig and Robinson.[69] Joe Waz of *Jazz Forum* liked Mary Osborne's uncluttered, vintage sound and Fettig's "crisp tantalizing playing."[70] Yet all critics felt the selections were somewhat stale and too basic for this groundbreaking concert. Feather's expectations were not met by the "tired jam session repertoire."[71]

Original or more innovative tunes would not have served the group better. Their function in the lineup was to demonstrate the truth that an ensemble of women jazz players, even if they hadn't played together as a group before, could inspire each other and perform with as much creativity, drive, and command as any collection of male players. The first Women's Jazz Festival All-Stars were uniquely qualified to do just that.

Marian's easy-going and gregarious personality, as well as her superb playing, had made her a well-respected, visible player for decades. But two other members of the All-Stars had also spent years carving out their reputations and paying gig dues along with their male counterparts.

Mary Osborne, born in Minot, North Dakota, in 1921, started playing ukulele when she was four, switched to violin to play in the school orchestra, then took up banjo in her father's band. By the time she was a teenager, she had settled on her chosen instrument. "When I picked up that first guitar, that was it. I knew that's what I wanted to play the rest of my life."[72]

After moving to New York City in the late thirties, Mary attracted the attention of Coleman Hawkins, Ben Webster, Dizzy Gillespie, and Art Tatum at jam sessions. The calls started coming and she was never without a gig. She also recorded extensively with Hawkins, Mary Lou Williams, Meryl Booker, Billie Holiday, and Mercer Ellington. In the fifties, television audiences heard her regularly on *Arthur Godfrey's Talent Scouts*, and she did a ten-year stint on *The Jack Sterling Show*, a daily morning radio show on CBS. Like Charlie Christian, her first mentor, Mary incorporated hornlike phrasing into her playing, making her guitar a solo instrument as well as a rhythm instrument.

Although she always gave Christian credit for her original inspiration, her hard-driving, soulful sound also made her a favorite with rhythm and blues bands.

During these early days in New York, Mary met Leonard Feather, who helped her get recording dates, and Marian McPartland, who followed Mary at the Hickory House. She also met trumpeter Ralph Scaffidi, whom she soon married. The couple worked—Scaffidi as a staff musician at CBS—in New York until 1968 when they moved to Bakersfield, California, to open the Osborne Guitar Company.

When Marian called Mary for the Now's the Time gig, Mary was still playing and teaching. "Never once in my life did I say, 'I'm not going to play. I'll just become a housewife,'"[73] she told author Linda Dahl. Her three children, all musicians, were grown, and she was ready to rejoin the scene. The fact that she was a woman hadn't hindered her before, and it wouldn't now. "People would say, 'Gee, you don't *look* like a musician.' Well, what are musicians supposed to look like? I never got jobs because I was a girl; I never kept them because I was a girl. Everything I accomplished was because this was the business I was in and this was what I was—a musician."[74]

"There isn't any gender to music," Dottie Dodgion says. "I know I upset a lot of people by being a girl drummer, but it never seemed strange to me at the time. I played with a lot of guys—Al Cohn, Zoot Sims, Ruby Braff, George Mraz, Hank Jones, Joe Venuti. They didn't hire me because I was a girl. They hired me because I could play the way they liked."[75]

Dottie started out as a singer, and with no less a jazz legend than Charles Mingus, but she had grown up watching her father play drums. "My father never showed me one lick. I sat and watched him. He did tell me that if someone asks you to sit in, do it. Be there when you're needed."[76] So if a drummer was late, Dottie made a practice of grabbing a pair of brushes and a magazine to play along. The bass player Eugene Wright, who encouraged her interest in drums early on, told her guys would think that was cute, until she started taking their gigs away from them. Which she did.[77] Her drumming career took off, although not without some hindrance.

> In the old days, when I first came to New York, it was like this: There'd be five male drummers after me, [at jam sessions] and all five of them would get to play first. I would stay there until last, and they'd let me come up and play a tune. You had to prove yourself all the time, everyplace. A woman drummer—you think they were going to differentiate? But I really listened, tried not to get an attitude, tried not to be bitter because of that. Bitterness wouldn't have helped me at all to improve myself. So I really tried to take it and learn and listen.[78]

By 1964 Dottie was playing a trio gig with Marian McPartland and a very young Eddie Gomez at a New York Club called Strollers. Dottie and Marian had matched views of how to make it swing, supporting each other and helping Gomez find the groove. "Stick with me, baby," Dottie was known to shout as she accented the bass drum when she thought Gomez was dragging.[79]

Marian and Dottie had something else in common. They had both had disastrous, short-lived gigs with Benny Goodman. In both cases their pink slips had come after they received more applause than the King of Swing. The night Dottie got her notice, Gene Krupa sent her roses and a note that said she was in good company—Benny had fired the best.

Dottie knew very well that to be a serious player you have to leave your ego off the stand. "I had polio when I was fifteen, and I thought I would never walk, let alone play the drums. That puts things in perspective. You don't have to be big and powerful to play the drums, but you do have to have a desire, and you have to listen. Everything is in your wrist and your placement of the beat. The rest is stamina."[80] In her long career Dottie had seen too many musicians, both women and men, destroyed by rancorous egos. "If your heart is in it and you can play, nothing else should matter."[81]

It also doesn't hurt to keep a well-tuned sense of humor. When once asked about what she thought of Buddy Rich's playing, Dottie's rim shot answer was, "He plays good for a man."[82]

The jazz roots of baby boomers Janice Robinson, Mary Fettig, and Lynn Milano found fertile ground in 1960s scholastic jazz programs. An increase in high school, and even junior high, jazz bands gave rise to jazz camps and festivals catering to this age group. Not only did this generate more interest and excitement about the music, it gave young players more exposure, girls as well as boys. Mary Fettig met Marian McPartland in 1976 at a jazz education festival in Kansas City where McPartland was playing with Mary's then father-in-law, saxophonist John Park.[83] After Alec Wilder introduced Marian to Janice via telephone,[84] Janice played with Marian at a Youth and Jazz Day at the Newport Festival.

Mary Fettig, who started out on marimba but took up clarinet and alto saxophone to play in her Concord, California, grade school band, remembers how her high school band director, Bill Burke, changed her life. "He was a classical trombonist, but an excellent teacher no matter the genre. He didn't allow his musical preference to get in the way of being the best concert band, marching band, jazz band teacher. I was learning traditional theory from the orchestra teacher, Lea Maples, but in spite of that, I played by ear. Mr. Burke hooked me up with the Stan Kenton Camp in Redlands, California, because he loved Kenton's music, and it gave me an opportunity to learn jazz. That was the summer before I started to play in the jazz band at school."[85] Mary attended the Stan Kenton Camp for three years and was lead alto in the top band for two of them. "I got to sit in on the Kenton band when they needed another alto to read new music for educators."[86]

While still in high school Mary met jazz education pioneer Jamey Aebersold. "Mr. Burke brought in a number of great jazz musicians to play with us, and he was one of them. Jamey was very kind and generous, sending me material right after he had played with us."[87] The Ygnacio Valley High School Jazz Band, under Bill Burke's direction and with Mary as his lead alto player, won the first Monterey Jazz Festival High School Competition in 1971. Mary was also voted outstanding jazz saxophonist.[88]

A year later, while Mary was a music education student at UCLA, she and some friends went to hear a Kenton concert at Disneyland. Just as in a Disney movie plot, Kenton talked to her on break, told her he remembered how well she played, and asked her to join the band; he'd call her with details. "I was so excited. Here I was at Disneyland—where my dreams really could come true." But his call the next day wasn't what she had hoped for. During the night Kenton had been admitted to the hospital. "He called from the ICU to tell me that he would be in the hospital for a while and that my joining the band was on hold. I finally joined the band a year later, in 1973."[89]

Janice Robinson's academic career took her to the Eastman School of Music where she studied classical trombone. Born in 1951, Janice grew up in a suburb of Pittsburgh, Pennsylvania. She started off on trumpet but had trouble with high notes, so her band directors switched her to trombone. Begrudgingly, she went along with the switch, although at first she felt the trombone was somehow a lesser instrument than the trumpet and too easy. By high school, and after a turn on the Ted Mack Amateur Hour where she played an arrangement of "A Taste of Honey," that attitude had changed. She followed her Amateur Hour spot with an appearance on a Bill Cosby television special. "I got to see a lot of the music world *very* quickly." [90]

While at Eastman, Janice got in on the ground floor of their jazz program, which "had been underground for some time before the formal class offerings."[91] She had the opportunity to do some writing for the jazz ensemble while pursuing a degree in music education and preparing for an orchestral career. She received NEA grants for composition in 1978 and 1981. After graduation she played at the Santa Barbara Music Academy, for the National Orchestral Association, the Dance Theater of Harlem Orchestra, the Symphony of the New World, and the Brooklyn Philharmonic, as well as for Oliver Nelson, Frank Foster, and the Jazz Composers Orchestra.[92] By 1974 she was playing in a group called Jazz Sisters, which included bassist Lynn Milano, also an Eastman graduate. This New York-based group played an eclectic book of jazz, blues, and jazz-rock. She also got a call to join the Thad Jones/Mel Lewis Jazz Orchestra. It was then she made her choice to pursue jazz. "I think the last audition I took was for the Metropolitan Opera. I was in Boston with Thad and Mel, and I was supposed to go for a Boston Symphony audition, and I called them and didn't go."[93]

Mary Fettig and Janice Robinson were two of the first women to play in the new breed of 1970s big bands. "Although the Kenton band had female vocalists, I was the first woman to *play* in the band," Mary recounts.[94]

As a testament to the uniqueness of their musical situation, both women were guests on the popular television game show, *What's My Line*. "We had just returned from a six-month European tour," says Mary. "We had been on the road constantly, and when we finally got back to the Bay Area in California, my home, I was told the day before that I had to fly to NYC to tape *What's My Line*. I was very homesick, finally had a chance to see family and friends, and was pulled away to do the show. Not a happy camper to have to leave."[95] Janice's stint on the show came about under happier circumstances. She had as her co-guest

Marian McPartland.[96] "I was introduced as a protégé of Marian's, but Jimmy McPartland 'coached' me a little behind the scenes."[97]

Both Janice and Mary relate that their fellow band members were accepting and protective. "Discipline and hard work doesn't have a gender," says Janice. "Every guy in the band had a different approach to the changes, a different sound." Some of the guys in the band helped her find her own approach. "One of the guys, Billy Harper, used to say, 'Why don't you try this? This is something that trombone players usually do. Try that, . . . see how it sounds.' . . . I learned a lot."[98]

About this time Janice also started playing in Clark Terry's Big Bad Band, where again she was the only female. In 1976 she, along with drummer Sue Evans, was hired for a European tour with the Gil Evans Orchestra. All the while Janice discovered that there was a lot of growing room within the definition of "professional musician." "I found it's one thing to listen to the music or to play and have a general appreciation and another to really be closely involved with the directions that one goes within the music."[99]

Mary Fettig remembers the guys in Kenton's band "certainly looked out for me, and when audience members seemed a little too friendly off-stage, I could count on someone to intervene for me."[100] As far as having to prove herself as a musician, Mary always had musical goals in mind. "I have always felt that I need to play as well as or better than those around me to be accepted. It only serves to improve my musicianship and hire ability, so I prefer to think of [playing like a man] as a positive aspect."[101]

Mary remembers having more hassles from the press than any musician. The novelty of a very young woman with long, blond hair and a girl-next-door smile who played with as much moxie as any seasoned man was too much of a temptation. All too often reporters gathered around her after concerts to ask the same tired question—"What's it like to play with all these guys?" Mary preferred not to think of herself as any different musically. "I remember with Stan that I would come down front for a solo, and there would be cheers before I played anything, and I didn't like that. But the cheers were bigger after I played, so I hoped it was for the music."[102]

Janice felt that extra applause for women could cause jealousies. Audiences sometimes paid more attention to the look than the sound and in a way that insulted not only the men playing at their highest skill level, but also the woman who joined them. The audience didn't always think of the band as a single unit. Janice saw it happen too many times. Men playing at the top of their level were ignored while women were wildly applauded regardless of what they played.

Both horn players agreed that, in music that is improvised, everyone brings a unique voice to the tune. Their pioneer positions in big bands were an improvisation of another kind. "Improvising is difficult," Janice concludes. "It's like life, you know. You try to prepare yourself to meet all the different circumstances in life."[103]

John S. Wilson of the *New York Times* remarked that the most outstanding feature of the All-Stars was the contrast in what all these women brought to the group. He mentioned to his readers that Mary Osborne played with "light, dancing grace," and Janice Robinson provided a "swaggering, lusty sound on trombone that provided a strong, deep-toned lead for the ensemble."[104]

Wilson was most impressed with Lynn Milano's "firm rhythmic foundation."[105] In his *Kansas City Star* review, Steve Paul remarked that, although Lynn was "a frail-looking bassist" who was reportedly plagued with back problems, her "size belies her finesse on the upright."[106] Leonard Feather reserved most of his praise for this former student of Ron Carter's. "The surprise of the set was Lynn Milano, whose sound and style on upright bass is big, bold and flexible. [She] kept a strong bass line going throughout the group's five tunes and soloed very impressively."[107]

Shifra Stein, in her *Kansas City Times* review, opined that Mary Fettig had provided the "most outstanding solo work" and called her a "gem of a player who put on a superlative performance."[108] Improvisation took on a new twist for Mary right before this set. "I was hanging with Jamey Aebersold, who I had known since I was in high school, when someone came up to me to tell me that someone had gone into my dressing room and knocked over my alto. Jamey went with me to assess the damage. It was knocked onto a cement floor, unplayable. Jamey took a cab to his hotel and brought me his horn to play the concert." [109]

Despite this and the fact that it took part of the set to get her microphone working, Feather, who had first heard Mary playing in her high school jazz band at the Monterey Jazz Festival said, "Her alto is almost in a class with Phil Woods and her flute playing shows maturity and fluency."[110]

"I feel like we bonded instantly as a group," Mary remembers. "Even though I was playing a completely foreign horn and trying to adapt, I was on cloud nine the whole time."[111]

So was the audience.

After a brief intermission, Mary Lou Williams took command of the stage.

In addition to providing festival goers with a wide range of eclectic musical styles, the performing artists also carried in their gig bags a plethora of egos. Jazz musicians can't survive professionally without a healthy dose of self-confidence. The technique gymnastics they have to perfect, and the grasp of harmonic concepts that has to become second nature, must be absolutely secure if they are to hold their own and be ready when any tune is called. Playing jazz is not for the timid. Arguably, one of the greatest benefits of the first Women's Jazz Festival was proving that that trait was not masculine, or more to the point, not un-feminine.

As euphoric as the festival atmosphere was, there were as many different approaches to the politics of jazz as there were players. Female musicians who were most firmly established in their careers had fought the battle for equality for years, sometimes decades, and had passed the point of intimidation long ago. Their talent combined with perseverance had put them on equal footing with any player, male or female. Some, although happy to play with anyone who was good, preferred to play with men. Mary Osborne, Dottie Dodgion, and even Marian McPartland had made public statements about their hesitancy to play with all-female groups and the pitfalls of forming a group based on gender. All had insisted that music should always come first, that women should get their fair turn, but that, just like when playing with men, there were inherent problems playing with women.

No one was more outspoken on this topic than Mary Lou Williams. At a press conference held Saturday of the festival, Mary Lou stated, "I'm very feminine, but I think like a man, and I've been working around them all my life. I can deal better with men."[112] She went on to praise Mary Osborne, and no one could doubt her affinity with bassist Carline Ray, both on her mass and the Sunday night trio set, but Leonard Feather interpreted her press conference comments as "defensive and almost antifeminist."[113]

That Mary Lou had a soft spot in her heart for Kansas City was apparent. "I've lived through four eras of jazz," she told the press, "and I've played the styles of all of them. The greatest era of them all was Kansas City in the thirties." When talking about her early career, she was known to tell people, "Nobody ever got homesick for New York when they visited K.C."[114] She was thrilled to have her mass performed in her adopted town and to give the city this Palm Sunday treat. Board member and pianist/singer Sylvia Bell was assigned to pick up Mary Lou, who traveled with her manager, Father Peter O'Brien, at the airport. "I took her to her hotel and rehearsals and gig, and she was very nice to me. We had some good conversations. I drove her to the street named after her—around 10th and Paseo—which she was very pleased to see."[115]

But she also made it clear that she had no loyalty to the Women's Movement. Nor to Leonard Feather or Marian McPartland, for that matter. In Feather's review for *Melody Maker*, he finds it curious that Mary Lou "paid tribute" to Mary Osborne but didn't mention Marian McPartland, who he said was a "virtually unpaid public relations person for the event." [116]

In her biography of Mary Lou Williams, *Morning Glory*, Linda Dahl states that after the WJF, Mary Lou wrote Feather a letter "trembling with anger" because she felt he had "championed" Marian while chiding her for being "antifeminist."[117] Their animosity was long standing. In the late forties, when Leonard Feather was producing all-women recordings, which Mary Lou felt tended to be "gimmicky," they had their first run in. Mary Lou didn't like that Feather insisted on certain side women for her recording. She was used to picking whom she played with and felt his choices would not meet her standards. She also wasn't pleased that he expected her to record some of his tunes. Her fear of less than professional attitudes from the players came true at the first session. "It was the cattiest session I'd ever encountered; the girls talked more music than they played."[118] Not known for her forgiving nature, Mary Lou hadn't forgotten and called Leonard manipulative and cold.

There was also a surprising amount of animosity in Mary Lou's attitude toward Marian McPartland. Linda Dahl traces this back to early in Marian's career when she was getting record contracts at a time when Mary Lou was not. She was jealous of the attention Marian got and her easy manner with the press and public alike. In a letter to a friend, Mary Lou said, "She wants to be the Queen of the ivories. Me, I don't care—I pray for her. Anything I do she tries to ape me."[119] Mary Lou was affronted when Marian took over her gig at the Cookery in NYC. She felt Marian had come into the club to hear her just so she could steal her arrangements.

The two women had shared a bass player, too. Brian Torff had played for Mary Lou in the early seventies. Mary Lou's frustration toward sidemen was legendary, and she was particularly hard on bass players. Carline Ray, her bass player for the WJF, summed it up. "She liked a bass player who would play down in the lower reaches of the instrument and lay down a nice musical swinging cushion and let her do her thing—in other words, stay out of her way."[120] She liked to hire bass players who were relatively inexperienced and train them the way she wanted them to play. She was known to call out the notes she wanted to hear and growl, "Play them changes,"[121] but as Marian told *Down Beat* readers, "On the bandstand Mary was demanding and intolerant, but also like a mother, praising the good."[122]

In the *Down Beat* article, written a decade earlier, Marian had described Mary Lou as "conscientious, introspective, sensitive, fragile, . . . a woman vulnerable, . . . a woman hurt so many times she tends to withdraw from and be suspicious of others." To Marian this, along with her "unconditional commitment to the art of jazz," made Mary Lou "irresistibly fascinating."[123]

When Marian's NPR radio series, *Piano Jazz*, debuted seven months after the first WJF, Marian asked Mary Lou to be her first guest, as the most important woman in jazz. Because of Mary Lou's partiality to Baldwins, the taping took place at the Manhattan Baldwin showroom. The taping started off with Mary Lou turning to Marian's producer and commenting, "I should be doing this show." Mary Lou's mood didn't improve. When Marian asked her what key she preferred, Mary Lou curtly answered, "Depends on my mood," to which Marian asked, "What kind of mood are you in now?" Mary Lou answered, "Oh, I could just be in a flat mood, period." Mary Lou's playing on the show was brilliant by all accounts, but Marian later summed up Mary Lou's attitude as "snotty." The episode's airing was postponed, and Billy Taylor became the first broadcast guest on *Piano Jazz*.[124]

The crowd knew nothing of this tension, and any direct contact Mary Lou had that night with Marian or Leonard, or Marian's bass player Brian Torff, was distant but cordial. Mary Lou's hesitancy to embrace the women's lib element of the evening didn't affect the music, except perhaps in what Linda Dahl called the "perfunctoriness of her performance."[125] Critic Steve Paul referred to the set, which included "My Blue Heaven" and "My Favorite Things," as "effortless" and "less than challenging for the trio."[126] Leonard Feather innocuously stated, "Mary Lou Williams played a relaxed set of blues and standards, supported again by Carline Ray and Everett Brown."[127] Mary Lou may not have presented any new tunes, but her arrangements were fresh and impressive. Her version of "Over the Rainbow" was dense and rich in texture and beautifully phrased. Her spirited interpretation of "Surrey with the Fringe on Top," which showed off her lightning-fast left hand, gave the audience exactly what they wanted. Regardless of what was going on in Mary Lou's complicated psyche, she held reign in Kansas City hearts.

The Toshiko Akiyoshi-Lew Tabackin Big Band presented a stunning contrast to anything heard earlier that night. Despite the fact that this sixteen-piece, all-male big band tipped the balance toward more men than women performers at the first Women's Jazz Festival, it was very much Toshiko's band. The forty-nine-year-old, diminutive piano player told the audience, "There is some talk about this women's festival having too many men. But my particular band could not exist without my music."[128] As composer, arranger, and pianist for the group she ran along with her husband, tenor saxophonist and flutist Lew Tabackin, Toshiko was what critic Steve Paul called the group's "guiding light." He proclaimed the band "the freshest, most energetic big band anywhere."[129]

Although Japanese, Toshiko grew up in Manchuria, where her piano training was strictly classical. When her family moved back to Japan after World War II, exposure to G.I. radio gave Toshiko a taste for jazz. She listened to everything she could but was particularly influenced by Teddy Wilson and Bud Powell. She found work playing in coffeehouses and on television, and by 1956 she was the highest paid free-lance arranger and studio musician in Japan.

With the endorsement of entrepreneur Norman Granz and pianist Oscar Peterson, Toshiko won a full scholarship to Berklee College of Music. It wasn't an easy transition. She told Leonard Feather in a *Ms.* interview, "I dealt with both racial and sexual prejudice. I played clubs and TV wearing a kimono, because people were amazed to see an Oriental woman playing jazz."[130]

During the sixties most of her work was with small groups, but in 1967 she made her debut as a composer-conductor at a Town Hall concert in New York. It was there her big band compositions were first heard in public.

In 1969 she married Lew Tabackin, and the couple formed a quartet, but when Lew got the call to play in the *Tonight Show* band, they moved to Los Angeles. Formed as a rehearsal band to showcase Toshiko's prolific library of compositions, Toshiko's band offered challenging, tightly orchestrated ensemble work along with extended, improvised solos that featured primarily Lew.

Her musical blending of east and west gave her compositions their unique flare. "I came to think that being Japanese was not a negative aspect. I could draw something from my own culture and perhaps return to the jazz tradition something that might make it a little bit richer than before."[131] Her use of Japanese percussion, vertical voicings, extended forms, accents that are unusually placed, and frequent meter changes, all grounded in a bebop tradition, made for interesting listening.

The Women's Jazz Festival audience couldn't agree more. Although the program was already running well past the contracted 11:00 end time, the crowd insisted on two encores. "We started paying overtime at 11:01," Dianne told the exuberant crowd after the first encore. "They might as well play one more."[132]

The group opened with "Strive for Jive," an up-tempo piece with plenty of the vertical ensemble work Toshiko did so well. The energy unleashed in Lew's tenor solo on "Hangin' Loose" brought an audience that should have been tired to its feet.

Toshiko's writing for woodwinds was particularly striking on this set. During her piece "Kogun," Lew took one of his characteristically long and ambling flute solos with a background of four flutes. Leonard Feather called Tabackin "the only male hero of the evening" and said that his unaccompanied solo swung "monumentally on its own."[133] Leavenworth, Kansas, native and KU graduate Gary Foster, featured on an ethereal piece premiered that night called "Illusive Dreams," played alto on top of a five-flute section, which created what Feather called "a pastoral image of rare beauty."[134] In his article for *Down Beat*, Chuck Berg referred to Dick Spencer's alto solo on "Road Time Shuffle" as "gritty" with plenty of room for his "aerial alto acrobatics."[135]

Kansas City Star critic Steve Paul reserved his highest praise for this group. "Toshiko is the most innovative arranger and bandleader since Duke Ellington."[136] They offered a perfect yin and yang ending to this marvelous evening of music.

It was 12:30 Monday morning before the last chord was heard and the applause died down. Already there was talk about who to have for next year. The general consensus was that the first Women's Jazz Festival had been a rousing success. The weekend had proved that the jazz gene was not gender based. Chuck Berg put it this way: "The International Premiere of the Women's Jazz Festival was a joyous happening. Without rancor or rhetoric, it was a celebration to improvised music by women."[137]

The evening was not without glitches. By all accounts, the sound, provided by Sound Dynamics, was uneven and at times muffled. The Bösendorfer piano donated for the evening was miked so poorly its rich tones were all too often dulled. Some microphones were reported dead. There were times when the amplification cut out altogether.

Potentially the biggest crisis of the event was averted by someone there as a fan. When an aggressive group of feminists learned that men would play at the main concert, they organized a protest. Just before concert time, San Francisco feminist and pianist Margie Adams learned of this and asked to speak to the women. She told them the exclusion of men was never the intent and that protesting what was clearly a remarkable opportunity to promote women musicians would be counterproductive. The protesters disbanded. Carol and Dianne didn't know anything about the hubbub outside the Hall until it was over.[138]

The hope to fill every seat in Memorial Hall fell short. Of the available 3,600 seats, 2,000 were occupied, although the enthusiasm of 2,000 more than filled the space. For a first year festival, the numbers were better than usual. The organization was able to break even, thanks in large part to the National Endowment for the Arts grant. "Better than Newport and Nice and others," Leonard told readers, "all losers the first time around."[139]

The intent was never to make money. Board member Marie Spearing summed it up. "We didn't make money, we made history."[140]

Chapter 3

The Second Year

March 23–25, 1979

"Jazz is a peculiarly male music for which most women lack the physical equipment, to say nothing of the poise."
—Whitney Balliett, Jazz Critic, *New Yorker* magazine, 1977

LIKE A PICK-UP NOTE INTO THE NEW DECADE, 1979 belonged more to the eighties than the seventies. Names that jostled for headlines throughout the eighties and beyond—Iran, Afghanistan, Ayatollah Khomeini—started making noise in 1979. In fashion, a harbinger of an indulgent decade, sleeves, pant legs, and hair got bigger. "Rapper's Delight" gave The Sugar Hill Gang their first commercial rap hit, showing the world that this edgy street music could explode in a recording studio.

The hope generated by early successes toward the passage of The Equal Rights Amendment took a negative turn toward the eighties as well. Throughout the late seventies, state after state ratified the amendment until thirty-five of the necessary thirty-eight were counted. But by the initial ratification deadline, March 22, 1979—one day before the start of the second Kansas City's Women's Jazz Festival—five states had rescinded their votes. Through a joint resolution in Congress, the deadline was extended, with little effect.

As always, there were women who didn't wait for a constitutional amendment to give them permission to be themselves and to do what they saw needed doing. In 1979 Jane Byrne became the first female mayor of Chicago. That was the year an exclusive team of women operated a railroad train from Port Washington, New York, to Penn Station. The Navy assigned its first female naval commander. Not to be outdone, the Army produced a 1979 ad stating, "Some of our best men are women."[1] Yet, a prominent, generally respected jazz critic still maintained that women didn't have "the physical equipment" to play jazz.

All of Me

Two weeks after the first WJF, the Board of Directors met to start planning the second. They gave themselves a few minutes of self-congratulatory time then started outlining the challenges that would face them in 1979. Finances loomed large.

By 1979 the gas crisis had opened the nozzle on escalating prices on everything from asphalt to plastics. Like it or not, higher gas prices were here to stay, and by extension all travel was more expensive. Providing transportation for the artists took a large chunk of the budget before a note was played.

With the first-year NEA grant check pending, and the list of board members to be reimbursed for fronted money growing dusty, Carol and Dianne and treasurer Debbie Williams knew the financial viability of the organization had to be constantly addressed. At the first post-festival meeting on April 16, WJF had a balance of $571 in the bank.

Carol reported she had already submitted the next year's application for the Missouri Performing Arts Council grant, and board member Maggie Weed added that she was working on the next NEA grant application, due on June 1. The Kansas Arts Council would be approached again as well.[2]

But none of these agencies would even consider another year of support without proof that the festival could raise additional money, both corporate and private. Now with accolades and endorsements to speak for them, board members approached more local businesses for financial support. Henry Bloch of H&R Block answered the phone this time and offered to underwrite the scholarship. The Powell Foundation of Yellow Freight committed to a second year donation, as did the *Kansas City Star*, Hallmark, and Kansas City Southern. Butler Manufacturing and Tension Envelope added their support. Many business owners gave personal donations rather than corporate, but names like Jerry Berkowitz of Mr. Guy's clothing store, Dave Metheny, owner of Burton Motors, Marty Nichols of J.C. Nichols, and real estate tycoon and band leader Warren Durrett appearing on the donor list helped get the attention of the business community.

The continued endorsement of the Kansas City business community was indeed a healthy sign of support. Business leaders were well aware of the fact that Kansas Citians were conservative with their entertainment dollar and that their professed love of jazz didn't always translate into ticket sales. The 2,000 attendees of the first Women's Jazz Festival—1,500 fewer than the hoped-for goal—came from thirty-six states. For any jazz venue to survive in Kansas City, a fan base had to be identified and nurtured.

No one learned this lesson more tragically than local jazz connoisseur and Friends of Jazz board member, Howard Rittmaster. For years Howard, who worked as a court reporter, dreamed of bringing big name jazz players of different generations and genres to Kansas City for a three-day festival. The five groups he envisioned would be composed of players who hadn't necessarily played together but played the same style. He saw it as a three-day jam. Encouraged by the success of WJF, Friends of Jazz concerts, and the Summer Jazz Concerts in the parks, Howard enlisted the noted jazz writer Ira Gitler as a co-sponsor. What became known as the Jazz Olympics was held in the Radisson Muehlebach's Imperial and Grand Ballrooms on June 1–3, 1979. Howard was confident that if he presented top jazz favorites, all in one place, as if his extensive record collection had come to life, the fans would come. He believed in his dream so deeply, he put up most of the money himself.

The result was a jazz party extravaganza. For the musicians it was more a jam reunion than a gig. Before the first segment, billed as "New York 1930s," drummer Jake Hanna told Shifra Stein, "I never heard of a lineup like this in my whole life. It's like playing in an all-star game."[3] Off the stand, Stein found it difficult to pin the players down for interviews. Their enthusiasm for the event and each other kept interrupting. "I gotta say hello to these cats,"[4] trombonist Carl Fontana told her.

For three days a who's who of jazzmen gathered at the hotel, and in concerts billed as "The New York Scene Today," "Kansas City Sound," "West Coast Style," and "Tribute to Charlie Parker" brought together some of the best jazz the city had ever heard. Al Cohn and Pepper Adams were there, along with Jimmy Rowles, Shelly Manne, and Buster Williams. Jay McShann, Doc Cheatham, Earle Warren, Herbie Mann, Milt Hinton, Dicky Wells, Nat Pierce, and Gus Johnson played tunes like "Take the A Train" and "Moonglow" and reminded everyone why there was so much joy in the Kansas City sound. The segue into the Charlie Parker tribute brought together Billy Mitchell, Red Rodney, Charles McPherson, Barry Harris, Ray Drummond, and Leroy Williams. The rhythm section of Hal Galper, Jim Hughart, and John Dentz, along with Jimmy Knepper, Gary Foster, and Lee Konitz made for perfect West Coast chemistry. Hearing Gary Foster, Kansas native and altoist for the Toshiko Akiyoshi/Lew Tabackin Big Band, for the first time at the Jazz Olympics, Lee Konitz hired him on the spot for a Japanese tour.

To critics and players alike, Jazz Olympics was an artistic success. Old friendships were renewed and new ones established. The weekend had created an atmosphere of spontaneous creativity and what Shelly Manne called "breathing in unison."[5] Howard's dream had come true. With the help of Ira Gitler, he had assembled an astounding collection of jazz players. He had earned the thanks of some of his jazz heroes. With the exception of Art Pepper, who was in the hospital with pneumonia, the turnout of those heroes was complete.

The musicians came. The audience did not. At no time were the two ballrooms more than half full. Some of the concerts had only a smattering of people in the audience. The total of tickets sold came to only a few hundred. Some fans, fully intending to buy tickets, changed their minds at the ticket counter because they felt prices were too steep.

Too many who were aware of the concerts were astounded at the high ticket price. At a time when WJF charged seven dollars and eight dollars for the main concert, the Jazz Olympics charged twenty dollars per concert or one hundred dollars for all five. Potential audience members reportedly complained that, as much as they loved jazz and thought the visiting musicians were worth the money, they weren't willing to pay New York City concert prices. Plainly, they felt they couldn't afford it. Shifra Stein wagged her finger at readers for not putting their money where their mouth was. She felt that without the city's support and a heightened level of sophistication, events like this were sadly destined to failure. "Poor planning and bungling sponsorship is getting to be tiresome. The rumors of failure filter back to the big cities we seem so bent on impressing."[6]

Howard and Ira had hoped to recreate the type of jazz party popular in New York City where well-to-do jazz lovers thronged to hear their favorite players. Howard had predicted the Jazz Olympics would turn out to be the "greatest jazz happening ever held in Kansas City."[7] He made the somewhat naïve assumption that the money would follow. He trusted the lineup would sell itself without extensive publicity, and because he was sure he'd be able to pay himself back, he didn't solicit funds to finance the $75,000 in expenditures.

Once the music-induced euphoria dissipated, Howard admitted that he was "hurt badly in the pocketbook." He told Shifra Stein, "The Jazz Olympics took a lot out of me, not only financially but as far as my health and peace of mind are concerned. It totally took over my life, and it's something I'm going to have to come out of both mentally and financially."[8]

He didn't get the chance. His health and bank account decimated by the Jazz Olympics' financial failure, Rittmaster died tragically two months later at the age of fifty-two.

Work Song

All of this underlined that fact that soliciting financial support from various sources was vital to the success of WJF. Carol, Dianne, and the Board had done their homework and follow through with Kansas City business leaders, but there was more to the underwriting process than that.

Women's Jazz Festival Incorporated was a committed equal rights organization and wanted jazz fans, friends, and family to have as much opportunity to donate to future festivals as the fat cats did. They also had the connections to make fundraising events musically memorable. On a very hot August evening, an invitation-only Jazz Cruise gave two hundred fans just that. What better way to promote music than playing music? The Jazz Cruise successfully raised money, kept WJF in the public eye, broadened the fan base, and gave local musicians a chance to show their support by doing what they loved best. To the sounds of Jay McShann, Claude "Fiddler" Williams, Milt Abel, and drummer Paul Gunther, fans took a three-hour riverboat ride on the Missouri River. The complimentary food and drink made the cruise a floating party, all for a WJF donation of twenty-five dollars.

Board members and musicians couldn't wait to do it again. On November 12, they brought the party inside. Invitations were again sent out to interested fans and potential business donors. A round robin of performers kept the cold, blustery evening out by stoking warm sounds throughout the Essex Apartments Clubhouse. Milt Abel, Mike Metheny, Mike Ning, Tommy Ruskin, all quite happy to be playing their instruments rather than basketball, joined Carol and Scotty Robinson, John Leisenring, Frank Smith, Corky Brown, Abel Ramirez, Russ Godbey, and others. Seven hours of non-stop jamming furthered the cause.

To keep the WJF "running baby"—so named when someone declared that the festival was born running—happy took the combined nurturing of everyone involved. To keep it healthy so it could continue to grow took a lot of outside help. All of this fundraising went a long way toward feeding the hungry infant.

In the midst of the planning, the problem solving, the waking-up-in-the-middle-of-the-night-with-a-new-thought, the phone calls at all times, came a surprise. In January, Carol and Dianne received word that they were co-winners of the 1978 Golden Feather Award for Women of the Year in Jazz. This annual award, given by Leonard Feather and announced in his *L.A. Times* column, paid tribute to not only the idea of WJF but all that went into producing such an event. Of course Leonard had seen first hand what went into the final product and appreciated how that came about. "Carol Comer and Dianne Gregg . . . overcame the problems of apathy and financial inadequacy to mount this venture." He acknowledged that the pair was in the final stages of planning the second year.

WJF was well connected to others in Leonard's class of '78. Man of the Year in Jazz, Tim Owens had recorded the 1978 festival for his NPR show, "Jazz Alive." Competing with the bands of Thad Jones-Mel Lewis, Count Basie, Maynard Ferguson, and

Buddy Rich, the Toshiko Akiyoshi/Lew Tabackin Big Band, WJF's first closing act, received the Golden Feather Big Band Award.

Blues Melba

"One of the things we were most proud of concerning the Women's Jazz Festival was bringing Melba Liston out of retirement."[9] Dianne goes on to mention that it took a year of telegrams, letters, and phone calls to convince the soft-spoken, statuesque trombone player and arranger that she should take a break from her teaching job at the University of the West Indies in Jamaica to come participate in WJF. Melba had made a name for herself in the late forties, a time when female horn players were virtually unheard of and female composers often had their credits stolen. She had had her heart broken more than once by the music business, and when Dianne first contacted her, Melba wasn't sure public performance was where her talents were best applied.[10]

Kansas City was part of the lure. Kansas City was where Melba's love affair with music and the trombone began. She was born there in 1926, and although she grew up just blocks away from the incubator of Kansas City Swing, her only exposure to that sound was through the radio. She remembered her grandfather listened to "things that were swingin'."[11] Melba listened too. As a very young child she developed a complicated number system, which assigned numbers to pitches to help her remember the tunes.

Then at the tender age of seven, she discovered the trombone. "It was the most beautiful thing I had ever seen. It looked like a statue in the music store window. I had to have it." She remembered sitting on the back porch later that night with her grandfather, picking out church tunes and folk songs by ear on her beautiful, new golden statue. Although she was tall for her age, it still took a while before she could reach sixth and seventh positions without turning her head.[12]

By the next year Melba was playing on a local radio show. After she and her mother moved to Los Angeles when Melba was eleven, she started playing in Melodic Dots, a WPA after-school youth jazz band program run by Mrs. Alma Hightower.

"Melba's just always been an advanced musician. We had to struggle to keep up with her,"[13] remembers saxophonist Vi Redd, Mrs. Hightower's great-niece and another member of Melodic Dots. By then Melba was teaching herself to write and arrange music. She moved the family piano into her bedroom and came out only for meals. Her mother would call out to her school friends to come entice Melba to leave her room. "I didn't pay attention to anybody that didn't love music." Not a "frilly girl" as she called it, she considered herself an outsider. "I was good friends with anybody that loved music, and it was only there that I had any friends."[14]

When Melba was sixteen, she began playing in the house band at the Lincoln Theater, a movie house that included a nightly stage show. There she met Gerald Wilson, who was so impressed he took Melba under his wing and gave her writing assignments and jobs copying parts. It was under his tutelage that she learned to be an arranger. Playing in Wilson's band in 1947 and 1948 was her musical coming out. He introduced her to Count Basie, whom she played with briefly, and Dizzy Gillespie, with whom she had a life-long working and personal relationship. Dizzy's 1948 band included John Coltrane, John Lewis, Jimmy Heath—and Melba Liston.

Even when playing with these top professionals, Melba was never far away from her shy, little-girl self who would rather write in her room than be in the spotlight. Melba didn't like going to jam sessions, and she wasn't aggressive about soloing. "I didn't work toward being a front line soloist. But I was the girl in the band, so I was expected to show what I could do, and that included solos."[15] She preferred ballads, where her soul could sing through the trombone. She liked being in the middle of the band, where she was surrounded with the harmonies and complexities of the tunes. According to Melba's friend Vi Redd, the fact that Melba wasn't competing with others for solos helped her standing with her male bandmates. "I have a theory," says Vi. "I think men will accept a woman in the band who is sitting down, like a piano player, but once a woman horn player stands up next to the males, she's saying she's on equal footing, and they don't like that."[16] By all accounts, including her own, Melba was a somewhat introverted person, domestic and nurturing in nature—all characteristics that delighted Eisenhower-era chauvinists. The guys in the band "were callin' me Mama back then, 'cause I used to fuss with them about smokin' their cigarettes or drinkin' their wine," she recalls.[17]

When Billie Holiday hired Gerald Wilson to be her musical director for a 1949 tour of the south, Melba joined them as assistant director and arranger. "I think we were stranded longer than we worked,"[18] she remembered. The audiences were skimpy and disgruntled. They wanted swing they could dance to. Audience indifference and the grueling, hostile travel conditions imposed on black musicians, combined with the general loneliness of the road, were more than Melba could live with. She remembered being stranded on the road with no money and a two-day wait for a Western Union wire. "We ate a lot of oatmeal."[19]

When she returned to Los Angeles, she packed up her trombone. Disgusted with the business side of music, she wanted to try working somewhere with a steady paycheck, so she took a clerical job with the Board of Education and moonlighted as a Hollywood extra. For a brief time, the same luminous smile and quiet regal beauty that charmed jazz audiences could be seen on the silver screen. In the 1956 movie *The Prodigal*, Melba plays the harp behind Lana Turner. She's in the palace orchestra in *The Ten Commandments*. Although she was encouraged to take more bit parts, Melba wasn't interested. She told a friend, "They're all crazy out there."[20]

Making a living as a jazz musician, in any decade, for either gender, creates a life booby-trapped with financial and emotional challenges. Not many make it to the top. Those who do, with few exceptions, are expected to spend time on the road to promote recordings and their current bands. It takes a particular temperament to adapt to prolonged periods away from family and one's own bed, as Melba discovered on the Billie Holiday tour.

Making a living as a female jazz musician during the fifties was nearly impossible. It was a decade when the cultural perception of American womanhood swung as a sharp-edged pendulum from *Playboy* centerfolds and Marilyn Monroe to Harriet Nelson and June Cleaver: the sex kitten or the angel. The relative freedom women experienced in the workplace and the music world during World War II quickly disappeared when the GIs came home. Economic conditions were never better than in the fifties, and memories of Depression-era deprivation faded. In many households it was no longer necessary for women to work. All this meant attitudes toward women jazz musicians, especially horn players, were more hostile than ever.

But Melba Liston could no more stop creating music than she could stop breathing, regardless of what society told her she was supposed to do. In 1956, Dizzy "Birks" Gillespie lured her back into playing (she had never ceased writing and arranging) on a tour of the Middle East for the State Department. Always Melba's champion, Dizzy had called her in California to say he wanted her to play the tour and to be sure to bring her arrangements. Then he told his New York-based band that he was hiring the best person for the job. The band's response epitomized the ingrained assumptions and prejudice women jazz musicians constantly faced. When Melba arrived at the first rehearsal, they verbally made their displeasure known. Melba told the story to author Linda Dahl. "They said, 'Goddamn Birks, you sent all the way to California for a *bitch*?'" Dizzy told them that indeed he had, and that they were going to start with her arrangements, and that he didn't want to hear any mistakes. "And of course they got about two measures in and fell out and got all confused and stuff." Known for writing intricate rhythms and close, dense harmonies reminiscent of Ellington charts, Melba had the ability to make a few instruments sound like many. Her arrangements quickly transcended any musical prejudice. "After that they were calling me Mama again."[21]

She played with Dizzy at the Newport Jazz Festival in 1957 and recorded with Art Blakey and the Jazz Messengers that same year. In 1958, she produced her only album as a leader, *Melba and Her Bones*, and began a forty-year collaboration with Randy Weston. In 1959 Quincy Jones brought Melba into his band as both a player and arranger for a European tour. She wrote—as a ghostwriter—for Motown. She became the house arranger for Riverside Records. Her arrangements enhanced the careers of artists as varied as Johnny Griffin, Milt Jackson, Abbey Lincoln, Diana Ross, Marvin Gaye, and Tony Bennett. She played with Charles Mingus at his 1962 Town Hall Concert.

Now at the peak of her career, she defied employment odds and won over the musical minds of a generation. Critics and other players tried to analyze her writing style, but that only amused her. "I like it and I write it. It's very simple."[22]

If anyone had told her in 1959 that she was helping to lay the foundation of a movement that would speak out for women's rights, she might have scoffed. She didn't play and write music to prove a point, although it had never occurred to her that her music wasn't equal to anyone else's. But she was still very much a woman of the pre-World War II generation. When her fellow band members asked her to cut their hair and sew buttons on their gig shirts, she was happy to oblige. She was creating, enhancing, and preserving art. She fought only for the music and the respect it commanded. To Melba Liston's way of thinking, "If it wasn't for the women there wouldn't be no culture a-tall."[23]

The More I See You

The baby began wailing for attention again on Friday, March 23, 1979, as the second year got under way. Starting with Leonard Feather's presentation of vintage jazz movies, the Friday night collegiate and high school concert, and Signboard jam session, the festival continued on Saturday with clinics and more jam sessions at Crown Center. Following the format of the previous year, the 1979 clinicians were an eclectic gathering of top-notch players and educators: Joanne Brackeen, piano; Monnette Sudler, guitar; Sue Evans, percussion; Carol Kaye, electric bass; and Dr. Karen Fanta Zumbrunn, improvisation. To accommodate more audience members, each clinician presented two workshops this year, one for beginners and one for professionals.

The ever popular jam session, which ran from 4:00 p.m. on Saturday until 1:00 a.m. Sunday, was fronted this year by the local, almost all-female group, Airhart. Drummer Ira Wilkes joined Patti Breitag on alto sax and keyboards, Joan Griffith on bass, and Jerri Johnson on vibes and percussion. With plenty of opportunity to display their chops, the three women dissipated any myths about the lack of staying power in female musicians. Along with Wilkes they held command of the eight-hour gig. Despite the spontaneity inherent in a jam session format, Airhart provided consistency of quality.[24]

As a special treat, Big Apple Women in Jazz, the traveling branch of Cobi Narita's Salute to Women in Jazz, performed between jam sessions. With bassist Carline Ray acting as musical director and Cobi as emcee, the sixteen-piece group exploded with New York energy on tunes ranging from "I Can't Get Started" to a bluesy "You Promised." Evelyn Blakey, a pediatric paramedic and Art Blakey's daughter, sang what Leonard Feather called "a satirical quasi-blues" feature, "Put on a March for My Dime." Jane Ira Bloom, who had stolen the audience's attention away from band leader John Lyman at the Signboard jam the night before, set the crowd clapping along on "C Jam Blues." Jane Ira's original, "Dorian Blues," a fast tempo, contemporary piece written specifically for the festival, proved a highlight of the evening. Although not all the band members were professional musicians, and all volunteered to come to Kansas City, the overall effect was one of enthusiasm and sisterhood. The entire group, which consisted of Amina Myers and Jill McManus on piano, Barbara Merjan and Paula Hampton on drums, saxophonist Jean Fineberg and flutist Barbara London, Nancy Hildegarde Pratt and Jean Davis on trumpet, vocalist Janet Lawson, and the vocal quartet Joy Spring, as well as Carline Ray, Evelyn Blakey, and Jane Ira Bloom, closed their set with a wailing blend of "Anthropology" and "Oleo."

Like Carol and Dianne, Cobi Narita listened to her heart's logic more than to critics. She saw that a showcase for women jazz musicians was needed, so she organized one. She told author Linda Dahl. "I felt that women needed something like that Kansas City Women's Jazz Festival to give them an opportunity to show that they can play."[25] The first Salute to Women in Jazz took place in New York City on June 26, 1978.

Not a player herself, Cobi fell in love with jazz from listening to the radio. Although this California-born, Japanese American spent much of her teenage years in the World War II Gila River Detention Camp in Arizona, it didn't diminish her spirit and strong ambition. She started the camp's newsletter as a way of keeping everyone there connected. "It was in my cultural background never to complain."[26] Besides the newsletter, Cobi started a debating society, a theatrical company, and a jazz group.

During the two decades after the war, Cobi went to college, married, had seven children, divorced, and worked for The International Council of Shopping Centers in the marketing department. After a time, they sent her and her family to New York City.

On her first weekend in New York City, in 1966, Cobi struck up a conversation with some jazz musicians playing in Central Park, which led to a volunteer job with an outreach program for jazz musicians, which led to her job as executive director of Collective Black Artists.[27] She thrived for two years before the board of directors decided "a male black person should be in that job."[28]

Never one to be deterred from a new opportunity, Cobi won a scholarship to study new community activist techniques at MIT and moved to Boston. Armed with new ideas and a renewed spirit, she returned to New York and founded Universal Jazz Coalition. Paul Ash, brother of music storeowner Sam Ash, joined her there and much later became Cobi's husband. Enlisting jazz giants Dizzy Gillespie, Herbie Hancock, Art Blakey, Dave Brubeck, Clark Terry, George Wein, Leonard Feather, Nat Hentoff, Dr. Robert Moog, Mary Lou Williams, and others for her coalition board, Cobi set out to provide places to play and opportunities for education. She organized workshops, set up lectures on self-promotion and the business end of music, and even hired a "house band" for singers to practice with so they could receive constructive criticism.

It didn't take long to see that women players were often overlooked. "A lot of women have 'made it,' a lot of women are 'making it' now, but a lot of others don't get the opportunity to perform as much as they should."[29] Disturbed by this obvious inequality, she felt the next logical step was to do something about it.

Cobi's ideas for a women's jazz festival in New York began taking shape in January 1978. "There was no list of women artists or list of special women to be honored. The list came about because of interest expressed by musicians and music listeners both, with people calling in with names and/or telephone numbers of artists, or telling each other about an artist who should be contacted."[30] By June the lineup included, among many others, Jane Ira Bloom, Patti Bown, Barbara Carroll, Jay Clayton, Sharon Freeman, Alberta

Hunter, Sheila Jordan, Jill McManus, Janice Robinson, Hazel Scott, Carline Ray, Lynn Milano, Marian McPartland, Nina Sheldon, Maxine Sullivan, and Mary Lou Williams.

Halfway through the four-night festival, Salute to Women in Jazz was almost aborted. Cobi had rented Casablanca, the midtown club that had once been Birdland, for all four evenings. After the second night the club owner was in no mood to say "play it again." With standing-room-only crowds, he decided he needed a larger cut of the profits and changed the contract for the remaining two nights. Cobi and the Coalition refused to accept his new terms, so when the musicians and audience arrived, they found themselves locked out. Paul Ash, at this point not only deeply involved in the organization but Cobi's gallant fiancé as well, approached the owner of a parking garage next door. Using the garage's power, they turned the festival loose in the street. Because instruments were locked inside Casablanca, Sam Ash also helped save the day by sending over instruments from his store. Roseland loaned them a truckload of folding chairs. The spontaneous atmosphere added to the excitement and turned the night into a jazz party.[31] Janice Robinson remembers Mary Lou Williams sitting on a crate eating beans and rice.[32] The solidarity of these women musicians playing for the sheer joy of it and each other made the evening as comfortable as a backyard barbeque.

But they were to have their elegant evening as well. When George Wein arrived and heard what had happened to their original venue, perhaps chagrined at losing Marian McPartland's 1977 challenge to produce a night of women players at the Newport Jazz Festival, he donated Carnegie Hall's Recital Hall for the next night. "Wasn't that nice!"[33] Cobi remarked to reporters.

The Universal Jazz Coalition went on to support countless musicians, male and female, throughout the eighties. Each June until 1987, they sponsored the Salute to Women in Jazz. A new generation of female musicians grew up with that June promise.

Sax player Carol Sudhalter summed it up. "It's a tremendous thing that Cobi did, a pioneering thing that gave women a chance for the exposure they needed, deserved, and might not otherwise have gotten."[34]

Big Apple Women in Jazz was the most ear-catching and visible all-women band at the Kansas City festival, and Airhart was the hometown favorite, but they were by no means the only ones. Joy Spring, the four-piece vocal group cocooned inside the Big Apple Women's band, consisted of Carmen Barnes, Lionelle Hamanaka, Hazziezah Hazziez, and Nancie Manzuk. Their depth and blend in "Little Willie Leaps" and Clifford Brown's tune "Joy Spring," from which they took their name, added fresh perspective and character to the set's diverse mix.

Some groups, such as Ad Lib from Houston, came to jam and listen. They felt the opportunity to play with and listen to musicians from all over the country was so advantageous, they got their local union to underwrite the cost of the trip.

Of course there was a sense of sisterhood and discovering together with friends and strangers alike that they were opening a new chapter of musical history. But the vibe went far beyond that. The music, the sounds that reached out to each individual as they vined their way through Crown Center, bound souls and opened hearts. Faceless, genderless, everywhere and in everyone, the music was all there was.

Building on the success of the first Women's Jazz Festival, the 1979 festival included a Combo Contest. Fourteen combos from nine states submitted audition tapes to the WJF board and competed for the coveted first spot on the Sunday night performance. The winner, Aerial, a New York City-based female quartet, shimmering with new musical possibilities, opened the Sunday night program with "strong imaginative harmonies that swung ferociously."[35]

The group, led by pianist Nina Sheldon, had come together specifically to try out for the WJF contest. Nina told Shifra Stein, "We still haven't achieved the amount of technical expertise we are capable of, but that's only because we haven't been performing together very long."[36] Nina, bassist Carline Ray, drummer Barbara Merjan, and flutist Barbara London had met the summer before at the Salute to Women in Jazz festival. All but Nina played in Cobi Narita's Saturday night Crown Center Big Apple Women in Jazz concert. This was their first major public performance, save one. After hearing Aerial's audition tape, Carol and Dianne had written a letter of recommendation for them to play at the National Association of Jazz Educators (NAJE) convention in Philadelphia earlier that month. That initial outing had gone so well, Irv Kratka of Inner City Records[37] approached them to make a record.

In a letter to Carol a week before the festival, Nina said she was looking forward "with glee" to meeting everyone and being a part of the weekend festivities.[38] She elaborated for the *Star*: "It's inspiring to know that musicians like myself will have an opportunity to reach an audience and critics that we might never have reached before. Besides, nothing makes me happier than meeting other women who can really play. It just knocks me out."[39]

There was plenty of reason to be knocked out by her bandmates. Carline Ray, who performed with Mary Lou Williams at WJF the year before, had spent over thirty years building a stellar reputation in concert halls, recording studios, and clubs where she played with the International Sweethearts of Rhythm, Benny Powell, Erskine Hawkins, and Joe Newman. The addition of Barbara London's flute gave Aerial's sound a refreshing color and balance. Her outstanding technique and warm tone, which her original compositions gave advantage to, wove the group together. She had previously played with Richard Davis, Joe Newman, and Jill McManus. As the youngest member of Aerial, drummer Barbara Merjan, a student at Ithaca College, was a rising star. A student of Joe LaBarbera, she had already played with Jay Clayton and Janet Lawson.[40]

The set started off with Cedar Walton's "Ugetsu," followed by Emmy Kemp's heartfelt ballad "Tomorrow's Woman" sung by Carline Ray, at Kemp's request. Written in the style of a Broadway show tune, Carline's rich throaty tones told the audience, "I'm writing this song for all my sisters." Leonard Feather told his *Down Beat* readers that the tune "symbolized the spirit of the entire festival."[41]

Getting comfortable with their groove, they launched into Nina's original tune "Aerial." The melody flew along as if on its own sparked current of joy, with just a flavor of "Return to Forever," proving author Linda Dahl's assessment. "[Nina's] playing is characterized by layers of airy runs built by her right hand while her left hand feeds firm rhythmic chords. She is also noted for her witty melodic compositions."[42]

Leonard Feather stated in his introduction of Barbara London that he didn't like it when he heard her described as a female Hubert Laws. "She is herself, definitely a person and stylist in her own right. Barbara London is a real discovery."[43] Aerial closed out their set with a Barbara London original, "Superflutity," a flute feature that proved his assertion without a doubt.

Being compared to male counterparts was only one of the sexist challenges all female jazz players faced in the seventies. Nina was very forthcoming about others. Although by 1979 she had already played with Sonny Stitt, George Coleman, Woody Shaw, and Bobby Hackett and had been leader of the house trio at the Village Gate for three years, she fought the same discrimination battles over and over. "Not only does a woman have to know how to play as well as her male contemporaries, but she has to be so good—so special and so much better—that she'll be called on to perform regardless of her sex."[44]

Nina worked her way into incredible opportunities. "I was trying to stand up with the big boys."[45] She felt she had to grab the chances given her, even if it meant a variety of uncomfortable situations on the stand. Sometimes it was a condescending musician or a hostile club employee. At one of her first professional gigs Nina asked the bartender what she should wear, and he just said, "Show your tits."[46]

But Aerial's music and their (clothed) exposure to the jazz scene were helping to change the paradigm. When George Wein heard the group in New York after their NAJE and WJF gigs, and after the addition of Jane Ira Bloom, he signed them up to play at the 1979 Newport Jazz Festival—the first women's group to do so.[47]

Shifra Stein said it best. "The group's capabilities seemed unlimited."[48]

You and the Night and the Music

No one could claim that WJF's lineup was narrow-minded. Already that weekend, audiences had attended collegiate concerts, workshop performances by top jazz educators, a grass-roots concert of New York women, a Sunday afternoon Gospel Songfest of local gospel choirs and soloists, also held at Crown Center's International Café, and a set introducing a quartet of very talented women setting a new bar of possibilities. But nothing compared to what came next on the Sunday night lineup.

Richie Morales's up-tempo drum intro to the first tune, Kenny Kirkland's "Shenkansen," set the level of anticipation as if he were waiting for the perfect moment to release the kaleidoscopic, psychedelic, kinetic force that was Urszula Dudziak. Her husband Michal Urbaniak's electric violin, Kenny Kirkland's synthesizer, and Marcus Miller's electric bass blended with Urszula's exquisite voice, both acoustically and enhanced by a ring modulator and echoplex, to create a type of "Future Talk," the name of their album released just the month before.[49]

Urszula, a thirty-five-year-old native of Staconka, Poland, with a four-and-a-half octave range, had started singing as a teenager after hearing a Radio Free Europe broadcast of Ella Fitzgerald. Although she sang acoustic jazz when first touring Europe, trouble with languages and a fascination with new electronic possibilities prompted her to create her own vocabulary of rhythmic syllables. Shifra Stein called it "vocal pyrotechnics."[50] Linda Dahl said Urszula's singing could "scrape the stratosphere" when she was traveling on her "ethereal excursions."[51]

In 1973, *Jazz Forum* named Urszula "Best Female Vocalist"; in 1975 she was "Most Promising Female Vocalist" in *Down Beat's* Critics Poll; and Leonard Feather honored her as "Woman of the Year" in 1977.[52] Her abandonment of lyrics in favor of accented growls and screeches, as well as soaring adventurous melodies, transcended scat. Frequently it was difficult to tell where her voice, with its impeccable intonation, left off and Michal's violin began.

Throughout their set of originals, all featured on *Future Talk*, the Polish pair's unique style was bellied by the rhythm section's contemporary yet not-quite-fusion accompaniment. It wasn't all a musical acrobatic circus. After flying to the stratosphere, the group settled down to a delicate little swing tune, written by Urbaniak for the couple's young daughter, entitled simply, "Kasia's Dance."[53]

The couple's exotic appearance added to the mood. Urbaniak's long dark hair and droopy mustache and Urszula's peasant dress and her flowing hair accented with tiny braids, glistening with light, visually defined the gypsy sounds incorporated in their electric jazz.

Dianne remembers being charmed by the down-to-earth manner of the talented couple. They had traveled to Kansas City with Urszula's mother and their baby daughter and were proud of the bargain airfare they had arranged. "I remember them saying they had saved us money by getting 'Super-saver' tickets."[54]

They were even forgiven for going past their allotted time, always a concern for festival planners. Carol tells the story:

> Kansas City had never heard anything like it. The place went absolutely wild. But we were already running long and we really didn't want to have to pay stagehands overtime. But Urszula didn't get off the stand because the audience was loving the band and they were loving the audience. Finally we had to give the cue to the board member backstage to cut the lights. It broke the spell and the house fell dead silent. Then very softly we heard, "do-ka-chick-a, chick-a." Urszula told the audience she liked the effect. We gave up.[55]

At the end of the set, emcee Feather came out and announced, tongue in cheek, that if audience members sent a self-addressed stamped envelope to Post Office Box 1979, Warsaw, Poland, they could get back the translation of all Urszula's lyrics.[56]

No one could have ended the first half of the concert with more grace than Marian McPartland. She brought the adrenaline-charged vibe of the crowd back down to earth and replaced it with the cozy intimacy of a club. Accompanied only by the magnificent bassist Brian Torff, who had played with her at the festival the year before, Marian seemed to caress the Bösendorfer into singing just the nuances and shadings she wanted. Diane Lewis, of the *Wichita Eagle and Beacon*, told her readers that "her personal joy in the turn of a musical phrase can be felt in the first balcony."[57] It was as inspiring to watch Marian play as it was to listen to her.

Stripping the sound down to piano and bass made Marian's harmonic brilliance pure and clean. Torff, who at twenty-five had already toured with Cleo Laine and Mary Lou Williams besides Marian, had been coached by the best on how to blend his accompaniment without losing his voice. Leonard Feather called his playing "astonishing."[58]

The duo opened with "You and the Night and the Music," followed by Herbie Hancock's lovely "Tell Me a Bedtime Story." Marian introduced her two original tunes—"Time and Time Again" and "Silent Pool"—in a friendly, relaxed manner, as if she had just dashed them off and was trying them out before a group of friends. She made a point of telling the audience that "Lullaby of the Leaves," which featured Torff, was written by female composer Bernice Petkere. With the remaining tunes "Emily" and Duke Ellington's "Cottontail," the set had the effect of a complex, gourmet dish perfectly prepared by practiced, enthusiastic chefs.[59]

"The artistic directions of the players were pretty diverse."[60] That's how Jane Ira Bloom diplomatically assessed what happened after the intermission.

The idea behind the Women's Jazz Festival All-Stars was straightforward enough. Just like men, women should be able to come together in a pick-up ensemble and let the music speak for itself. In 1978, that idea had worked beautifully. As leader, Marian McPartland assembled the players she wanted to play with. But the fact that Marian's Now's the Time rhythm section—Dottie Dodgion, Lynn Milano, and Mary Osborne—provided the core and horn players Janice Robinson and Mary Fettig were protégés of Marian's gave the '78 All-Stars the advantage of familiarity. There were no wild cards. Everyone was comfortable with each other's playing.

A different approach was used the second year. In April of 1978, the WJF board compiled a list of possible All-Stars and voted. Whoever received the most votes per instrument was contacted for the gig. This system, although fair, didn't take into account styles and personalities. The results led to WJF's first real discord.[61]

Jane Ira Bloom was one of the first musicians contacted for the '79 All-Stars. This twenty-four-year-old Berklee School of

Music and Yale graduate had impressed everyone who heard her at the 1978 jam sessions. She had come to Kansas City after seeing a notice about WJF in *Down Beat*. "I came on my own for the opportunity to meet other musicians and to play in new settings."[62] In the WJF program, Carol Comer described her playing this way: "Jane mounted the stage in March '78 and proceeded to blow the walls down with her superlative technical facility and originality."[63] Having received her masters in music only two years before, Jane Ira had already worked with George Coleman, the Mercer Ellington orchestra, Sheila Jordan, and Jay Clayton. By 1979 she was listed in *Down Beat's* poll of Talent Deserving Wider Recognition.[64] Nat Hentoff wrote of the finesse of her clear, full sound.

Even as Jane Ira's list of accolades grew she felt "there was covert discrimination, phone calls that didn't come, opportunities that didn't arrive and should have. And in the 1970s, anyway, the young artists weren't being recorded, and it was hard for any of us to get hired in clubs. So I had to develop my own direction."[65]

That direction was born of a concentrated focus on the pure sound of the soprano sax and how it could be altered by motion. What some called "idiosyncratic gyrations on stage" Jane Ira called "Doppler-like arcing motions." She even got her sometimes-bass player, Kent McLagan, to design a velocity sensor she could attach to the end of her bell that intertwined motion with sound. Jane Ira's developing style was intellectual and contemporary, visionary and sincere.[66]

Of the four drummers receiving votes on the '79 All-Stars ballot, Sue Evans got twice as many as anyone else.[67] Because of her wide range of experience and exposure, many of the board members had some knowledge of her playing. At twenty-seven, she had the distinction of being recognized three times by the *Down Beat* Talent Deserving Wider Recognition poll (1975, 1977, 1978).[68] She had toured with Judy Collins as well as the Gil Evans Orchestra, recorded with Hubert Laws, Jeremy Steig, and Lee Ritenour, and at Radio

City Music Hall, she backed Sammy Davis Jr., Nancy Wilson, and Barry White. She was first call sub for many Broadway shows. She had also worked with Steve Kuhn, Urbie Green, George Benson, Art Farmer, and Roswell Rudd's Jazz Composers Orchestra.[69] She also got calls as an extra from the New York Philharmonic, the Brooklyn Philharmonic, and the New Jersey Symphony Orchestra. "If I had to choose one thing that has helped to make me successful, it would be the variety of things I do."[70]

Although Sue had a reputation in the jazz world of playing "with authority and taste,"[71] she was thought of by other players as primarily a commercial world percussionist and studio player.[72]

"Janice Robinson told me about the WJF, and she must have told them about me,"[73] says guitarist Monnette Sudler. She was the only guitarist the WJF board considered for the '79 All-Stars.[74]

Monnette remembers friends of her step-dad playing guitars at her house when she was a teenager and being smitten with the sound. She asked them to teach her to play, but because they played by ear, they declined. Curious, she asked friends and her Aunt Marlene how to find jazz on the radio and began listening to everything she could. She was particularly drawn to the music of Yusef Lateef, John Coltrane, and Wayne Shorter. "I guess I should have been a sax player,"[75] she quips.

Monnette's mother discouraged her from playing guitar—she was already taking piano lessons—because she didn't want Monnette to end up in a rock & roll band. "Until we saw Jobim on television. I said, 'See, guitar can do that too.' After that my mother was better with my decision to be a professional guitarist."[76]

Throughout the seventies, Monnette attended Berklee and Comb's College in Philadelphia, but frequent, extended gigs, first with vibist Khan Jamal's group, halted her academic career. She also performed with Byard Lancaster, Sunny Murray, and Sam Rivers. At the 1976 Newport Jazz Festival, she appeared with Rivers, Dave Holland, and drummer Warren Smith.[77]

"I played with mostly men," she says. "I never played with just women except in Kansas City. Musicians never made me feel patronized, although some promoters did. Promoters sometimes felt women would be a lot of trouble on the road. On a Berlin tour once, a promoter told me, 'Everyone said you would be a lot of trouble, but you're no trouble at all. It's the guys who are getting on my nerves.'"[78]

Linda Dahl wrote that "Sudler tends to the meditative and reflective, playing in the octaves style first formulated by Wes Montgomery."[79] Shifra Stein referred to her "rock-like sound."[80] Later Monnette was identified as the guitarist hired "anywhere they wanted a guitarist with an attitude full of sass and an angelic smile to soften the edge."[81] As a '79 All-Star, her style was a work in progress.

The veteran electric bassist Carol Kaye holds the distinction of being the most recorded bass player, male or female. Not only can she be heard on records such as Barbra Streisand's *The Way We Were*, Sonny and Cher's *The Beat Goes On*, and Isaac Hayes's *Shaft*, she's also on the soundtracks of *Butch Cassidy and the Sundance Kid*, *Sweet Charity*, *The Poseidon Adventure*, *The Thomas Crown Affair*, and *Airport*. She did extensive studio work for television in the sixties and seventies as well. She's credited as the bass player for *Mission Impossible*, *M*A*S*H*, *Get Smart*, *Hogan's Heroes*, *The Love Boat*, *Peyton Place*, *Lost in Space*, *The Brady Bunch*, and *Soap*, to name a few.[82]

Nowhere was she more entrenched than in the pop music recording scene. Although she built her reputation playing jazz, then studio guitar, with artists such as Sonny and Cher, Ed Ames, Shelly Fabares, Wayne Newton, Sam Cooke, and Herb Alpert,[83] in 1963 she switched to bass to help out at a Capitol Records session when the bass player didn't show up. "I'd been in the studio doing guitar dates for five years, always thinking I'd have played the bass parts differently, and now I had my chance. It was fun to groove, and feel that power and responsibility as the basement of the band, so I started even a heavier work schedule playing electric bass from 1963 on."[84] Because she applied her pick technique to the bass, she became known as the "chick with the pick." She did extensive studio recordings with The Beach Boys, including *Pet Sounds*. She recorded with Lou Rawls, Joe Cocker, Glen Campbell, Nancy Sinatra, The Righteous Brothers, Quincy Jones, Mel Torme, Frank Zappa, Cannonball Adderley, and Lalo Schifrin. As a first-call studio musician, Carol backed countless big-name groups, sometimes without credit. The many records she played on for Motown in L.A. led to controversy about credit. "Mostly we got paid in cash—good money, just in cash. Everyone did those dates non-union, . . . but the music was certainly much better than the surf-rock stuff we were all cutting by then." The lack of a paper trail made it difficult to prove who played what. Regardless, Carol is credited with over 10,000 pop, jazz, and movie recording sessions.[85]

Because throughout this time she was supporting her three children and her mother, she took all the gigs she could, except those on the road. "George Shearing asked me also to join his group, but when you have a family, . . . you don't want to lose money by going on the road, not even with the great George Shearing, so I had to turn him down."[86]

Although she enjoyed "doing the movie calls from 1963 on . . . recording every day, playing side-by-side with the greatest musicians in Hollywood . . . playing the scores of great composers,"[87] she missed playing jazz. "I resumed my jazz career in the 1970s doing concerts with Joe Pass, and later with Hampton Hawes while purposely cutting down on studio work, never doing rock dates again, only working movies and TV film for genius-composers and record dates of my own choosing with Mancini, Ray Charles, etc. in the 1970s so I could play real music again."[88] In his *Encyclopedia of Jazz in the Seventies*, Leonard Feather refers to Carol's "full, clear sound and exceptional technique."[89] She could cover it all.

WJF board members "discovered" pianist Dr. Karen Fanta Zumbrunn during a 1978 jam session. What first impressed them was the way "Karen took total command of the stage when she began to play."[90] She had extensive, and geographically expansive, academic credentials that had taken her from Ohio to Harvard to California to Paris. She was the only All-Star pianist on the 1979 ballot.[91]

Although Karen hadn't played with big name groups, now at thirty-nine, she had very successfully straddled the academic and jazz worlds. She had played in a variety of clubs, including the Blue Note in Paris. She led house bands or did solo gigs. Whether the bandleader or professor, she was usually in charge. Her degrees were in music education, where she broke ground as a jazz lecturer and clinician. Her most popular clinic was on improvisation and the role of each instrument in a jazz combo. This was the clinic she presented at WJF 1979.[92]

WJF was always a work in progress, adapting to whatever board members thought would best promote the art form and please fans, but encouraging new female talent was consistently at the top of the list of goals. WJF was a platform for exposure. A spot with the All-Stars could be the looked for break. That's what the board offered Dr. Karen when they contracted her for the All-Star band.

Add to this interesting mix Melba Liston's comeback. Still apprehensive about becoming vulnerable again in a business that had burned her more than once, Melba agreed only to play with the All-Stars. Those who hoped to see her at jam sessions were disappointed. A Melba Liston clinic on jazz arranging remained unrealized as the shy trombone player focused on ensemble playing.[93]

Carol Kaye remembers having long talks that weekend with Melba about their careers. Quincy Jones had spoken glowingly about both of them to each other, and they had plenty of notes to compare. One of their more revealing conversations was about their Motown experiences. Carol knew she had been hired as a ghost-player, but she hadn't realized it worked on the arranging end too. "Melba told me some fascinating stories about ghost-writing the very Motown arrangements that Gene Page had conducted on our Motown dates. [He] used to make us laugh on the dates as he looked at the music like he never saw it before in his life, couldn't answer questions about the music, except with 'ahhh' or 'ohhh,' and then couldn't find the spot we'd ask about. After staying up half the night with Melba talking about those recording dates, I knew why. Motown had her in the back room, supplying her with whatever she needed, writing those arrangements day and night. I was out front recording them. This included some of the greatest hits with Stevie Wonder, The Supremes, The Four Tops, and The Miracles. But we had never met."[94]

Both women were hidden parts of the process, but their Motown experience taught them to respect the art, if not everyone in it, and to focus on presenting themselves as professionals. "The music note knows no gender," Carol states. "As long as you're professional, that's all that counts. Being a fine musician solves 99.99999% of any problems, and not attacking the men, or feeling sorry for yourself too." [95] Melba had spent six months convincing herself that she was ready to be a part of the performing world again, even the distasteful parts. If she trusted the musical instincts of those she played with and kept it about the music, everything would be fine. Carol's words were just the pep talk she needed.

"I was seeing to last minute details that Sunday afternoon when I got the call," Dianne recalls. "It was Linda Whitaker, our board member who was in charge of artists getting their rehearsal time. She just said, 'You better get over here. We have a problem.' We already knew Melba was apprehensive about the gig. We had been cajoling her for six months. But when I got over to the hall, I found out it was much worse than that."[96]

The All-Stars had an hour to run through their chosen tunes for tempos and form. None of them had played together before. They represented two different generations and six different styles. Although they all had jazz as a common denominator, it wasn't an effortless mix. Right away Dr. Karen took over, to the surprise of veterans Carol Kaye and Melba Liston.

"We had a terrible time with her," says Carol Kaye. "Melba and I just rolled our eyes when that teacher/pianist tried to teach us where the coda was and other petty things."[97]

Dianne found Melba profoundly upset. "She was threatening to walk."[98] She, along with Carol Kaye, was displeased not only with Karen's bossy attitude but with her playing. It was over-powering and loud with no sign of the finesse that someone who lectured about ensemble playing should incorporate into her own playing. No doubt Karen was nervous too, playing with two heavyweights and three up-and-comers the same age as her students, but the last thing the group needed was a teacher.

Hastily, plans were changed. Dianne and Carol Comer consulted with Marian McPartland and came up with a solution for the concert. After the first tune, Monnette Sudler's aptly named original "Transitions," in which Melba would only play on the head, Marian replaced Karen on piano, and Barbara Merjan, who had already played with Nina Sheldon and Aerial, replaced Sue Evans. The group was reduced to a trio to accompany Melba on her featured tunes. Whether the extensive personnel changes were part of Marian's terms or Melba's is unclear. Most of the audience was none the wiser.[99]

Not so Leonard Feather. He announced the personnel changes from the stage, but told his *Down Beat* readers, "One wonders why they [Jane Ira Bloom, Monnette Sudler, Sue Evans, and Karen Fanta Zumbrunn] were brought so far to play one number."[100] He answered his own question. "The attempt to mount an all-female Jazz Festival All-Star group failed to come off, mainly because the rhythm section didn't jell." He attributed this to a drummer who thought like a percussionist and to Dr. Karen's insensitivity and "heavy-handedness."[101]

Now secure with a rhythm section she could trust, in front of a hometown crowd that already loved her, Melba made her trombone sing. Although she started out her set "gingerly,"[102] she soon got her gig-legs and gave the audience a helping of what Clark Terry, Quincy Jones, Dizzy Gillespie, and Randy Weston had dug so much about Melba's playing.

Slower than normal tempos on "Donna Lee," "Night in Tunisia," "Come Sunday," and "Morning Glory" gave Melba an opportunity to stretch out without technical demands and make the most of her gutsy tone, swinging hard the whole time. "She was having the time of her life," Dianne remembers. "Look at the pictures. She's radiant."[103]

Although there had been a minimal amount of disruption to the concert's pacing, it was an unsettling experience for Dr. Karen. Ironically, as a teenager Karen had first decided that she wanted to be a jazz piano player after hearing Marian McPartland perform live. Now her idol was usurping her. Carol Kaye remembers arriving at the sound check and seeing the educator off in a corner crying. "There she was bawling her eyes out, because she was only playing one tune with us. You never cry over something, you act PROFESSIONAL no matter what."[104] Carol felt strongly that first you become the best musician you possibly can, and then you show no weakness. In her clinic the day before, she had said, "You've got to be able to cut it with the best, and cut it so that the best will reach down and help you." Carol's tough love approach turned into an unexpected lesson for the doctor. "They'll nail you if you can't make it," she told clinic attendees, "and you get toughened up that way."[105]

Carmen McRae paced irritably backstage. The concert was running quite late and she was getting impatient for her set to start. Board member Linda Whitaker, assigned to take care of Carmen's needs, cheerfully told the matriarch of song, "Well, you know they always save the best for last." Carmen took Linda's face in both of her hands and sweetly cooed, "Bullshit, Baby."[106]

Carmen took command of the stage with all the grace and charm that made her the consummate performer, a singer's singer. All signs of impatience dissolved, she wasted no time launching into an up-tempo version of "If I Were a Bell." Along with her trio—Marshall Otwell, piano; Ed Bennett, bass; and Frank Severino, drums—her singing reminded the crowd why standards are so timeless. Almost without stopping, she sang "Yesterdays," "On Green Dolphin Street," and "The Night Has a Thousand Eyes." After some light banter about how happy she was to be back in Kansas City for such an important event, she sang "The Masquerade" "Autumn Nocturne," and "No More Blues."[107]

Leonard Feather wrote in his *Down Beat* review that Carmen McRae was almost beyond criticism.[108] Although she swung, and swung hard, and played her voice like the quality instrument it was, some in the audience felt it was too professional, almost cold. Her set lacked spontaneity and flexibility. The late hour and a restless crowd (those Memorial Hall seats were hard) no doubt played into this. It wasn't until she sat down at the piano and explained that she wanted to play and sing a couple of tunes for them that the audience warmed up. "I'd like to do something I really have a lot of nerve doing, because there have been some heavyweights up here on this stage and sitting at that piano. And I'm going to sit there. Just remember, I ain't no piano player, you understand."[109] She closed her set with "More Than You Know" and "This Is the End of a Beautiful Friendship," and as she walked off the stage, everyone there felt she had left a little bit of herself with them.

"Her recent efforts [show Joanne Brackeen's will be] as important to the 1980s as Herbie Hancock's and Bill Evans's were to the 1960s and McCoy Tyner's and Keith Jarrett's were to the 1970s."[110]

The hour was late. The crowd was thinning. But all those who stayed for the last set knew what Leonard Feather was talking about. Joanne Brackeen and her extraordinary sidemen, Eddie Gomez and Billy Hart, promised to fulfill Leonard's bold statement. A native of Ventura, California, the largely self-taught Joanne—her college career at the Los Angeles Conservatory of Music lasted three days—learned to play by listening to records and spending long hours transcribing Frankie Carle solos note for note. She traded the classroom for L.A. clubs, where her "professors," Dexter Gordon and Harold Land, let her sit in. She designed her own advanced seminars by transcribing the solos of Charlie Parker, John Coltrane, and Bud Powell.

In 1960, when Joanne was twenty-two, she married saxophonist Charles Brackeen and had four children in almost as many years. While her children were young, she stopped going to clubs and performing, but Joanne never stopped writing music and practicing. "I was never a careerist. . . . My attitude was that I played just for the fun of it."[111] When the couple moved to New York City in 1965, she found the New York jazz scene "much more stimulating than the West Coast."[112] Always drawn to the avant-garde, she loved the experimentation and openness she heard.

Linda Dahl explains how this total focus on listening propelled her into the Art Blakey group—literally. "She was sitting in the audience at Slug's, a Lower East Side jazz club, listening to Blakey's group. The pianist was so lost, because the music was too difficult for him, that he stopped playing. Joanne got on the bandstand. When Blakey looked up, he saw her playing the piano. 'After that we went to Japan,' Joanne recalled."[113] She played with the Jazz Messengers for three years.

From 1972 to 1975, she was Joe Henderson's pianist, and from 1975 to 1977, she worked with Stan Getz (along with Gomez and Hart). As much as Joanne loved playing with Getz and the fact that he encouraged her to stretch out into her experimental style, after a couple of years she was ready to immerse herself in her own music. "Different songs are like babies, and I feel better playing one that I created and nurtured than one I adopted, no matter how good it is."[114]

At Bill Evans's suggestion, his agent, Helen Keane, who hadn't planned on another pianist client, took over the management of Joanne's career. "It was exciting for me," Helen told Leslie Gourse. "I loved her work, because she was so different, something new. Technically, melodically, and harmonically, she had it all together."[115]

Joanne's music is full of complicated and complex time changes that collaborate with the rest of the rhythm section. "My music uses rhythm as its basis and demands a lot from the bassist and drummer. It's nothing that I necessarily plan. It just happens when I write." Her musical affinity with bassist Eddie Gomez ran deep. "With Eddie the music comes so naturally, and we have this strong inner feeling on stage. I can play anything I want and he's ready for it. We can move and weave while maintaining the structure."[116]

The Joanne Brackeen Trio's abbreviated set of three tunes took the second annual Women's Jazz Festival right up to the midnight curfew. Five hours of intense, diversified, enlightening jazz showcased an amazing array of musical talent that just happened to be female. Still, the musical interrupt-us of Joanne's set left the audience wanting more.

Chapter 4

The Third Year

March 20-23 1980

"I'd never hire a chick to play in my band."
—Buddy Rich

WHEN THE BOARD MET ON APRIL 1 to assess the second WJF, there was good news and bad. That the festival was a success was undeniable. Fans and performers alike were delighted with the lineup and its diversity. Performers told Carol and Dianne they loved the audience. Unlike the first WJF, the second attracted national media attention from all three major networks (NBC, ABC, CBS), as well as a complete taping for NPR's *Jazz Alive* series. Network and print media sang the praises of excellent clinicians and top-notch school bands, as well as the main acts. No other local arts organization had offered its performers this kind of national exposure. The artists were very vocal about their royal treatment and how much it meant to them to have someone assigned to assist them through the weekend. They couldn't have been happier about their Crown Center accommodations. Urszula and Michal told one board member that it was the best festival they'd ever played. More than one artist told board member Marie Spearing they were amazed with the board's conscientiousness and attention to detail.

Not only the musicians were pleased. A Crown Center director told Mike Ning that the shops at the center had made more money the Saturday afternoon and evening of the festival than ever in the history of Crown Center. Shop owners felt confident that shoppers would come back to the urban shopping complex now that they had had a positive experience there.[1]

But with success came growing pains. As audience members happily left Memorial Hall humming Joanne Brackeen's last tune, *San Diego Union* entertainment writer, Robert P. Laurence, took notes. He concluded that "the Women's Jazz Festival has barely passed its first birthday, but it has already reached the awkward age." Focusing on the Saturday jam sessions held in the atrium lobby of the Crown Center shops, he felt the space was inappropriate for the size of the crowd. Food stands, tables, and potted trees made the space uncomfortable and confined. In the interview, Carol told Laurence that the intent was to keep the sessions intimate and informal. He replied that because of the growth in popularity of the sessions, it was too late for that.

Laurence noted that besides those there to hear the open jam sessions, musicians from dozens of states signed up for a chance to play. Not all were familiar with jam session etiquette. Complaints and frustrations surrounding the sign-up process were audible. Instead of sticking strictly to the order in which players signed up, "the list was often ignored as spots on the stage went to those with the chutzpah to take them." Laurence felt the cramped space made cutting in line easy. Whichever board member was assigned to patrol the sign-up list and keep it organized had an impossible task. All too often those who ignored the sign-up order were men, some who tended to play chorus after chorus. Women who had looked forward to a chance to play with a group—often from towns that didn't have regularly scheduled jam sessions, as Kansas City did—and had traveled hundreds of miles for that chance, sat on the sidelines feeling that once again men had bullied them out of playing.[2]

All of this illustrated the fine line that WJF had drawn for itself. By not wanting to exclude men, was WJF alienating a significant portion of its female fans and players? If it became strictly a women-only event, would it be accused of separatism and hurt its general appeal? A concession to ERA had been made in the choice of the main concert venue being in a state that had passed ERA. No one could doubt WJF's commitment to securing both well-known and emerging female talent. Yet, hardcore feminist groups still argued that the festival was selling out. On the lookout for offensive moments, they even attacked lyrics that suggested—in typical love song fashion—that the vocalist can't live without her man. Some walked out in the middle of Carmen McRae's set as she sang "More Than You Know."

None of this was anything the board wasn't aware of. The Sunday after the second festival, the same day Laurence's article appeared in the *San Diego Union*, their first scheduled post-festival meeting was held. Board member Bill Shapiro had a laundry list of suggested improvements. High on the list was the "lousy" acoustics in the Crown Center shops lobby. Many of the musicians on the board had additional comments about the acoustically inappropriate jam session space. Although there was plenty of viewing space along the two levels of balconies, the architecture was clearly not meant for quality sound production. There was nothing to contain the sound, and the musicians all too often had trouble hearing themselves and the players around them. No one had trouble hearing the crowd. The acoustical situation was all too common in many places that accommodated live music, but board members talked about ways of splitting up the sessions or moving them to ballrooms.

Carol reminded them that the working relationship between the Crown Center shops and WJF was very important to their financial success. Additional ballrooms would not come free. She did feel WJF was "in a position to do a bit of bargaining" because of the business the festival had brought to the shops. At their next meeting with the merchants, they would ask for a better sound system and additional session space. They were pretty sure that at least they could get the potted plants moved.

The male vs. female debate proved more persistent. Marinka Robinson, mother of the now twelve-year-old drummer Scotty, stated, "Young male musicians feel alienated and won't come to [our] concerts or jam sessions." Others countered with the fact that there were plenty of (some thought too many) local, male musicians of varying ages at the sessions, even some who had previously dismissed the idea of women being good enough to play with men. Male, as well as female, musicians received national media attention via the sessions. Mike Ning was even on the *Today* show. But the complaint underscored the need to revamp the sessions. One consideration was to have a session exclusively for women and a second for mixed players. Top priority was to make sure any woman who came to Kansas City for a chance to play at a session got that chance.

But the feelings of discrimination didn't end there. The fact that pianist Phil DeGreg had won the scholarship for the second year in a row disturbed some. When Phil's name was announced during the main concert's intermission, there were audible hisses. Board member Anita Butler asked if it would be possible to make the scholarship available only to women, but Dianne reminded her that would be illegal. To comply with the articles of incorporation and the statement of purpose, they must be careful not to be exclusionary in any way. That worked for both sexes. The scholarship recipient selection process assured anonymity. A code number was assigned to each submission tape before the tapes were distributed to the judges. No one knew Phil had won again until after his tape had been selected in a blind listening review by each judge.

Over one hundred high schools and colleges had received notices about the scholarship contest and follow up calls had been made to jazz band directors and administrators. Advertisements in the National Association of Jazz Educators publication, *Educator*, had reached hundreds of female members. Only nine submissions from five states were received. "You can't yank them out of their seats and force them to apply," Carol commented. "There must be a certain degree of motivation, talent notwithstanding."[3]

The momentum the Kansas City Women's Jazz Festival had gained gave it a life that, like the running baby it was, had to be trained as well as nurtured. Well aware that these problems had to be addressed and solved for the festival to retain the positive reputation it had earned so far, the board buckled down for another year of planning and problem solving.

All the Things You Are

In May at the second planning meeting for the 1980 WJF, the board took on the Main Concert venue problem. Reconsideration of Memorial Hall seemed to be on everyone's minds. Although the musicians were happy with the acoustics and backstage accommodations were satisfactory, now that Memorial Hall had housed WJF for two years, the board was familiar with its shortcomings. The seats were irritatingly uncomfortable. Board members had heard a multitude of complaints, and many fans had made it clear they would not return to Memorial Hall for a third festival. There had been talk before the 1979 festival about WJF providing cushions for all the seats, but the idea was dismissed because of the labor and cost involved.[4]

There was one glaring problem the board could do nothing about: the location. It was an undeniable geographic and sociological fact that many Missouri residents would not go to Kansas City, Kansas. Except for the fact that on the Missouri side the numbered streets run east/west and in Kansas City, Kansas, they run north/south, there is visually little to separate the two cities, the two states. Although neighborhoods on both sides of the state line resemble each other, all too often there is a pervasive prejudice of one against the other that goes back to the Civil War and Border Wars. None of this had anything to do with jazz, but far too many potential ticket buyers, particularly African American fans, had voiced that they were not comfortable planning an evening at Memorial Hall.

Add to that the fact that the ERA advantage was now a moot point. The delayed vote hadn't helped pass the amendment. There were no more states prepared to ratify in June than there were in March. Kansas no longer held a feminist advantage over Missouri.

Layered on this larger picture was an unpleasant bit of business with the Memorial Hall management. Their ticket count came out 375 higher than WJF's count. Because the Hall took a percentage of tickets sold, and they had destroyed all unsold tickets, WJF was forced to go with the Hall's figures.[5]

Exercising the kind of creative thinking that the WJF board excelled at, the new venue discussion started with Municipal Auditorium. Home to the Kansas City Jazz Incorporated festivals of the 1960s and early 1970s, it seated 10,000 people, and the availability of refreshments made it a crowd-friendly facility. Although WJF hadn't broken the 3,000 ticket mark yet, they felt better control of ticket sales and the draw of big names could fill the larger hall. However poor acoustics had plagued the KCJI festivals. Municipal Auditorium was also where basketball games were played, and it served as the big top when the circus came to town. Better, state-of-the-art sound systems would help, but the cavernous space would challenge any sound engineer.

In addition, only the biggest names in jazz, specifically Ella Fitzgerald, could justify the risk of renting such a space. Revived discussions about presenting Ella Fitzgerald brought up the point that Ella would perhaps attract fans that hadn't been to either of the Memorial Hall concerts. Not only was Ella the gold standard of potential artists, she would solidify WJF's legitimacy and keep the attention of the press. As WJF moved into its third year, many board members felt an increased fan base was crucial to securing larger funding. The group decided the idea of corporate sponsorship of Ella's $25,000 fee was worth exploring. All agreed that "Ella would draw like crazy."[6]

With so many variables, other options were discussed. When board members thought of concert venues on the Missouri side, the gold star went to the Music Hall, home of the Kansas City Philharmonic, in downtown Kansas City. Part of the 1935 Art Deco and Streamline Modern Municipal Auditorium WPA project, the grand concert theater, adjacent to Municipal Auditorium, had a seating capacity of 2,400. Described as one of Kansas City's "shining jewels," the hall had all the charm and ambiance, albeit Depression Era, that the veterans' Memorial Hall lacked. Italian marble walls and floors, classic Art Deco chandeliers, and floor-to-ceiling murals lent an air of class without pretention. Rich, maroon velvet curtains, which helped soak up the sound that bounced off the surrounding hard surfaces, cocooned the stage. The matching padded seats were comfortable.

Backstage there was plenty of room. Besides a comfortably large green room, there were both "Star" and "Chorus" dressing rooms. Lighting and sound systems in the Music Hall were the best in the city. In short, there was nothing about this venue that would disappoint out-of-town performers and fans. This was a grown-up concert hall for a grown-up festival. This was a venue worthy of the Queen of Jazz.

Just to make sure all their possibilities were covered, Dianne brought up the idea of having the Main Concert in one of the larger ballrooms of Crown Center. With seating for 1,600 to 2,000, it was a much smaller venue and would require "an entirely different kind of scaled-down program," but the convenience alone made it worth considering. No more buses to transport artists to the Main Concert, far less hauling of equipment. With fans and artists staying at the Crown Center Hotel, and restaurants and bars handy, everyone would benefit from the convenience. Dianne reminded everyone, perhaps a little longingly, "Logistically, it would be heaven."[7]

By July a decision had been made. Although Dianne had initially made a deposit on Municipal Auditorium, she reported to the board, "Our deposit has been transferred to the Music Hall." The risk of basing rental of the 10,000-seat venue on Ella Fitzgerald's appearance was emphatically too much. Besides the $25,000 fee, the number one-rated jazz singer had a 120-day escape clause built into her contract. With the "danger of having our main act back out," reserving Municipal Auditorium was not only imprudent, it was seen by some as suicidal.

Also at the July meeting, Carol and Dianne reported on their successful talks with representatives of the Crown Center shops. Promises of a better sound system and an added band shell satisfied acoustical concerns regarding the lobby jam sessions. A separate, second jam session room with a "holding area" where performers could wait to go on was agreed upon. A more efficiently manned (or womanned) ticket booth would be relocated away from jam session crowds, but still accessible to fans. Crown Center maintenance agreed to take out the trees and tables for the festival weekend. Their feeling of clout and earned bargaining power had given the board everything they asked for.[8]

Another award came soon after the second WJF. Carol and Dianne traveled to Tulsa, Oklahoma, in June to accept the prestigious "Women Helping Women" award from Soroptimist International. Citing the pair as the organizers of the "only organization of its kind in the nation," Soroptimist International praised them for bringing women jazz musicians to the attention of the country through the festival events and media coverage in the *New York*

Times, the *Los Angeles Times*, *Rolling Stone*, *Billboard*, *Down Beat*, and all major television networks.

A working trip to New York City, also in June, proved fruitful. Besides tightening media and other publicity connections, Carol and Dianne were able to secure Joanne Brackeen for the 1980 Main Concert—this time in an earlier slot—and talk to Barbara Carroll about a possible appearance. More importantly, Dianne gave a speech at the now annual Jazz Coalition Salute to Women in Jazz, and both Carol and Dianne served on a B. Dalton Books-sponsored panel discussion on women in jazz. Both Linda Dahl and Sally Placksin, who were independently writing jazz women books, interviewed them.

All of this confirmed their reputation, the importance of what they were doing, and how essential it was to keep doing it.[9]

Swing Is the Thing

Being on the Women's Jazz Festival Board of Directors meant there was never a shortage of things to think about, and if it seemed like there was, it probably meant something was being overlooked and should be quickly identified. That list of things to do and figure out snuck into stray moments, as well as assigned times for discussion. But undoubtedly the task that gravitated to the center of everything was the selection of artists. There was a long road between thinking a particular musician would be perfect for the upcoming year's lineup and actually making it happen. Three a.m. phone calls to Japan for Toshiko's convenience, well-spaced, carefully worded calls and letters to Jamaica to coax Melba out of retirement, a personal favor request to a supporter for his Baldwin piano (because that's the only kind Mary Lou would play), and special arrangements so Mary Lou could take the train (because she hated to fly), had all become business as usual.[10]

But as plans for the third WJF took shape, with Marian's help, Carol and Dianne took on a different kind of scheduling challenge. It started as a wouldn't-it-be-cool-if moment, the kind that Carol and Dianne were so good at turning into reality. When Marian mentioned she was working on a book about women jazz musicians and wanted to tell the story of the International Sweethearts of Rhythm, the idea of assembling the surviving original members for a salute was born. From Marian's research, they knew that nine of the original seventeen Sweethearts were still alive and healthy enough to travel. It had been over thirty years since they had seen each other, and it was impossible to know up front how they'd feel about a reunion. Now in their sixties and seventies, most of the original Sweethearts had retired from playing, but all nine accepted the invitation to be guests of honor at a salute.[11]

In the 1930s, when far too many all-girl bands were clichés wrapped in taffeta and satin, the International Sweethearts of Rhythm offered fresh faces, understated outfits, and a sound that earned them the nickname "Darlings of Swing." Formed in 1938 as a fund-raising group by Laurence C. Jones, founder and principal of Piney Woods Country Life School, a boarding school near Jackson, Mississippi, the original members of the Sweethearts had first played in the school's forty-five-member, female marching band. With a school philosophy of "earn while you learn," all the students at Piney Woods were required to contribute to the financial operations of the school. After seeing Ina Ray Hutton and her Melodears, Dr. Laurence decided Piney Woods needed an all-girl dance band. The fourteen- and fifteen-year-olds who made up the original band were enthusiastic about earning their credit by playing for dances in the surrounding small towns, even if they'd never played jazz before. Music teacher Consuella Carter would see that they were prepared.

"I had played the piano before I came to Piney Woods," recalls Willie Sims. "Consuella Carter was our music teacher, and she said to me, 'I need another trombonist [for the jazz band] and you are it.' At that time we did what we were told." Judy Bayron had a similar story. "My sister and I came to Piney Wood as orphans. My sister already played saxophone, so they looked for a hole in the band and said okay, you can play guitar. For six months I played three chords. Then a spot in the trombone section opened up, so I was moved to trombone."[12] Miss Carter, who had attended Piney Woods herself, understood first-hand the power music could have in forming a productive life. First a violinist, then a dedicated trumpet player, Miss Carter became the school's first band director. With a successful and attention-grabbing all-girl concert band and marching band under her baton, she cultivated the most syncopation-savvy of her female students for the new jazz band.[13]

The work ethic instilled in the girls at Piney Woods held a seat in the band as well. "When you left Piney Woods, you were equipped for life," recalls Sweetheart trumpet player Sadie Pankey. "Dr. Jones made sure we had training for our heads, our hearts, and our hands. You could learn any skill at Piney Woods: typing, shorthand, making shoes. We had a dairy; the boys mostly built the bus we traveled in. Every year we all made Christmas decorations to sell."[14]

"Education came first and foremost. We had so much fun playing, but we always had to remember that we represented the school." Trombonist Willie Sims was well aware of the high reputation the boys' jazz bands had in the area, but as young ladies, they were expected to remember all the "don'ts." Drummer Pauline Braddy remembered it this way:

> Young ladies don't smoke.
>
> Young ladies don't sit at the bar.
>
> Young ladies always carry their gloves and wear their hats.
>
> Young ladies never dance with fellows without jackets and ties.

It was kind of rough on the fellows, but it was rough on the girls too.[15]

In 1941 the International Sweethearts of Rhythm turned pro. By now their ranks included a Mexican girl, a Chinese girl, and a Native American girl, as well as African Americans and three white girls. Dr. Jones was proud of the integration and prouder still of the reputation of excellence the musicians had earned.

As their popularity grew so did the radius of their gigs. The bus was equipped with eighteen bunks to eliminate the issue of lodging for a racially mixed group. A tutor and chaperon were hired. Because the Sweethearts played tours of one-nighters, driving time was school time. It truly was a school bus, complete with girl talk behind their books. Forty-plus years after the fact, they didn't remember chatter about boys or clothes, but they did remember that drummer Pauline Braddy knew trivia about any movie. Helen Jones Woods remembered that their schedule consisted of schoolwork until they got to the night's venue. Their band class, in a different city every afternoon, was the only preparation they had for their performances.

The trouble started, as it so often does, with money. The girls were each given eight dollars a week, although the armories, dance halls, schools, and theaters paid full price for their shows. Mrs. Rae Lee Jones (no relation to Dr. Jones), the band's chaperon, saw to it that the girls got plenty of sleep, stayed away from boys, and drank their milk, but she also encouraged them to question whether Dr. Jones had their best financial interests at heart. He soon got wind of the fact that he was losing control of the band and threatened to hold back their diplomas unless they returned to the school. He also fired Mrs. Jones.[16] The teenage Sweethearts decided that they would rather stay with Mrs. Jones than return to school, sparking what the April 26, 1941, edition of the *Afro-American* called "the wild flight to Washington." Still traveling in the school's homemade bus, the band "escaped pursuers in Florida and eluded a whole army of highway patrolmen in seven Southern States to reach Washington and freedom."[17]

Not used to being crossed and feeling that the girls were violating their "earn while you learn" status, Dr. Jones alerted the police to be on the lookout for the "stolen" bus and to detain the girls when found. The band surrendered the bus in Montgomery, Alabama, and sent it back to Piney Woods with the driver. Contacts in Washington, D.C., secured their passage via Greyhound bus, and all ties to the school were severed. "Overnight we became professionals,"[18] remembered Pauline Braddy.

The Sweethearts, along with Mrs. Rae Lee Jones, set up housekeeping in Arlington, Virginia, not far from the National Cemetery. Sadie Pankey remembers hearing "Taps" from their yard. The band entered their most productive period, rehearsing every day, sometimes for as long as six hours, in the "Sweetheart House," working up new tunes with composer Eddie Durham and, later, their coach and arranger Jesse Stone. Stone's connection to the Sweethearts would be lifelong. Early on he noticed the band's singer, Evelyn McGee. "I had a crush on her then, [but] I had to wait. The girls were protected by Rae Lee Jones from everybody but me. Mrs. Jones trusted me and I never mixed business with pleasure."[19] Stone did wait. The couple finally married in 1975.

World War II's decimation of male bands proved a boon for the Sweethearts. They played the Apollo Theater in New York, where, as one Sweetheart put it, "They cheered us as though we were the Brooklyn Dodgers."[20] Despite gasoline and rubber rationing, during the first two months of 1943, they played one-nighters in Texas, Oklahoma, Tennessee, Alabama, Mississippi, Louisiana, and Arkansas. Hundreds of fans, almost exclusively black, waited in line for hours to get in to their shows. Personnel changed as life on the road took on a harder edge. They were taking care of themselves now, with Mrs. Jones's help and financial guidance. New players were more experienced and proved to be strong additions. Saxophonist Viola Burnside and trumpeter Ernestine "Tiny" Davis had played together in the all-black Harlem Playgirls. Alto saxophonist Roz Cron joined in 1943 fresh from the Ada Leonard, all-white, female band. She noticed a difference right away.

> In all the theaters when the Sweethearts started playing, the audience would come in dancing down the aisle. Black audiences were always like that. But if you'd go hear Tommy or Jimmy Dorsey or Ada Leonard, people just walked to their seats and sat down.[21]

Roz soon noticed other differences in approaches to style. As a classically trained musician, she was surprised how quickly some of the girls learned to play.

> Many girls had problems reading [music] because they had learned the hard way. [The instruments] were just put in their hands and it was like now or never—learn it and fast. But they played in a more relaxed way of interpreting the music. Their beat was different than our uptight white rhythm.[22]

Off the bandstand the new girls had to keep in step with that endemic Piney Woods self-discipline that had characterized the Sweethearts from the beginning. They knew how to play well together—and in 1944 were named Best Female Big Band in the *Down Beat* poll—because they understood the importance of creating a musical unit. Unlike many female groups, they also knew how to live together. When singer and musical director Anna Mae Winburn joined the group, it was with trepidation about getting along with so many women. She needn't have worried. Evelyn McGee declared, "We were like sisters. We loved each other."[23] Roz Cron added, "There were some you liked better than others, but as a whole we just meshed. I think it was because we loved playing music so much and we sounded so great."[24]

By the end of the war, the State Department had received so many G.I. requests for the International Sweethearts of Rhythm that a USO tour was inevitable. Their music had been playing over USO radio broadcasts for some time, and they had acquired a very enthusiastic following. That the State Department would okay the Sweetheart's tour was testament to their popularity. Now international in travel as well as personnel, the Sweethearts arrived in France in July of 1945. Although the European war was over, thousands of American troops remained, most with what Antoinette Handy called "occupation blues."[25] Nothing diminished those blues quicker than the swinging sounds of the Sweethearts. The troops' enthusiasm was uncontained.

Building on the show that had been so well received at the Apollo, they added G.I. favorites and, as *Afro-American* reported, "It was too much to ask the men to sit quietly . . . so [they] simply got up from their seats and danced to their hearts content in the aisle. The theatre was rocked in good old American fashion as it has never rocked before."[26]

Trumpeter Tiny Davis recalls that they played to mostly black servicemen, because the troops were segregated. One of their most memorable concerts was in the badly damaged Nuremberg Opera House. "I played 'I'm a Big Fat Mama' in the Nuremberg Opera House and Hitler haunted me all night."[27]

The girls didn't have to go to Germany to face racial prejudice. "I fought my way through the south," remembers Roz Cron, "as if I were fighting another civil war. Sometimes I lost." During southern tours, Roz Cron, as the only completely white girl, remembers using dark makeup. "I always turned orange. It never turned out right. I always looked freakish and not quite right."[28] Vocalist Anna Mae Winburn adds, "We could put dark makeup on the white girls, but we couldn't change the color of their eyes."[29]

Once the tour bus was stopped because word had leaked that a mixed-race group was coming through. "The white girls had to sneak out the back of the bus and get a black cab driver to take them to the train station where they would wait for us,"[30] Helen Jones recalls.

"I wasn't even white," saxophonist Helen Saine remembers. "My mother was black and my father was Italian, but I snuck out with the white girls. The cab driver was scared. He really didn't want to have us in his cab. But we convinced him to take us to the station by staying on the floor of the cab where no one could see us."[31]

The Sweethearts arrived home at the end of 1945 to a record deal with Leonard Feather and more proposed tours. They stayed together, albeit with multiple personnel changes, until 1948. Musical tastes were swinging away from dance bands toward listening bands. Bebop and smaller ensembles dominated. The girls were older now, and many were ready to marry and start families. In a postwar climate that emphasized home-centered values, some were compelled to pack up their horns.

It had been an exuberant run. The International Sweethearts of Rhythm had shown the world that well-rehearsed young women with a strong work ethic could compete and win in listener polls and Battles of the Bands, against male musicians, narrow-mindedness, and racism. They packed their scrapbooks away and held their memories close, rarely talking about their teenage musical experiences . . . until the 1980 Women's Jazz Festival.

Confirmation

March 1980 in Kansas City became, by mayoral decree, Jazz Month. WJF's publicity committee, headed by Laurie Hamilton and Mike Ning, had tirelessly campaigned since the previous summer to add this exclamation point to preparations for the 1980 festival. Getting Mayor Richard L. Berkley's endorsement was only the beginning. In true Women's Jazz Festival fashion, Laurie and

Mike's enthusiastic promotion of not only WJF but also K.C. jazz in general brought local jazz musicians to the attention of residents with a blitzkrieg of activities.[32] They were almost too successful.

The idea was not a new one. In the mid-sixties, under Dr. Charles Wheeler's mayoral reign, the KCJI festivals had been the culminating event of Jazz Week. Jazz trios played lunchtime gigs at local restaurants, and downtown department stores displayed jazz tableaus in their windows. Suburban shopping malls sponsored big band concerts. There were jazz parades with various bands on flatbed trucks that ran from downtown to the Plaza.

Jazz Month 1980 would be both more complex and more subtle. There were no parades to draw attention. The Jazz Hotline Dianne set up on a WJF phone line kept the public abreast of the month's events, as did the *Kansas City Star* and the *Times*.

Not only was Crown Center the logical location for Jazz Month's true north, it was the most accommodating. The John Lyman Quartet now had jam sessions at Crown Center's Signboard Bar on Mondays, Fridays, and Saturdays. Carol's group, Calico, the all-woman quartet formed the previous summer, had a steady Thursday night gig at the Signboard too. With Carol on piano and vocals, Joan Griffith on bass, Carol Williamson on drums, and Lynn Riley on flute and alto sax, it was clear Crown Center's support of female jazz went far beyond one weekend in March.

Other clubs took up the beat and added jazz brunches and lunchtime jazz mini-concerts. Stix, Baer and Fuller department stores featured Mike Ning at their Ward Parkway Shopping Center Garden Tea Room and Larry Cummings at their Independence Center branch. The Prospect in Westport added a Sunday jazz brunch with Sylvia Bell and Milt Abel. Every Wednesday in March, live jazz could be heard at City Center Square from 11:30 a.m. to 1:30 p.m. Kimball Music Co., who supplied the spectacular Bösendorfer grand for the Main Concert, started the month off with a Jazz Piano Party that was open to the public.

There was even a jazz party for the Village Presbyterian Church Singles Club.

Focus on performances at local colleges not only brought live jazz to a different venue, it broadened the fan base by opening the students' ears and imaginations. Ron Roberts's Concert Ensemble performed at Park College, Penn Valley College, and Longview College. This contemporary, avant-garde group took the Kansas City sound well beyond swing. Ron and his sidemen served as ambassadors for the future of jazz.

College jazz band concerts that had been planned long before were also added to the month's advertised events. As part of a larger Jazz Month event, Jay McShann's appearance with the UMKC Jazz Band, John Leisenring's faculty recital complete with rhythm section, and the Johnson County Community College Jazz Concert drew members of the public who otherwise might not have been aware that these performances were even happening.

Clubs that routinely supported live jazz most nights of the week received added publicity and kudos. The Mark IV Lounge boasted live jazz seven nights a week. The Pete Eye Trio at the Alameda Plaza, the Frank Smith Trio at Stephanie's, and The Greg Meise Trio at Eddy's South all had six-night-a-week gigs.

A plethora of other events loosely tied together by the definition of jazz rounded out the month and offered something for everyone. For those who liked jazz choreography, there was the Kansas City Ballet's "Spring in the City of Jazz" Benefit Ball. Theater League's production of *Ain't Misbehavin'* at the Lyric Theater in downtown Kansas City represented musical theater. A high school big band invitational took place a week before the start of WJF at Metcalf South Shopping Center. For those who liked their Kansas City jazz grounded in landmarks, a two-hour "Historic Jazz" bus tour, sponsored by WJF in conjunction with the Kansas City Landmarks Commission, hit all the high spots. Jones Store, Adler's, Halls Crown Center, and Woolf

Brothers department stores all featured elements of jazz in their window displays.[33]

Outside promoters had already made the connection between the annual WJF month of March and a heightened attention to jazz. Starting with a Midland Theater concert by Ronnie Laws and Lenny White on March 6 and ending with Chick Corea and Friends, also at the Midland Theater, on March 23 (the same night as WJF's Main Concert), big name performers swung, bopped, grooved, and burned their way all through the month. Rockhurst College sponsored, and UMKC hosted, a concert by the Swingle Singers on the eighth. Pat Metheny christened the Performing Arts Center at Lee's Summit High School—his alma mater—on the fourteenth.

On March 22, jam session night of WJF, "KOOL Super Nights," a spinoff of the KOOL Jazz Festival, set up shop at the Uptown Theater in mid-town Kansas City. With its lineup of power hitters (Dave Brubeck, Marian McPartland, and Carmen McRae), it could easily have derailed WJF by siphoning off audience members. But WJF's success and momentum, its out-of-town draw and multiple musical offerings kept it from running over itself while there were other players in town. Operating on the idea that what's good for one jazz organization is good for all jazz organizations, WJF organizers promoted all of it. They knew the jazz fans were out there. They just had to be persuaded to leave their cozy homes and come experience the smorgasbord of jazz the city had prepared for them.

KOOL Super Night's two shows, at 7:30 and 10:30, with ticket prices at $8.50 to $12.50,[34] coincided with the open jams at Crown Center. But for those fans not waiting to sit in, it was an easy drive down Broadway to the Uptown. That Carmen McRae had returned to Kansas City a second year in a row after being away for decades said something for the positive impression the audience had given her at WJF. For Marian, board member and steadfast advisor and supporter of WJF, to perform somewhere else in K.C. during WJF weekend wasn't seen as a rebuff but as a vote of confidence. By playing at the Uptown, Marian was letting go of the baby's hand.

Come Fly with Me

Although the majority of WJF board members had two festivals behind them, there would be no coasting through 1980's planning sessions. Always trying to keep the fans happy, they took seriously the criticism that the previous year's Main Concert was too long. The decision was made to add a Friday night concert to the lineup. This concert—Top New Talent (TNT), held in Crown Center—would showcase lesser known up and comers and give them a chance to shine. Designed to take the idea of the Combo Contest a step further, TNT's performers would be chosen from audition tapes. The program stated:

> There are a number of gifted women jazz artists in the world, many of whom are involved in a constant struggle for greater recognition and respect. There are limited opportunities for them to be heard, not only by mass media but by the jazz aficionado.[35]

Quintess, playing on the word "quintessence," proved the perfect group to begin the new concept concert. This five-piece Los Angeles group, formed specifically to audition for the 1980 WJF, beat out eighteen other groups from twelve states (although the program assured readers and listeners that there were no losers). Quintess played with what *Kansas City Star* reviewer Terry Teachout called "a Horace Silver flavor," but with a "gentler, floppy-hat feel."[36]

Ruth Kissane, who led the quintet and played trumpet and flugelhorn, personified the spirit of the new renaissance woman by combining careers in two predominately male spheres. Besides playing in the Bruce Wells Jazz Octet, the Roz Cron Big Band, and Maiden Voyage in L.A., she was a successful and respected Hollywood animator. Called "one of the top women animators of the modern age," this Disney-trained animator and layout designer was best known for her work with Bill Melendez and the *Peanuts* television specials, including *It's the Great Pumpkin Charlie Brown* and *A Charlie Brown Christmas*.[37]

Pianist Janet Jones, with stints in the bands of Benny Powell, Blue Mitchell, and Chet Baker, played both acoustic and electric piano with a versatility that made her a favorite in San Francisco and Boston, as well as L.A. Her "uncluttered and loose" style let in "a lot of air"[38] for the other Quintesses to build on.

Like Ruth Kissane and Janet Jones, tenor saxophonist Kay Blanchard had played with Maiden Voyage. Her experience teaching instrumental music in public schools and playing orchestral oboe, as well as traveling with several combos and big bands throughout the country, made her a consummate listener and a top-notch player. In his review Teachout referred to the two-horn front line playing with "crackling unisons."[39]

The versatility of both electric bassist Carrie Barton and drummer Marilyn Donadt provided the group with a solid foundation. Most of Carrie's work experience was in clubs, such as the Troubadour and the Starwood, and recording studios for both commercials and studio demos.[40] Marilyn's inventive percussion instincts brought to the sound not only her solid trap set drumming but the unique addition of handmade instruments from recycled materials. This percussion of the peculiar had earned her the attention of Hollywood. Her work can be heard on the soundtracks of *Black Hole* and *Meteor*.[41]

The intent of featuring new artists who were on the rise and deserving of a larger audience was exquisitely realized in the second TNT performer. Dianne Reeves had stolen the show at the 1979 Wichita Jazz Festival and now promised to do the same in Kansas City.

The Denver native caught the attention of Clark Terry when her high school jazz band performed at the 1973 National Association of Jazz Educators conference in Chicago. Charmed that he had discovered such fresh talent, he decided to take her under his wing, as Terry did with so many he saw promise in. He hired her later that year to perform at the Broadmoor Hotel in Colorado Springs with Grady Tate and Tommy Flanagan. Dianne lived up to Terry's confidence in her and referred to that gig as her "first grand encounter."[42]

Music had always been a part of Dianne's life. Her father, who died when she was two, had been a singer. Her mother, Vada Swanson, was a trumpet player. She had an uncle in the bass section of the Denver Symphony, and George Duke was her cousin. Early on, the recordings of Betty Carter, Carmen McRae, Ella Fitzgerald, Billie Holiday, and Sarah Vaughan enchanted Dianne. She had a particular fondness for Sarah Vaughan.

Dianne heard stories in songs, and she instinctively brought out the nuance of a lyric so the listener heard the story too. She was drawn to African and Latin music and how those rhythms, as well as call and response, had influenced modern jazz. She developed her own style of scat that incorporated all that she took from other cultures. "I'm a chameleon. When you put me in certain soils, musically speaking, I will be in that place."[43]

She couldn't have found a better place than Kansas City to dazzle her audience. Dianne's chosen standards, "My Funny Valentine," "On a Clear Day," "Who Will Buy," "Touch Me," "Here's That Rainy Day," "God Bless the Child," and an improvised "Blues in G," warmed the audience with her rich tone and controlled dynamics. Leonard Feather said she "looks and sounds like a taller, humanized Diana Ross."[44] She told the story of each tune as if she were telling it for the first time. She displayed a more theatrical stage presence than some listeners preferred. Leonard reported she occasionally "bordered on theatricality."[45] *Billboard*'s Paul Hohl called her vocals "emotional-laden."[46] Terry Teachout said she "oozes . . . overflows with excitement."[47] But her musical assurance held everyone's attention and more than filled the room. Leonard concluded, "Her exhibition of dynamic contrasts, of aural and visual charm, convinced many in the audience that she is unquestionably destined for stardom."[48]

Three hometown musicians backed her up with seasoned perfection. Pianist Paul Smith, bassist Greg Whitfield, and drummer Ron Vincent each had the equivalent of a PhD in jazz vocal accompaniment. Collectively they had worked with Marilyn Maye, Carol Comer, Kay Dennis, Julie Turner, and later Oleta Adams and Karrin Allyson. Smith remembers that Dianne was, even at her young age, very confident and a total pro. "She had everything charted and they were easy to read, which made things go very well."[49] Terry Teachout said it best: "It's pure pleasure to note that you simply will not find a better rhythm section anywhere."[50]

After the intermission, the Mary Watkins Band took the stage. Mary's experience included working with Les McCann, Donald Byrd, and Grover Washington as a singer, songwriter, arranger, and piano player.[51] Immersed in music from an early age, she was drawn to the diversity of American music. Her personal tastes ran from pop to jazz to gospel, and her writing "interweaves these elements, highlighting one aspect or another as suits the content of her statement."[52] The band of women she brought to WJF was an amalgam of styles that synthesized into mellow fusion. Terry Teachout put them into the category of "grandchildren of Ramsey Lewis" and called the music "cocktail fusion."[53] That wasn't surprising considering the band's credentials. Joy Julks, the group's bass player and sometime French hornist, worked with John Handy and Pharoah Sanders. Linda Tillery on drums was the lead singer and drummer for the San Francisco rock band Loading Zone. Tucki Bailey was a member of Country Joe and the Fish. Mary hoped to create a new sound born of our common cultural heritage by using multiple synthesizers and visceral rhythms. The critics weren't in the mood (or Moog). Leonard Feather referred to the group as an "r&b combo [that] trundled out tiresome funk clichés."[54] Paul Hohl called the set "less than satisfying."[55] The excessive use of varying sizes of triangles and a vibraslap only led to fusion confusion.

All of these women went on to have distinguished careers as studio musicians and educators. Their time with this experimental band was short-lived. Individually they composed operas, children's works, chamber music, and orchestral pieces. They were very active in Women's Music movements and Afro-American Women Composers groups. None of them chose a strictly jazz path; each of them developed her own voice. The Top New Talent concept wasn't meant to promote a strict and narrow jazz. Its root system ran deep and sent out shoots into a variety of musical gardens.

At a time when the big bands of Stan Kenton, Buddy Rich, Woody Herman, and Thad Jones-Mel Lewis were thriving with young blood and innovative charts, an all-girl big band was a good idea, because with few exceptions, women did not play in these well-known bands. The male bands traveled all over the world to play at colleges, concert halls, and festivals, even State Department tours. The girls could do the same, only this time without the fancy dresses, high heels, and Mercurochromed lips.

Drummer Bonnie Janofsky and alto saxophonist Ann Patterson brought that good idea to fruition by forming their own band in September 1979. Most of the members had been in Bonnie's band with Roz Cron, but this new band formed with the idea of someday playing at the Kansas City Women's Jazz Festival. That day was March 21, 1980.

Leonard Feather told the audience that Maiden Voyage, the re-named Bonnie Janofsky-Ann Patterson Big Band, was the first all-girl big band since the forties and, in his opinion, the best one.[56] He wasn't alone in his thinking. Maiden Voyage would appear on the *Tonight* show with Johnny Carson a month after their performance at WJF. Both bandleaders acknowledged, but did not accept, the notion that girl bands were still—or again—a novelty. They knew they would sometimes be hired specifically because they were all women, but their playing standards and excellent presentation could go a long way toward combatting prejudice. "We don't disappoint anyone musically,"[57] Ann told *Down Beat* writer A. James Liska. Well rehearsed and focused, they displayed as much power as their male counterparts, with none of the societal limitations that plagued their antecedents. Charts by Bob Brookmeyer, Tommy Newsome, and Ladd McIntosh, whom Ann playfully introduced to the crowd as president of the band's men's auxiliary, filled in the gaps between tunes by Nan Schwartz and senior band member Betty O'Hara.

Maiden Voyage started off their set with a piece called, "Sweet Georgia, Upside Down," which made use of what was quickly becoming the band's signature: vibist Judy Chilnick's doubling of the main melody line. The band danced through Nan Schwartz's up-tempo arrangement of "All Blues," and made Ladd McIntosh's arrangement of "You Are the Sunshine of My Life" glow. Valve trombonist and flugelhorn player Betty O'Hara sang as well as soloed on her arrangement of "God Bless the Child." Stacy Rowles, featured on "Spanish Gypsy," played with a warm lyricism that was smoky yet sweet.[58]

Ann Patterson, with a masters in oboe performance, felt there weren't many top-notch women saxophonists because "the saxophone is a very free-blowing horn—you have to be very aggressive to play it."[59] Ann's command of her featured tune, "Summer of '42," demonstrated just how to use that power without losing finesse.

Through it all, Maiden Voyage lived up to the definition of what Ann and Bonnie felt a late twentieth-century, all-women's big band should be. Ann wanted the band to be about more than just money. To survive, she felt the goals should be "to give women who have incredible potential some experience; to give women who are doing their thing and doing it well some exposure; and to give women musicians some work."[60] No one at WJF could argue with that. To be competitive with the guys, women had to have the same playing experiences, and that meant steady work in a big band. "It's funny," Ann, repeating what many women felt, told Liska, "but a male musician is just assumed good until proven otherwise. For women, it's just the other way around."[61]

The Friday night Top New Talent Concert was actually the fourth event on the second day of the third WJF. With a full concert on Friday night, the Student Big Band Invitational moved to Thursday night. As it had for the previous two years, a four-hour jam session in Crown Center's Signboard Bar heralded the start of the festival, this year with Dianne Reeves sitting in and, later in the evening, members of the International Sweethearts of Rhythm. The more-than-capacity crowd then moved down the hall to the International Café to hear school bands.

Both sides of the state line were represented in the high school category. Entering its third decade of excellence in jazz education, Raytown South High School from Raytown, Missouri, directed by Carroll Lewis, led off the concert. Shawnee Mission East's band, from Prairie Village, Kansas, led by Al Hanna, followed. Next John Leisenring, Director of Jazz Studies at UMKC and charter WJF board member, brought out that college's band. The Yes M.A.A.M. (Musicians Ain't Always Men) Band from North Texas State, under the direction of Jodi Gladstone, closed the concert.[62]

To perpetuate WJF's commitment to jazz education, each student group featured female soloists. Raytown South brought out Valerie Fidmont on flute and Stacy Shoemate on trombone. Shawnee Mission East featured Robyn Wilk on flute and Diane Fitzcharles on piano. For high school girls to have a chance to play at a large venue, big band concert, in front of an audience made up of far more fans than just their parents, and to stand up to solo with their bands gave forward motion to Ann Patterson's goal. These girls, along with their college sisters from UMKC—bassist Carole Brown, trumpet players Lisa Reif and Barb Reifsteck, violinist Laura Seaton, and trombonist Angie Wellman—were getting the experience and exposure that would take their generation one more step toward musical equality and acceptance.[63]

Highlighting this evening of fresh, enthusiastic jazz in what Paul Hohl called "a varied, up-tempo performance,"[64] the Yes M.A.A.M. Band proved that cooperation between the sexes paid off musically. Representing a school that was, and is, known for its outstanding professional quality One O'clock Lab Band, a band that in 1980 was all male, the Yes M.A.A.M. Band, made up of fifteen girls and four boys, demonstrated that music has no gender. They had traveled from Denton, Texas, at their own expense to participate in the concert because they loved to play, but they also proved a point.[65]

For the second year, Leonard Feather presented films from his collection of rare jazz cinema. Held at White Recital Hall on the campus of UMKC on Friday afternoon, this was an entertaining and educational way to spend a couple of hours and to relax before the swingin' and boppin' evening ahead with the TNT concert.

The selections for 1980 featured Billie Holiday and Bessie Smith along with saxophonist Vi Redd. In this pre-YouTube era, when researchers and collectors were usually the only ones who saw vaulted films such as these, this component of WJF was a treat. Accompanied by Leonard's lecture, the films added historical perspective to the weekend.[66]

As always with WJF, if there were a few unscheduled hours available, a jam session was added. After Leonard's films and lecture, the Genesis Jam Session, also in White Recital Hall, gave beginner jazz students an opportunity to play in "a comfortable, non-intimidating atmosphere wherein . . . improvisational skills could be explored and practiced."[67]

As explained in the program, the opportunities for young players to stretch out with their newly honed chops were few compared to earlier days in Kansas City's jazz history. As jazz education moved from the after-hours clubs to the classrooms, players in their teens and early twenties no longer had the exposure to the jazz greats still playing around town. Because most live music clubs adhered to a twenty-one and over policy, "the younger musician has been deprived of the chance to learn how to play solo choruses, trade fours, comp, etc."[68] The Genesis Jam filled the void, albeit for a day. Members of Quintess provided the house rhythm section, and Kay Blanchard drew on her years of teaching public school band to help with instruction and encouragement. WJF truly had something for everyone.

Saturday, as in the past, was set aside for clinics and workshops in Crown Center, then two marathon jams. Following the format of the previous year, clinics were offered for both beginners and advanced players. This year's All-Stars, Jill McManus, Louise Davis, and Barbara Merjan, took on the rhythm section clinic. The expertise of area college professors, reeds specialist Dr. Jean Lansing of Wichita State and Dr. Betty Scott who covered brass at the University of Missouri at Columbia, gave clinic goers unique insights into their instruments. New York singer Janet Lawson, also an All-Star, tackled the subject of vocal jazz.

New in 1980, the clinics included a session on the topic of the Business of Music. Aware that it takes more than talent and musical motivation to make it in the music business, a stellar panel of experts—Leonard Feather, Helen Keane (who managed Bill Evans and Joanne Brackeen), Carla Bley (all-around entrepreneur), and WJF's own Dianne Gregg and Carol Comer—addressed the problems and pitfalls of becoming professional.[69]

Hoping to stave off criticism and accusations of unfairness, the 1980 jam sessions included a "Jazzwomen" jam in the International Cafe. Calico, a quartet Carol fronted and that included Joan Griffith on bass, Carol Williamson on drums, and Lynn Riley on reeds, provided the core band. The 4:00 p.m. to 1:00 a.m., female-only jam format left plenty of room for everyone to get a chance at multiple choruses.

For those with more egalitarian tastes, the Mike Ning Quartet, made up of Mike on Piano, Scott Robinson on drums, Carole Brown on bass, and Angie Wellman on trombone, set up in the Meeting Place of Crown Center. The hours for both jam sessions were the same, and so was the groove.[70]

Come Sunday

"This is unbelievable. I never dreamed we'd be all together again."[71] Singer Evelyn McGee took the stage at the Meeting Place in Crown Center for the tribute to the International Sweethearts of Rhythm. Although not strictly an original Sweetheart, Evelyn had joined the band while it was still affiliated with Piney Woods School and thought of this event as a school reunion. She and her husband, former arranger for the band Jesse Stone, had come at their own expense to be a part of the afternoon. As Evelyn launched into "Unforgettable" at the Sunday afternoon tribute, she couldn't help but make it more personal. "Carol Comer, you're unforgettable," she sang out. "Dianne Gregg, you're unforgettable. All my Sweetheart sisters, you're unforgettable."[72] Marian McPartland, who had played at another venue the night before, accompanied Evelyn. Initial contact with the Sweethearts had come through Marian, and she told the crowd she wouldn't have missed this. Her awe of the older women was apparent. To the crowd's delight, drummer Pauline Braddy, who hadn't played in twelve years, and trumpeter Nancy Brown Pratt, who borrowed a trumpet from a Maiden Voyage member, joined Evelyn and Marian mid-tune and finished with them on "I Cried for You."

Carol and Dianne had made it clear in a letter to each Sweetheart earlier in the year that there would be no pressure to perform, but that all would welcome a spontaneous jam. "We are bringing you in to honor you and not put you on display. If you want to perform, we would LOVE it—but we don't want any of you to think that performing is part of the deal. . . . We only want you to have a super time."[73]

A big part of that super time was to hear Maiden Voyage and to see first hand what an all-girl band, circa 1980, could do. Ann Patterson told the audience that none of what they did would have been possible without the trail the Sweethearts blazed forty years before. From the Friday night concert, they reprised their original "Pretty Good for a Girl" with the bitterly tongue-in-cheek lyrics, "You'll learn to cook and to sew, once more you'll like it, I know,"[74] sung by the entire band. For the rest of the afternoon, the band stuck to stock arrangements rather than playing covers of Sweetheart tunes. The afternoon juxtaposed then and now.

Wearing nametags decorated with large red hearts, each Sweetheart was called to the stage to receive a sweetheart rose from emcee Leonard Feather. "This is an emotional afternoon,"[75] Leonard, visibly touched, told the audience. Besides recording the group in the late forties, he had done publicity for the band. In a casual manner, he asked each Sweetheart questions about their time with the band. Willie Mae Wong, baritone saxophone, told about her time as treasurer and the meager eight dollars weekly stipend each girl received. Helen Saine recalled that, although she "turned pro" along with the other girls, when the band set up housekeeping in Virginia, the juvenile authorities sent her back to the Piney Woods School until she turned sixteen. Right after her birthday, she was back with the band. Helen Jones recounted for the audience the rehearsal schedule they stuck to on and off the road and how their various musical directors drilled them on basics. For Evelyn McGee, sitting in with the band one night when she was a teenager convinced her she wanted to go on the road. Remarkably, her mother gave her permission, and Evelyn left with the band that night. "I didn't even have a real suitcase. I carried my things in a cardboard satchel."[76]

Undoubtedly the most sobering of the stories belonged to alto saxophonist Roz Cron. Although she tried to disguise herself during gigs to keep the southern authorities at bay, they caught up with her in El Paso. As she walked to an after-gig restaurant escorted by an African-American GI who had just attended the Sweethearts' performance, police circled, then stopped the pair. After hassling the serviceman and sending him on his way, they focused on Roz. "I wasn't supposed to fraternize with blacks. I tried my usual story of being mulatto, but the policeman looked through my wallet and found the picture of my very white Jewish parents standing in front of an obvious New England house, white picket fence and all. I spent the night in jail."[77]

Not even memories of the Jim Crow south could squelch the delight of renewed contact after so many years. "I can't believe this is happening," Anna Mae Winburn told the crowd. "I feel like I'm in the Twilight Zone."[78]

The only unhappy moment of the afternoon came without warning when Ruth Kissane, the Maiden Voyage trumpet player who had led Quintess on Friday night, fell. While Leonard Feather read congratulatory telegrams from Clark Terry, Carline Ray, and Norman Granz, a leg of the chair Ruth was sitting on slipped off the top riser and she fell four feet to the floor. Medical personnel in the audience attended to her immediately, and an ambulance was called. Carol, more than a little unnerved, updated the crowd and told them Kacee, as the band called her, had asked that the tribute proceed without her. "Make things good with my band," Carol quoted Ruth. "All Kacee wants is for you to have a good time."[79]

Meanwhile, all-around utility player Marian McPartland once again offered a solution to an unforeseen predicament by playing a jaunty stride piano piece called "Little Rock Getaway." Maiden Voyage regrouped as Stacy Rowles, back from the All-Star rehearsal, took up her position in the trumpet section and her sub took over for Ruth.[80]

Keeping the focus on the Sweethearts and the mood light, Maiden Voyage finished the tribute with another couple of tunes. That the memorable afternoon had renewed the spirits of these old friends and reunited their musical souls was clear. They had plenty to be proud of. Leonard Feather later told *Down Beat* readers, "It has been a long way from the Sweethearts of Rhythm, born 1938, to Maiden Voyage, born 1979, and the old-timers were thrilled to hear what, in effect, their pioneer efforts had wrought."[81]

Ruth Kissane's fall turned Carol and Dianne's worst nightmare into reality. Although WJF had insurance for such things, they were distraught at the thought that a performer would leave the weekend in worse physical shape than when she had arrived. Taken to nearby St. Mary's hospital, Ruth's prognosis wasn't good. Ann Patterson had assured the crowd and the band that Kacee would be okay, but surgeons worked into the night to repair a severed artery and "multiple compound fractures of the right arm and elbow."[82] Bad news indeed for the right-handed, prolific Hollywood animator.

The Main Concert of the 1980 WJF, or as Leonard Feather announced to the crowd, "the eleventh event of the fourth day of the third annual Women's Jazz Festival,"[83] began with Leonard reading a congratulatory telegram from President Jimmy Carter.

> You have done so much to highlight for all of our citizens the truly significant achievements of women in the history of jazz. . . . Rosalynn and I welcome this opportunity to salute your important service to our nation's cultural vitality and to the leisure hour enjoyment of our citizens.[84]

Only four groups made up this last night of jazz in the roomier, more acoustically appropriate Music Hall. Although many in the crowd had packed their ears with jazz for four days, the largest Sunday night audience yet happily paid up to $9.50 per ticket. With the exception of the Main Concert, TNT, and the clinics, all WJF events were still free. *Billboard* critic Paul Hohl told his readers, "Those which did cost helped to generate much needed revenue at a seemingly modest price for the quality of the artists involved."[85]

In the lead-off position, the All-Stars played with an assurance that sounded practiced and familiar rather than born that afternoon at the sound check. Leaving nothing to chance, Carol and Dianne had asked Jane Ira Bloom to lead the All-Stars and to pick the band she wanted. Jane Ira had declined. She was concentrating on her own music and felt the sidemen—and some would be men—she would want would not exemplify what WJF wanted in an All-Star group.[86] Carol and Dianne next asked a young pianist they had heard during the 1979 WJF jam. Although asking someone they had heard only at the jam session had proved less than satisfactory the year before, Carol and Dianne had also heard Jill McManus in New York during the Universal Jazz Coalition's Salute to Women in Jazz. They were also familiar with Jill's group, Jazz Sisters, which included WJF All-Star alumni Janice Robinson and Lynn Milano. Although Jill had worked with Richard Davis, Michael Brecker, and Lee Konitz, she frequently put together women's groups for festivals and specific gigs. Carol and Dianne felt confident she was up to the challenge of fronting the 1980 All-Stars. Jill accepted.

Bassist Louise Davis brought a polished professionalism to the group. Predominately a New York recording studio player, Louise could be heard on countless commercials and radio and television shows. At the time of the 1980 WJF, she was the house bassist at Disney World, where she backed up name performers all year-around.

Barbara Merjan had become well known to WJF crowds. As the drummer for the 1979 Combo Contest winner, Aerial, Barbara's impressive playing caught the attention of audience and critics alike. She was asked to fill in with the '79 All-Stars when Marian, whom she had played with in New York, took the piano reins. Since then Barbara had become the first female drummer to play the Newport Jazz Festival when Aerial played there in the summer of 1979. She had also taken part in the week-long festivities of the Universal Jazz Coalition's Salute to Women in Jazz. Although still in college, Barbara's reputation spoke well for the upcoming generation of female jazz musicians.

The "technically flawless" voice of Janet Lawson added what she called "vocal instrumentation." Blessed with an almost four octave range, Janet made use of every note. Singing her own composition, "Woman," tastefully accompanied by the band, she carried on the theme started by Carline Ray's "Today's Woman" during Aerial's performance the year before. Her years of working with Art Farmer, Chick Corea, and Attila Zoller, and her involvement with the Universal Jazz Coalition's Salute to Women in Jazz added confidence to her already unique sound.

Another alumnus of the New York Universal Jazz Coalition's Salute to Women in Jazz, saxophonist Jane Fair, added Canada to the list of countries represented at WJF. Born in Ontario, Jane made her home in Toronto, where she appeared with the

Jim Galloway Big Band. Jane played a lyrical style full of nuance and charm without a hint of brashness. Not lacking in control or power, she chose to sing through the sax with her own voice. There was no need to try to "play like a man." [87]

Stacy Rowles's busy weekend included two Maiden Voyage performances, rehearsals, jam sessions, and the All-Star set—business as usual for Jimmy Rowles's daughter. Stacy started on the piano at age six, but was more interested in finding her own instrument. Both she and her father were happy with her choice of trumpet. According to Marian McPartland, Stacy once wrote her father this note: "Dear Dad, if you buy me a flugelhorn, I'll play the [expletive] out of it."[88] Along with her brother and sister, Stacy felt she always had the support of older musicians around her.

> There were several times when I was a teenager when he [Jimmy] would bring people home to show me off. He'd bring Snooky Young and all these trumpet players home in the middle of the night and wake me up and say, "Come down and play." And so I'd drag myself out of bed, come down and play some march or something which—being in junior high school or high school at the time—was all I knew.[89]

Despite a life-long musical collaboration with her piano playing father, the *New York Times* considered Stacy "perpetually under-discovered."[90] Nevertheless, she gained the attention of musicians and audiences west of the Mississippi. Before she was twenty she appeared at the Monterey Jazz Festival with her father, and Clark Terry featured her with his All-Star All-Girl Big Band at the Wichita Jazz Festival in 1976. Primarily a West Coast player, her "restful, melodic solos with a warm tone . . . sing in a wise, honest voice, shy but swinging."[91] Her early submersion into the world of sound gave her an edge in understanding jazz. "I listen to everyone I can and put something new into my brain from them. I'm spongy, and I take apart what I hear, and I change it, and that process keeps everything fresh and moving."[92]

Together the 1980 All-Stars presented a well-polished example of what a pick-up ensemble could do. After the previous year's shaky moments, this model worked.

"I think I like to be different. I think I like to offend," Carla Bley told *Jazz Alive* interviewer Chris Bosley. "As a kid I was always doing something outrageous to get attention. I guess it's just that immaturity in me."[93] Despite that self-assessment, Carla also has the reputation of being a brilliant businesswoman, innovatively relevant composer, and demanding bandleader. Carla's music, deeply original and visionary—Leonard Feather called it "Jazz of the Absurd"[94]—was, in 1980, also meant to shock, to thumb its nose at any expected response. "My audience expects something startling."[95] Feather, a generation older, didn't count himself in that audience. He referred to Carla's music as "Artistry in Bullshit."[96]

The most unconventional of any of the 1980 WJF artists, Carla had little formal musical training. Her father, a church organist and choirmaster as well as a piano teacher, started Carla on piano at three, but she rebelled against his instruction before her teen years. Carla says the badly played scales and elementary piano pieces she heard her father's students play implanted themselves in her ears as an early influence. She wrote her first piece of music at five to show to her father at her lesson. "I had just put a lot of dots on the page. He said there were too many dots, so I erased half of them, and that was my first composition."[97]

She left school at fifteen, she told Bosley, to take on the trade of dishwashing. Other interviews tell of her wanting to become a professional roller skater. She moved from her native Oakland, California, to New York City in the mid-fifties. Her first big job at Basin Street was not that of a musician but as the coat-check girl. She sold cigarettes at Birdland, where she heard many jazz greats. After hanging around musicians, she decided that playing music really could be a career path and started writing. A smitten Paul Bley, who bought cigarettes from her even though he didn't smoke, starting playing her tunes. Because she felt marriage gave her a way to move forward with her music, Carla married Paul and they moved to California. Paul associated with those forming the avant-garde movement in the sixties, exposing Carla to the music of Ornette Coleman, Don Cherry, and Charlie Haden. As a band wife, "I listened like I'm sure no musician could who played. I heard every note everybody played. Every wart on every note everybody played."[98] All this prompted her to expand her writing. "I was lucky," she told *Melody Maker*. "People started playing my music as soon as I began to write it." [99] She began to play piano again, discovering she loved being on stage and that her lack of technique was masked in avant-garde pieces she wrote herself. She also found she liked to travel, the wining and dining, all the attention her new lifestyle brought.

Along with her next husband, Michael Mantler, she organized the Society of Jazz Composers to support the avant-garde efforts of other New York bands. They also formed the Jazz Composer's Orchestra and a New Music Distribution Service.[100] Carla started her own record label, WATT records, and later a second called XtraWatt,[101] and formed the band that, by WJF 1980, had been together for five years. Although other versions of the Carla Bley Band included women (Karen Mantler, Carla's daughter with Mantler, frequently played organ), this band was all men save its leader. Standard instrumentation? Unthinkable. Both Carla and Arturo O'Farrill on keyboard; Steve Swallow, future spouse, bass; D. Sharpe, drums; Michael Mantler, 1980 husband, trumpet; Gary Valente, trombone; Vincent Chancey, French horn; Joe Daley, tuba; Carlos Ward, alto sax and flute; and Gary Windo, tenor sax[102] made up this troupe of musical jesters.

The Carla Bley Band's set—more aptly an act—ranged from playful and clever to angry and distasteful. Terry Teachout wrote, "Her works superimpose furious sonorities from the horns over a thunderous beat, with bizarre vocals woven in."[103] All tunes blended into the next without introduction. The opening, unnamed tune, characterized by kinetically syncopated horn rhythms and a cacophonous organ solo, set the tone. Well-rehearsed, tight, flawless playing, albeit laced with anarchy as if written by the spawn of Frank Zappa and Emma Goldman, tricked the audience into assuming this exciting avant-garde use of multiple horns and multiple rhythms would continue. Not so. A very staged brouhaha about needing an extra microphone for drummer D. Sharpe who was about to sing a song—a flip-side tune about Siam—invited the audience into the band's musical funhouse. A simplistic, mildly offensive, stereotypical, Asian, pentatonic, two-note melody (which sounded suspiciously like the one the Siamese cats sing in *Lady and the Tramp*) with silly lyrics such as, "All the fancy cats come from this area. Also got a lot of animals that scare ya," avoided being singsong by oddly placing accents and mixed-up syntax. The horns wailed. D. Sharpe's voice cracked into an out-of-tune yodel.

The hostility in the next tune would prove truly shocking in any setting but became appallingly inappropriate at a women's festival. Astonishingly misogynistic, insensitive lyrics, yelled more than sung by another, unnamed, band member contemplated ways to render a young lady unconscious so nefarious deeds could take place. Outside the realm of humor, this tune crossed the line into a place ruled by bad taste. Critics choose to ignore the song.

Vamping right into the last number with a whirlwind of chaotic chords, Carla broke into what would be remembered as the signature song of her performance—and her taunting raspberry to anyone who didn't approve of her set. In a talk-sing she explained that all they were trying to do was present new music and she didn't like it when people booed her. "When they boo at us you know what we do? We tell them Boo To You Too. That's what WE do." A quasi-Motown horn line and driving rhythm section accompanied Carla as she urged the crowd to "boo on cue," in a twisted call and response, so she could then yell back, "Well boo to you too." The crowd loved it. Her can't-you-take-a-joke smugness beat the audience to its outrage over the previous song as she charmed herself back into their favor.[104]

The ever-present, irreverent humor in Carla Bley's music continued to make her popular among musicians and avant-garde fans. Steve Swallow said, "I have a lifelong virus of Carla's music."[105] Over the years, Carla's music lost the anger but never the aggressive edge. She explained that to Marian McPartland during a *Piano Jazz* interview. "People think girls write pretty music and boys write interesting, aggressive music. I'd rather write like a boy. When you compose, you can correct your image."[106] The varied list of those who have played her tunes includes Art Farmer and Linda Ronstadt, Gato Barbieri, Gary Burton, John Scofield, and George Russell. Always in charge, Carla has succeeded in propelling music, particularly big band writing, forward into a new era. Her long-time partner, and even longer-time bassist, Steve Swallow, calls her "Bleytoven."[107]

From the absurd to the sublime, the jarring juxtaposition of Carla Bley and Joanne Brackeen defined the range of jazz. The intermission helped restore equilibrium in the hall before Joanne, bassist Eddie Gomez, and drummer Motohiko Hino took the stage. Because Joanne's set had been cut short in 1979, she was given seventy-five minutes in 1980 to stretch out and awe the audience with "a series of iridescent originals."[108] Using the full range of the Bösendorfer, Joanne was nothing less than dazzling. Nina Sheldon remembered Joanne's excitement the year before when she tried out the concert stage Bösendorfer. The low extension opened up new creative possibilities. "Joanne loved playing down there in the dark notes."[109] Her opening Impressionist cascade of sound, punctuated by those sub-bass notes, blended the line between European orchestral music and late twentieth-century, American jazz. Joanne composed and played with an orchestral musician's palette of dissonance and an intense, cerebral, diamond hard touch. Terry Teachout felt she played with "the leaping, flashing, evanescent texture of Ravel, the complex scalar constructions of Bartok, the furiously uneven ostinato of Prokofiev—recreated as jazz of the highest order."[110]

Bassist Eddie Gomez felt musically drawn to Joanne. "After I left Bill [Evans], I had made a conscious effort to stay away from playing with a pianist. . . . But when I played with Joanne, we had an incredible understanding."[111] When he first met her years before, he thought she had promise, but "she was just Mrs. Charles Brackeen to me."[112] Much later, hearing her again convinced him that "she had gone past the point of someone having promise, and that she possessed a really unique talent."[113] He was most impressed with her highly developed use of rhythms and how that emphasis "called upon the bassist to extend himself."[114]

Fully aware of the time it took to develop a personal musical voice, Joanne told Nelson George of *Down Beat* that as glorious as her time with Art Blakey and Stan Getz was to her growth as a musician, she knew she "had to tone down my approach to fit what they did."[115] By 1980 she felt she was finally free to "connect with the rhythms in the universe and to use that force."[116] She likened it to the feeling of being lost in the music with like-minded players. "You are aware of the music's structure, but it is no border: just a starting point. That in-sync feeling both with musicians and the world around you is so natural."[117]

While Carla Bley's use of dissonance and "clams" produced a thumbed-nose attitude toward convention in all things, Joanne's dense, lush dissonances, fleeting or extended, meant to expand past the very existence of convention. Heady music, too involved for some to absorb, it nevertheless introduced the audience to the future. As a final farewell to the piano and the music, the last note Joanne played on the last tune, a stinger to her performance, was double low C, the lowest note on the instrument.

It may have been the accent, it may have been the impeccable professionalism, it may have been the control she took of the stage, but when the spotlight turned to Cleo Laine, the audience felt the presence of royalty. Years later she and her husband, reedman John Dankworth, received the honor of becoming Dame Cleo and Sir John, the only jazz couple with that recognition, confirming what their fans already knew. The *Los Angeles Herald-Examiner* called her "the best all-around singer in the world."[118] The fact that she was (and is) the only female vocalist to receive Grammy nominations in the categories of popular, classical, and jazz underscored that assessment.

Cleo considered becoming a librarian, a hat-trimmer, and a hairdresser before auditioning for the Johnny Dankworth Seven band in 1951. The couple married in 1958 and continued to work with each other on various projects until John's death in 2010. Cleo's credentials were considerable. She starred on the British stage in the Royal Court Theatre, played the lead in various musicals throughout the fifties and sixties, made recordings with Ray Charles, gave concerts in Carnegie Hall, recorded *Shakespeare and All That Jazz* with John, and performed Arnold Schoenberg's *Pierrot Lunaire*.[119]

As the last artists of the night and of the festival, she and her husband, along with Paul Hart on piano, Bill LeSage on vibes, Daryl Brunswick on bass guitar, and Kenny Clare on drums, held the audience spellbound for almost ninety minutes. Her range of tunes ran the gamut from "Feeling Good," from the musical *Roar of the Greasepaint, Smell of the Crowd*, to a melodic Shakespearean tone poem. She started the set with "It Might as Well Be Spring," an evocative song for late March. A slow ballad version of "Tea for Two" proved charming but perhaps too subdued for the end of the weekend. Husband and wife followed a unison, lilting melody as perfectly as one in "I'm Shadowing You." Cleo introduced John as her arranger, her musical director, her husband, and her very best friend. Their interpretation of "Oh My Sadness, Oh My Joy," a vocal and clarinet duet, was saturated with a level of emotion that was almost too intimate. Lightening the mood, they swung into a medley of tunes with a musical theme: "Fascinating Rhythm," "I Got the Music in Me," "Jazzman," and "It Don't Mean a Thing." Dankworth introduced the medley as songs about music, "interwoven with a devilish, British, musical ingenuity." That this group could transform the feeling in this large hall to that of a personal performance in a familiar pub gave testament to the level of Cleo's talent.[120]

Leonard reported in *Down Beat* that a contingent of Maiden Voyage musicians, along with Mary Watkins and local male musicians, spent much of Monday after the festival jamming at the Mutual Musicians' Foundation. As the coda to this amazing few days of music, they then drove to Charlie Parker's grave in Independence, Missouri, where, he concluded, "It was a somber and unforgettable ending to a weekend in this city where so much jazz history was established and continues to be made."[121]

Four days of jazz: sophisticated and sweet, classy and crazy. Women had done it all.

Chapter 5

The Fourth Year
March 25–29, 1981

"If there are truly irreconcilable differences between the sexes as regards to jazz appreciation, blame it on some uncaring chromosomal imbalance, not on the music."

—*Fugue* magazine July, 1978

LEONARD FEATHER MADE THE ANNOUNCEMENT. Flora Purim and Airto Moreira, delayed by a snowstorm in Colorado, had only just arrived. They were in the building, but the concert would be further delayed while the band set up. Carol and Dianne were more than a little upset that the fourth WJF's Sunday night Main Concert's headliners had already held up the concert for over an hour, not to mention the fact that they had missed the sound check. Now they were setting up their own, cold-from-the-truck equipment rather than using the already-warm, WJF sound system. When Dianne received the call that afternoon from Colorado saying that Flora's band would arrive late, she had been stunned by the audacity of the Brazilian husband and wife. Months before, Flora had received half her fee and full transportation costs for all seven of her band members to fly from Los Angeles to Kansas City. Now it became apparent that, instead, the band had traveled by van from Denver and pocketed the difference. If it hadn't been for the snowstorm, no one would have known.[1]

Until that last afternoon of the 1981 festival when it became apparent to organizers that Flora's band wasn't going to make the sound check, it had been another stellar year for WJF. Building on what had worked in the past and enhancing the week with suggested additions, WJF '81 had tied up five days of an eclectic lineup. In the *Kansas City Star* the morning after the festival, Terry Teachout voiced that some in the music community thought that 1980's WJF had been such an outstanding success it should stop there rather than risk putting on a diminished festival. In spite of the unexpected Flora delay, Teachout sent out kudos to Carol and Dianne and company for putting on almost a week of top-notch jazz.[2]

As in previous years, Thursday night of the festival was devoted to student big bands. This year's crop spanned junior high to college and included Indian Creek Junior High Jazz Band under the direction of Helen Marquette, Winnetonka High School with director Charlie Menghini, the UMKC Jazz Band led by Walter Bryant (while John Leisenring was on sabbatical), and, because of its popularity the previous year, North Texas State's Yes M.A.A.M. Band.

The ever-popular jam sessions took place once again on both Friday and Saturday afternoon and night. Included in 1981, the Genesis Jam for the under-twenty-one crowd was co-led by Calico bassist Joan Griffith and Maiden Voyage's Ann Patterson. Ann also worked the Mixed Jam and Open Mike Jam along with Mike Ning, while Calico provided the house band for the women-only jam.

Saturday morning clinics, now a WJF tradition, gave the academic-minded plenty to think about. The year's clinicians included Brandy Anthony, guitar; Judy Roberts, Rosemary Galloway, and Marilyn Donadt, rhythm section; Jean Fineberg, reeds; and Ernestine Anderson, vocal jazz. There was also a Business of Music workshop run by Carol Comer, Leonard Feather, Barbara Edwards (manager of the TNT group ALIVE!), Dianne Gregg, and Kathryn Moses. Attendance at the clinics had declined over the years, and during planning sessions for the 1981 WJF, there had been discussions by the board about cutting back on clinic offerings. In the end, WJF's commitment to jazz education trumped those concerns.

Back by popular demand, Leonard Feather followed the clinics with another presentation of his rare jazz films. His followers had no other way to see these films in 1981, and some shown at previous festivals were shown again by request. The year's screening centered on Billie Holiday and Bessie Smith.

A new component added to WJF, Fun with Jazz, brought the basics of jazz to Head Start children and added Wednesday to the week's schedule. Carol Comer's frequent jazz vocal clinics at schools and institutions had convinced her that this get-them-while-they're-young approach could foster a life-long love of jazz. Aided by Jackie Weissman (Miss Jackie), a local children's celebrity and teacher, musician members of the WJF board and friends entertained preschoolers bused to the Jewish Community Center for the event. With familiar tunes such as "Pop Goes the Weasel" and "Yankee Doodle," the children were invited to jam with the pros using call and response, rhythmic clapping, and scat singing. By exposing children to the inner workings of the art form, WJF's board hoped to spark an interest in each child to play an instrument or to become an informed, interested audience member.

"The inclusion of jazz dance in the Festival format is a direct response to your requests over the past few years, one which we're excited to be able to present for the first time this year." Notes in the program go on to say that the Sunday afternoon production of Music in Motion, led by Vicki Allen Reid, Kathy

Bartosh Landsman, and Dennis Landsman, accompanied by Calico, "will endeavor to illustrate the history of jazz dance, from the Charleston, tap, and soft shoe, to the more modern classical jazz Terpsichore."[3]

Sunday afternoon's jazz-related offerings had come to serve as a musical sorbet between the intense Saturday jam sessions and the evening's Main Concert. Although some fans considered this pushing the parameters of jazz's definition, adding these events—Mary Lou's Mass in '78, the Gospel Songfest in '79, the Sweethearts of Rhythm reunion in '80—rounded out WJF's schedule with acts that exposed fans to musicians they might otherwise miss. The Sunday afternoon performances stood as proof that jazz's influence had a far reach and that women were propelling it forward.

Stories to Tell

A musician's recordings could make or break her career. Because live performances were concentrated in big cities and were sporadic elsewhere, records were the only way many fans kept up with their favorite artists. As a jazz show host, Dianne Gregg felt a responsibility to introduce up-and-coming, trend-setting new musicians. When that musician was a particular favorite of Dianne's, that responsibility became pure pleasure. "The unpleasantness with Flora Purim and Airto Moreira was all the more upsetting because I was such a fan," Dianne remembers. "We were so thrilled to have Flora because there were a lot of people in Kansas City who had never heard of her. She was a real standard bearer for contemporary music, and I made a point of playing as much of her as I could on my radio shows. I wore her records out. The needle wore through to the other side."

Carol always included Flora Purim in her kiddie clinics. "The kids loved Flora maybe even more than Ella [Fitzgerald] or Sarah [Vaughan] because her songs were so crazy."[4]

Chick Corea recognized that willingness to stretch the boundaries and take vocal risks when he asked Flora to sing on *Return to Forever*, the first album by the group with the same name. Flora remembers:

> In the early 70s, Chick Corea asked me to listen to some songs. None of his songs had lyrics. He had sent his music to Ella [Fitzgerald], Carmen [McRae], Sarah [Vaughan], and Nancy [Wilson], and they all sent it back saying the music was nice, but they couldn't take a risk to change their style from Bebop to that style of music called Fusion. So one day he asked me if I could come to his place and try to sing his new compositions. Then I took a chance and went.[5]

Both Carol and Dianne agree that, although the Brazilian husband and wife came as a package deal, it was Flora they had hoped to promote. Although many Americans heard Flora's six-octave-range brand of contemporary jazz for the first time on Chick Corea's 1972 albums *Return to Forever* and *Light as a Feather*, in Brazil she had been Hermeto Pascoal's lead singer. Along with Airto, she toured Europe with Stan Getz in 1968 and Gil Evans in 1971. Her unique style of blending lyrics with ethereal-sounding syllables caught the attention of fans and critics alike, and in the seventies she became a four-time winner of Best Female Jazz Vocalist in the *Down Beat* poll and was twice nominated for a Grammy in the Best Female Jazz Vocalist category.

Together Flora and Airto changed the flavor of Latin jazz. Flora's pure, clear flowing lines were undercut with an intensity that until then had been absent from bossa nova. Using Brazilian percussion as a foundation, Airto's work with Miles Davis and the early Weather Report albums not only spiced up the arsenal of instruments available but added fire and unprecedented excitement. The couple's work together on the Return to Forever albums left no doubt that Brazil's contribution to the jazz world had a new depth.

Flora was born in 1942 to a Russian émigré, violinist father and a Brazilian, pianist mother. She grew up in Rio de Janeiro. Her father forbade jazz in the house, so when he went to work, Flora's mother played Billie Holiday and Frank Sinatra records. She also introduced Flora to her favorite pianists: Bill Evans, Erroll Garner, and Oscar Peterson.[6] Flora not only learned an appreciation of jazz but this defiance of her father laid the groundwork for the political protest songs she later wrote against a repressive Brazilian government.

Flora moved to New York City in 1967. Airto soon followed. They married and quickly became involved in Fusion, the electric jazz movement that was trying to "re-educate discriminating musical minds." They also became involved with the New York drug scene. In 1971, not long after giving birth to the couple's daughter Diana, Flora was arrested for possession of cocaine.[7] During the nearly three years between sentencing and incarceration, Flora performed at outdoor festivals with Santana and Mickey Hart, took her own group to the International Jazz Festival in Montreux, Switzerland, and released her first American album, *Butterfly Dreams*. She then released six more: *500 Miles High* and *Stories to Tell*, two with Carlos Santana, and two with Airto. After the couple moved to San Francisco, Flora was sentenced to the Federal Correctional Institution, Terminal Island, in Los Angeles. Her year-and-a-half sentence began on August 24, 1974, hours after she had completed the recording of her second album, *Stories to Tell*. In his book *The Story of Flora Purim*, Edward Bunker recounts the closing moments of that recording session. "Flora stepped away from the microphone, her head bowed, her eyes closed, her body moving to the music. Then she moved back to the mike to reprise the final chorus. 'There's music all around. Can't you hear? Can't you see? I am free . . .'"[8]

The Best Is Yet to Come

Between her conviction and incarceration, Flora Purim secured her international reputation and again won the *Down Beat* readers' poll for best female vocalist. Her established contacts and credentials supported a career momentum that was out-of-bounds to newcomers. For the jazzwomen who participated in the 1981 Women's Jazz Festival's Friday night TNT concert, that level of professional achievement was still a dream.

Kansas City Star reviewer Terry Teachout called TNT "the Women's Jazz Festival's most important contribution to the cause of female jazz artists everywhere."[9] At a time when ERA had stalled out and female performers found themselves backlashed into a freshly conservative political climate, this opportunity for national exposure was unique indeed. In a *Kansas City Times* article two days before the TNT concert, author Letty Cottin Pogrebin wrote, "The Reagan administration is anti-women, and anyone who sees light at the end of the tunnel is probably looking in the wrong direction."[10] The TNT concert took steps to turn that tunnel around.

Combo Contest winner Sojourner, a seven-piece group from the Chicago/Detroit area with strong ties to Wayne State University, embodied the evolving face of contemporary jazz. A committee of eight WJF board members (Sylvia Bell, Joan Griffith, Ben Seagraves, Marinka Robinson, Marie Spearing, Mary Hodges, Carol Comer, and Dianne Gregg) selected Sojourner from among twenty submissions. The group's unique instrumentation, which included bass clarinet, harp, and sitar, as well as vocals and multiple percussion instruments, caught the committee's attention as an offering that would expose WJF's audience to adventurous new sounds and textures. The band's members—vocalists Rita Warford and Chavunduka, percussionists Sherri Weathersby and Aisha Hill, reeds player Elreta Dodds, harpist and flutist Kafi Patrice Nassoma, and sitarist Shanta Nurullah—had collectively studied or played with a powerhouse list of musicians: Woody Shaw, Pharoah Sanders, Anthony Braxton, LeRoy Jenkins, Art Blakey, and Lonnie Smith. This influence, and the group's mutual creativity, reflected, in their own words, "a culmination of all women's experience . . . the soul of women."[11]

One of the most rewarding aspects for everyone involved with WJF was to find and spotlight young talent. If that talent was right in Kansas City's own backyard, the reward was extra sweet. When Carol and Dianne heard singer Deborah Brown at the Crown Center Signboard Bar, they immediately invited her to perform at the 1981 TNT concert. Powerful and sensitive, playful and poignant, Deborah's voice wrapped itself around a tune and made it bloom. Whether scatting a bebop line or belting out a show tune ballad, Deborah's command of her vocal instrument had already made her a favorite in jazz clubs and hotels all over the country, Las Vegas in particular. But it was in her hometown that her cool blend of artistry and showmanship sparkled.

Making WJF truly international, the Swedish five-piece group Salamander appeared at the suggestion of Leonard Feather. With the instrumentation of two tenor saxes, bass, drums (the drummer doubled on trumpet), and piano, this group's sound reflected equal parts Ornette Coleman and Kurt Weill. Popular at festivals across Europe, Salamander's original music cut and pasted avant garde melodic and harmonic lines with the rhythms of jazz-flavored European music of the twenties and thirties, and did so without pretention or cuteness. Salamander's set may not have reflected the audience's idea of jazz, but it was authentic and mind-expanding. Marian McPartland put it this way: "Jazz is an indigenous music that reflects the culture and experience of the people playing it."[12]

To close out the evening, the San Francisco quintet ALIVE! brought yet another dimension of jazz to the stage. With roots in the growing women's culture movement, this all-acoustic band consisted of vocalist rhiannon (Terry Teachout calls this omission of a capital R "painfully trendy"),[13] pianist Janet Small, bassist Suzanne Vincenza, drummer Barbara Borden, and percussionist Carolyn Brandy.

"In the band we have an agreement not to use political rhetoric," bass player Suzanne told *Christian Science Monitor* writer and jazz pianist Amy Duncan. "We use experiences from our lives—we want to make ourselves as accessible as possible."[14] That those experiences were varied and happened in different parts of the country enhanced the ensemble. Suzanne spent the sixties involved with politics. Barbara had given up the drums and worked a day gig before making the commitment to a musical career. Before moving to New York to be a part of the musical comedy scene, rhiannon grew up on a farm in South Dakota. Both Carolyn and Janet started out on violin. Janet became a political science major, but her interest in reggae, funk, and the piano led her to a personal exploration of jazz composition. "I like the idea that we are saying something on stage that has to do with our lives and the world." Janet's music, in Amy Duncan's words, is "pithy, fascinating, and difficult, with complicated time changes and driving rhythms."[15] After giving up the violin, Carolyn became interested in African and Latin percussion. Her study of Afro-Cuban, Afro-Haitian, and Brazilian rhythms and instruments gave ALIVE! an energy all its own. With no declared leader, the band kept its objectives more cohesive and focused. Barbara explained, "I guess the goal with music is to have it be a way to help people tap into the highest universal resources in themselves and bring out the good, positive qualities."[16]

Time After Time

As the Main Concert got underway on Sunday, March 27, positive qualities abounded. All the worry about Flora and Airto's appearance remained unknown to the audience. As with any festival, the behind-the-scenes work, positively professional and organized, kept dreams of success from imploding. Nothing was assumed.

Holding the position, annually, as the most precarious segment of WJF, the All-Stars were a wild card. The first year Marian McPartland took the guesswork out of the equation by hiring the quintet she had recently worked with. In 1979 All-Star players were selected by board members' votes, and a clash of musical styles and personalities threatened to derail the set. Leader Jill McManus, to the satisfaction of musicians and critics alike, selected the 1980 All-Stars. Finding the perfect balance between understanding ensemble playing and showcasing the individual instruments didn't just happen. With all this as precedent, the 1981 All-Stars had high expectations to meet. Saxophonist Jean Fineberg recalls that the All-Stars had one quick rehearsal, typical of this format, and that everyone picked one tune. She had not played before with any of her bandmates.[17]

Once again the All-Stars came from a variety of backgrounds. Jean co-led Deuce, a jazz septet in New York, but had recorded with David Bowie, Laura Nyro, and Sister Sledge. Guitarist Brandy Anthony played with the Houston Pops Orchestra, as well as Bobbie Gentry, Sammy Davis Jr., Lionel Hampton, Benny Goodman, and Chuck Berry. Marilyn Donadt had played drums in the 1980 combo winner, Quintess, and was back to stretch the boundaries of percussion. The program notes tell us, "Her percussion work features special sound effects via original self-made instruments and found objects."[18] Both bassist Rosemary Galloway and reed player Kathryn Moses were from Toronto, Canada. Rosemary had backed numerous singers, including Lola Falana, and led her own band, the Swing Sisters. "Kathryn performs many styles of music and would like to avoid typecasting,"[19] but the program notes go on to say she was one of Canada's best-known and highly respected flutists. Pianist and vocalist Judy Roberts had already established herself in the Midwest as a performer who would pack a club and entertain audiences with her "extraordinary harmonies, instrumental virtuosities and all-around good feeling."[20]

As diverse as the All-Stars' backgrounds were, their musical experiences assured an interesting mix of sound. After a tenuous start, the group settled into a comfortable stride, wrapped themselves around Marilyn's inventive percussion effects, and presented a sterling performance.

When Ernestine Anderson took the stage after the All-Stars, she had been singing professionally for over thirty years and was once again gaining the attention she deserved. Yet most in the audience had never heard of her. Born in Houston, Texas, in 1928, Ernestine grew up around gospel and blues. At the age of three, Ernestine had astounded her parents when she began singing Bessie Smith tunes from their record collection. Besides listening to Bessie Smith, she favored Muddy Waters and John Lee Hooker recordings. Her father sang in a gospel quartet, and both grandparents sang in the church choir. "I don't even remember what my first experience with music was. I sort of grew into it."[21] Soon she was soloing in the church choir, and after winning a talent contest sponsored by a local nightclub, she had a steady, one-night-a-week gig—all at the age of twelve. Her grandmother had entered Ernestine's name in the contest on a whim. "I only knew two songs, 'On the Sunny Side of the Street' and 'So Long,'" Ernestine admitted. "The piano player asked me what key did I do these songs in and I just said 'C' for some reason and it was the wrong key. In order to save face I sang around the melody, improvised among the melody, and when I finished one of the musicians told me I was a jazz singer."[22] At eighteen she toured the West Coast with Johnny Otis and his popular rhythm and blues band. In her early twenties she became the vocalist in Lionel Hampton's band that also featured Jimmy Cleveland, Clifford Brown, and Art Farmer. In 1958 *Time* magazine called her "the best new voice in the business."[23] But the music business is a fickle business. More than once Ernestine's singing career took off only to stall.

After moving to Seattle with her family when she was in high school, Ernestine was recruited, along with a young trumpet player named Quincy Jones, to join Robert "Bumps" Blackwell's Junior Band. One gig led to another until, in 1952, she became Lionel Hampton's vocalist, replacing Betty Carter. When the demands of the road clashed with raising the family she now had, Ernestine settled in New York City. Still determined to make it as a musician, she worked in clubs and recording studios as she perfected her "tasteful, slightly gritty, moderately swinging contralto."[24] She found measured success as she built a reputation recording with bebop alto player "Gigi" Gryce. She resolved to blend family and career and be content staying in one place, but that often meant supplementing gigs with employment as a waitress or hotel maid. She marked time in New York, known as the girl who was a poor man's Ella or the one who sounds like Sarah. Anxious for an opportunity to establish her own identity, the road beckoned again, this time with trumpeter Rolf Ericson. After leaving her two children with her parents, Ernestine took off for a Scandinavian tour, which produced her first album, *Hot Cargo*.

In 1958 *Time* magazine puzzled why Ernestine Anderson, freshly back in the States, was under-appreciated. Too often compared to other better-known jazz singers, Ernestine's critical and popular success abroad didn't translate in her own country. Swedish crowds loved her and mobbed her concerts, seduced by the voice that "curls around the lyrics like a husky caress." Yet here at home she remained a jazz secret.[25]

Hot Cargo changed all that. With its American success, acceptance seemed assured. In 1958 she was invited to perform at the first Monterey Jazz Festival. *Down Beat* named her "New Vocal Star of 1959." Noted jazz critic Nat Hentoff said of her singing, "She phrases with intelligence, taste and a jazz musician's plasticity of line."[26] Quincy Jones said her voice sounded like "honey at dusk."[27]

As the sixties dawned, a change in the musical climate cut that momentum short. "A jazz person couldn't work in the United States when rock & roll became the music," Ernestine told author Brian Lanker.[28] She moved to London for two years only to find that the second wave of rock & roll—with the British Invasion bands leading the charge—had overshadowed American female singers. "As a singer who came of age performing with jazz orchestras in the 1940s," reported Andrew Gilbert for *Jazz Times*, "Ernestine Anderson was on the frontline when the seismic forces unleashed by rock swept away most of the American music market."[29] Accolades for Ernestine came less frequently, her gigs became less prestigious.

Flora Purim had come to the United States to nurture her style of singing. Ernestine Anderson left the United States for the same reason. But in Ernestine's case, a younger generation, impatient with songs from their parents' youth, made her style less relevant. "In order to keep working I had to leave the country. And when I came back, I stopped singing for a while. I just didn't want to go through the hassle of starting all over again. I decided maybe it was time for me to give it up, and that's what I did."

But by the time Dianne Gregg suggested Ernestine as a potential artist for WJF, her career was again on an upswing. Her old friend bassist Ray Brown had secured her a spot on the Concord Jazz Festival in 1976, which led to a recording contract with the new jazz label, Concord Records. By the end of the decade, she had produced three albums on that label. Her most current at the time of WJF, the Grammy-nominated *Never Make Your Move too Soon*, displays the voice that critic Ralph Gleason had championed for almost two decades. Eighteen years earlier, he had told readers of his *San Francisco Chronicle* jazz column, "She has good diction, time, an uncanny ability to phrase well, great warmth in her voice, a true tone and, on top of all that, she swings like mad."[30]

Accompanied by pianist Barney McLure, bassist Dan Dean, and drummer Moyes Lucas, Ernestine pulled out of her repertoire tried and true, if uninspired, tunes such as "Sunny," "Here's That Rainy Day," "Fly Me to the Moon," and "Summertime." The excitement and energy behind her distinctive voice and stage presence compensated for the threadbare, typical festival tunes and left the audience hungry for more. Fortunately for the audience and Ernestine Anderson fans, there was much more to follow. Partly because of her exposure at the 1981 WJF, Ernestine's career finally took off in earnest, and she recorded eighteen more albums.

After the intermission, Shirley Scott's playing reminded the audience how she acquired the title "The Queen of the Organ." Along with drummer Keith Copeland and tenor saxophonist Harold Vick, Aunt Shirley, as sidemen often called her, laid down a dazzling set. As far as Shirley was concerned, that dazzle reflected the trio. Shirley told Marian McPartland that she didn't like playing solo organ, that adding instruments was like adding food. The result, Marian acknowledged, was a "subtle and lyrical bebop style."[31] There was a more energetic flipside to that analysis. In his liner notes for Shirley's 1961 album, *Hip Twist*, Tom Wilson wrote, "Scottie casts aside her natural restraint on up-tempo selections to get right down to the nitty-gritty, building inspiring solos ablaze with febrile heat and an incandescent light, drawing the audience to her soulful flame, like moths to a candle."[32]

Forty-seven at the time of her WJF appearance, Shirley's earliest memory was of sitting on her mother's lap while she played piano. At three Shirley joined her mother on the piano bench. Her love of music, fostered on that bench, was always on the surface of her life.[33] Trumpeter Terrell Stafford, who played with Aunt Shirley much later, recalls that she always laughed when she played. Distracted at first—he wasn't quite sure where her laughter was directed—he soon realized that her laughter bubbled up out of pure joy.[34] Playing music was everything to Shirley, and that kind of pleasure was infectious to those who played with her.

Part of that joy came from the instrument she played. The Hammond B-3 organ, considered by many to be the Harley Davidson of keyboard instruments, is essentially a big band in a box. Although capable of producing delicate, pianissimo lines, the B-3, paired with a Leslie speaker, creates a fully balanced, soul-singing, surround sound. Its two sixty-one-note manuals equal five octaves. A foot pedal controls the volume, but each pitch is sustained until the key is released, creating a warm singing quality. The light action of the keys makes playing rapid passages much easier than on a piano.[35]

Shirley Scott took total command of the monstrous pieces of musical furniture that were the B-3 and Leslie. Her casual manner and soft-spoken voice contradicted the power she radiated and the energetic force field she created. After playing piano and trumpet throughout high school, Shirley had switched to organ in 1955. In 1956 she began a very long and prolific career playing in clubs (she was one of the few women to lead her own group at the Village Vanguard) and recording, initially with tenor saxophonist Eddie "Lockjaw" Davis. Davis had called her to fill in when his former organist abruptly left to form his own band.[36] Shirley had been playing the organ for six months. By 1960 she had recorded twelve albums. In 1961 she formed her own group but soon joined with tenor player Stanley Turrentine, whom she married in 1960, to establish the organ trio that sustained her throughout the sixties. That partnership resulted in another twenty-three albums.[37]

At the time of her WJF appearance, Shirley had taken her love of jazz to the classroom. That infectious joy she displayed while playing made a natural crossover when working with students at clinics and workshops. She had much to pass on. In the liner notes to Shirley Scott's memorial album, Harry Duncan, host of the San Francisco radio show *In the Soul Kitchen*, summed up her style: "She had a masterful understanding of dynamics and a keen sense for the myriad possibilities of the organ's voicings. Most of all she knew how to work a groove with conviction, imagination, and her insatiable sense of swing."[38]

Dr. Jive

All that joy, and the residue of pulsing swing, faded as the post-Shirley stage remained empty. Anticipation grew to impatient restlessness as the audience speculated on the cause of the delay. The hour was late, and everyone was anxious to hear Flora Purim, the Latin singer Chick Corea had introduced to jazz-fusion fans, live for the first time in Kansas City.

Until Leonard Feather made the announcement that Flora and her band had been delayed by a Colorado snowstorm, Carol, Dianne, and concert manager board members Ben Seagraves and Marie Spearing were the only ones who knew just how upsetting the group's absence was.

Carol and Dianne had fumed all afternoon. Besides never dealing with a tardy act before, they were flabbergasted that Flora and Airto would so blatantly swindle them out of transportation money. "We always paid the groups' transportation costs up front," Dianne explains. "One of our board members was a travel agent, so when we made up the contracts—and we had to have signed contracts before we could do any publicity, so you know that was months before the festival—we always worked with her. The artist's agent or manager would tell us what it cost to transport the group to Kansas City from wherever they would be right before the festival, and if the travel agent thought that was fair, that's what we paid, along with half their performance fee."[39]

"We didn't ask for receipts," Carol continues, "because all the travel expenses were reasonable. We just sent them the money for travel along with their front money. No one had ever given us any trouble about it."[40]

The same arrangement was true with Flora's group. Because they lived in Los Angeles at the time, Flora and Airto had requested, and were given, air travel expenses for seven band members from L.A. to Kansas City. Their performance fee included a sound check and full concert set.

"They came in defensive," remembers Dianne. "They knew they were very late, had cold equipment, and were facing an unhappy audience."[41]

Carol recalls that things went from bad to worse. "No one came up to us or Ben or Marie to apologize for being late or to check in or anything. We didn't see a manager, and neither Flora nor Airto sought us out. They just plugged their mikes and amps into the house system and started, which proved to be a problem."[42]

A couple of tunes into the set, the sound from their mikes started cutting out, and feedback from their amps sharply blemished the sound. This very electronic fusion group had eschewed the already-in-place and proven equipment for their own just out of the truck. Yet a surly Airto snarled into a working mike, "This Women's Jazz Festival needs to get new sound equipment. You'd think they'd have equipment that worked."[43]

"Well, we were livid," Carol says. "They had missed the sound check, which would have fixed any of the problems *their* equipment had. Our equipment had worked perfectly all night."[44]

Dianne had already made out the group's check. "Their check was $500 short of the original agreed upon amount because they missed the sound check and had already been paid more money than they needed for travel. We thought that was fair. But we were pretty sure Airto at least wouldn't see it that way."[45] Anticipating a confrontation, Carol and Dianne, along with board member Abel Ramirez, left the Music Hall and went back to wait at their suite at Crown Center.

Everyone seemed displeased with this concert finale. Terry Teachout reported that the band's "confused texture of sound" overpowered Flora's singing and "covered up the elaborate percussive fantasies conjured at the side of the stage by Moreira."[46] Teachout concluded that all of this could have been avoided by a sound check.

"Ben and Marie gave Airto the check at the end of the concert," says Dianne, "but of course he wasn't happy. He came to our suite to get that $500, but we stood firm."[47]

"Abel tried to reason with Airto, Latin man to Latin man," Carol remembers, "but Airto came in menacing and he remained that way. He really tried to bully us."[48]

When it became clear that Airto was not going to leave with another check, he left the room shouting, "We will never work this festival again!" Dianne shot back, "You've got that right."[49]

Even now disappointed in that segment, Dianne concludes, "It was a bummer of a way to end a year's worth of work. Everything else had gone so smoothly, but as much as we wanted to promote Flora, Airto turned it all ugly. I don't think we even talked to Flora."[50]

WOMEN'S JAZZ FESTIVAL

P. O. Box 22321
Kansas City, Missouri 64113

Women's Jazz Festival logo 1977–1983. IMAGE COURTESY OF MIKE NING.

Philharmonic ringers Dale Weddle and Chris Gekker save the day for the jazzers at the basketball fundraiser, 1977.
Reprinted by permission of Bob Barrett.

Jazz musicians on the bench, basketball fundraiser, 1977. Left to right: Tommy Ruskin, Horace Washington, John Lyman (on floor), Pete Eye, Mike Ning, Milt Abel, Scotty Robinson, unidentified friend, Steve Cardenas. Reprinted by permission of Bob Barrett.

Volunteers help Dianne (far left) and Carol (with megaphone) sell T-shirts, 1978. Reprinted by permission of Bob Barrett.

Marian McPartland and Leonard Feather at first Women's Jazz Festival, 1978.

Mary Osborne, 1978. Reprinted by permission of Paul Smith.

Lynn Milano, 1978. Reprinted by permission of Paul Smith.

Mary Fettig Park, 1978. Reprinted by permission of Paul Smith.

Betty Carter, 1978. Reprinted by permission of Bob Barrett.

Leonard Feather and Mary Lou Williams, 1978. Reprinted by permission of Bob Barrett.

Toshiko Akiyoshi, 1978. Reprinted by permission of Bob Barrett.

Toshiko Akiyoshi, 1978. Reprinted by permission of Bob Barrett.

Toshiko Akiyoshi/Lew Tabackin Big Band, 1978. Reprinted by permission of Paul Smith.

Aerial: Nina Sheldon, Carline Ray, Barbara London, Barbara Merjan, 1979. Reprinted by permission of Bob Barrett.

Joanne Brackeen's clinic, 1979. Reprinted by permission of Bob Barrett.

Joanne Brackeen, 1979. Reprinted by permission of Bob Barrett.

Urszula Dudziak, 1979. Reprinted by permission of Bob Barrett.

Marian McPartland and Brian Torff, 1979. Reprinted by permission of Paul Smith.

Jane Ira Bloom, 1979. Reprinted by permission of Bob Barrett.

Melba Liston, 1979. Reprinted by permission of Bob Barrett.

Melba Liston and Carol Kaye, 1979. Reprinted by permission of Paul Smith.

Monnette Sudler, 1979. Reprinted by permission of Bob Barrett.

Carol Kaye wearing WJF medallion, 1979. Reprinted by permission of Bob Barrett.

Altered 1979 All Stars: Marian McPartland, Carol Kaye, Melba Liston, and Barbara Merjan. Reprinted by permission of Bob Barrett.

Carmen McRae, 1979. Reprinted by permission of Bob Barrett.

Left: Carmen McRae at the piano, 1979. Reprinted by permission of Paul Smith.

Below: Stacy Rowles playing with Maiden Voyage, 1980. Reprinted by permission of Paul Smith.

Maiden Voyage, 1980. Reprinted by permission, f104, Women's Jazz Festival (K0314), The State Historical Society of Missouri Research Center-Kansas City, Photograph Collection.

Carla Bley, 1980. Reprinted by permission of Paul Smith.

Cleo Laine and John Dankworth, 1980. Reprinted by permission of Paul Smith.

Cleo Laine and Leonard Feather, 1980. Reprinted by permission of Bob Barrett.

Yes M.A.A.M. Band, 1981. Reprinted by permission of Bob Barrett.

Shanta Nurullah of Sojourner, 1981. Reprinted by permission of Bob Barrett.

Dianne Reeves, 1980. Reprinted by permission, f103, Women's Jazz Festival (K0314) SHSMO-KC.

Salamander: Cecilia Wennerstrom and Katarina Karlsson, 1981. Reprinted by permission of Bob Barrett.

Calico (left to right): Lynn Riley, Joan Griffith, Carol Comer (not pictured: Helen Marquette), 1982. Reprinted by permission, f103, Women's Jazz Festival (K0314) SHSMO-KC.

Swing Sisters (left to right): Rosemary Galloway, Norma Thompson, Jane Fair, Stacy Rowles, Jo Sarjeant, 1982.
Reprinted by permission, f103, Women's Jazz Festival (K0314) SHSMO-KC.

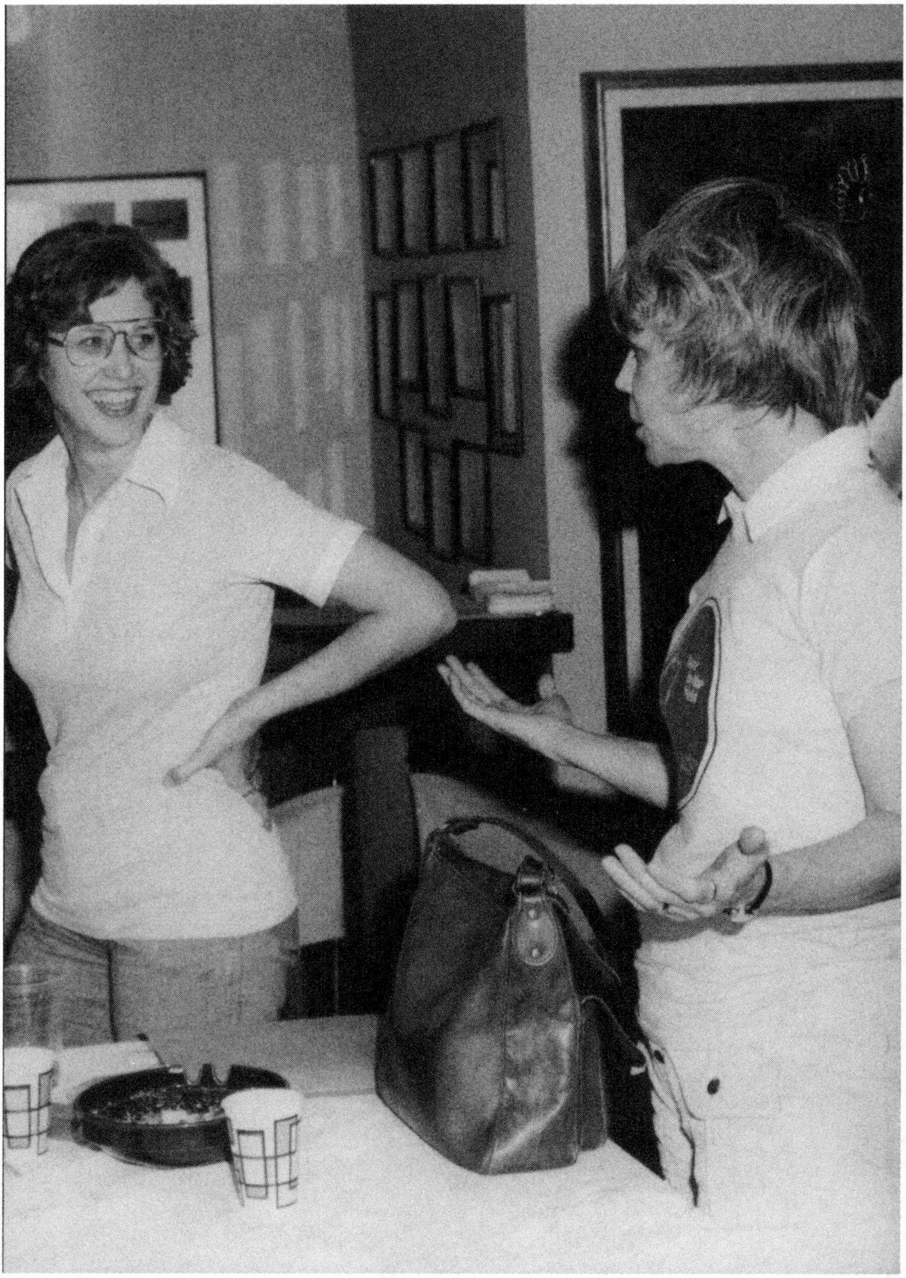

Dianne Gregg and Carol Comer at the WJF World Headquarters.

Reprinted by permission of Bob Barrett.

Alexandria's Ragtime Band, 1983. Reprinted by permission of Bob Barrett.

Above: Sheila Jordan and Harvie S, 1983. Reprinted by permission, f104, Women's Jazz Festival (K0314) SHSMO-KC.

Right: Susan Freundlich, 1985. Reprinted by permission, f102, Women's Jazz Festival (K0314) SHSMO-KC.

Chapter 6

The Fifth Year

March 24–28, 1982

"Is it possible that there is a mysterious element in the nature of musical creativity that runs counter to the nature of the female mind?"
—Aaron Copland

ON MAY 28, 1981, THREE WEEKS past her seventy-first birthday, Mary Lou Williams died of bladder cancer in her Durham, North Carolina, home. Throughout the country, jazz fans mourned her, but those in Kansas City felt they had lost a favorite aunt. In his *New York Times* obituary, jazz critic John S. Wilson referred to Mary Lou as "the first woman to be ranked with the greatest of jazz musicians."[1] For many, Mary Lou Williams embodied the sound of what a jazz musician was, regardless of gender. Her prodigious musicals gifts became obvious at a young age in her native Pittsburgh, but it wasn't until she moved to Kansas City in the late 1920s that her career took shape.

Although her time with the Andy Kirk Band is well documented, it began inauspiciously. Hired by an undertaker to drive a hearse, Mary Lou doubled as a chauffeur for Andy's band. "I'd wait outside ballrooms in the car, and if things went bad and people weren't dancing, they would send somebody to get me, and

I'd go in and play 'Froggy Bottom' or some other boogie-woogie number—and things would jump."[2]

Mary Lou's talents overrode social taboos concerning mixed-gender jams, especially in the middle of the night. "One night, around 4 a.m., I awoke hearing someone pecking on my screen. I opened the window on Ben Webster. He was saying, 'Get up, pussycat, we're jammin' and all the pianists are tired out now. Coleman Hawkins has got his shirt off and is still blowing.'"[3]

Tenor man John Williams, who later became Mary Lou's husband, spoke for the other male musicians in the first band the couple played in together. He was repulsed by the idea of a fourteen-year-old, girl piano player. Then he heard her play. "I never heard anything like that in my life. Terrific." Williams was most impressed with her left hand. The absence of the demure touch he associated with female pianists quickly got his attention. "She played note for note anything that she heard, Earl Hines, Jelly Roll Morton, and heavy like a man."[4]

Her genius, admired, respected, and sought after, directly influenced the careers of jazz greats Bud Powell, Thelonious Monk, and Erroll Garner, among others. But it was her compositions that propelled the art form forward. The arrangements she did for Count Basie and Duke Ellington endure as relevant pieces in any age. Her three masses demonstrate just how universal spiritual music can be. *Zodiac Suite*, a masterpiece of modern music with more in common with Norman Dello Joio than Fats Waller, defies classification even seventy years after it was written. "I change all the time," she told *New Yorker* jazz critic Whitney Balliett. "I experiment to keep up with what is going on, to hear what everybody else is doing. I even keep a little ahead of them." Regardless of the style or era, she remained "the lady who swings the band."[5] Fellow pianist Billy Taylor explains, "She has the most consistent way of swinging. Even with a rhythm section that isn't quite hanging together, she can make it swing."[6]

Yet, as with any pioneer, the path she forged wasn't always smooth. She felt she was passed over as a potential on-screen Hollywood player—a part Hazel Scott excelled at—because she was too black. Bad business advice meant that others repeatedly used her tunes without paying her royalties. Although Mary Lou never lacked in confidence, her jealousies toward other women pianists—particularly Hazel Scott and Marian McPartland—were legendary.

It was a volley from the State Department that hurt the most. During the Cold War, the State Department used jazz as a diplomatic tool, sending well-known jazz players on tour behind the Iron Curtain, to Africa, and to the Middle East. This soft propaganda worked beautifully in winning over the hearts and dancing feet of citizens from Ghana to Moscow, Iraq to Prague. Starting in 1956, bands led by Duke Ellington, Benny Goodman, Dave Brubeck, Louis Armstrong, and Dizzy Gillespie worked to promote democracy and dispel Americans' reputations for propagating racism. Yet when Mary Lou Williams proposed a group to join these tours, she was turned down flat on religious grounds.

Mary Lou's conversion to Catholicism had changed her life and given her a center she had longed for. It was a private decision that did not alter her commitment to jazz. Yet those on the State Department acceptance committee thought of her as a religious fanatic and too unstable for an overseas tour. Other jazz musicians—John Coltrane, Sonny Rollins, and even Dizzy Gillespie—had gone through periods of self-discovery that involved publicized religious conversions. To the State Department, those men were looking for ways to enrich their souls and art. In Mary Lou's case, they felt her commitment to Catholicism just left her unbalanced.

Crusty impatience often characterized Mary Lou's relationship with her sidemen, yet a strong affinity for teaching children the joys and mysteries of jazz brought her much pleasure. Concerned that jazz would die out without engaging a new generation of fans as well as players, she championed the idea that jazz be taught in public schools. She set up impromptu workshops on Harlem streets and taught kids to scat. She taught at a Pittsburgh high school and worked with children's choirs. Although she hadn't finished high school, Duke University offered her an artist-in-residency. Starting in the fall of 1977, she taught jazz history, led a jazz ensemble, and gave private lessons. Inspired by the students' enthusiasm for old as well as new styles of jazz—many she herself had helped to form—Mary Lou found a peace at Duke that had eluded her elsewhere. She was awarded Teacher of the Year, and until illness made it impossible for her to attend classes, she continued to find ways to connect students to jazz in pertinent and lasting ways.

Mary Lou was in her second year of teaching at Duke when she taped the infamous *Piano Jazz* segment with Marian McPartland. Marian began the interview by asking about Mary Lou's teaching: "How do you explain to your kids when you play a chord like this?" and Marian played a modern jazz chord. Mary Lou shot back, "I don't play a chord like that." The more Marian tried to engage Mary Lou in a casual but informative conversation, the more closed-lipped Mary Lou became. The strain between these two piano giants, too uncomfortable to be broadcast as the first *Piano Jazz* show, seemed to mark a deep breach.[7]

When she learned of Mary Lou's cancer, soon after the *Piano Jazz* taping, Marian sent Mary Lou a St. Cecilia medallion. Aware that Mary Lou was a devout Catholic, Marian hoped this symbol of the patron saint of music would offer her the healing power music can provide. That gesture went a long way toward softening the relationship between the two.[8]

Mary Lou Williams' funeral mass, at St. Ignatius Loyola Church in New York, was packed with fans and friends, as well as a who's who array of musicians. Sarah Vaughan sent flowers arranged to look like a piano. Benny Goodman sat near the front. Dizzy Gillespie and Buster Williams played tributes. At the personal request of Mary Lou's manager, Father Peter O'Brien, Marian played "What's Your Story, Morning Glory?" Marian's biographer Paul De Barros relates that Marian played "in honor of the woman she had revered since she was a teenager and with whom she had finally made peace."[9]

Others besides Marian had experienced Mary Lou's displeasure, as well as her generosity, her surliness, and her love. She came as a complete package, and her music would survive the same way. As she told *Down Beat* in 1964, "Anything you are shows up in your music."[10]

But Not for Me

By 1982, the taboos shattered by iconic role models like Mary Lou Williams and Marian McPartland made the environment for a new generation of female players more accepting, save one place: the big band. The 1970s saw a resurgence of big band popularity, but unlike the big bands of the 1930s and 1940s, these bands played in concert halls rather than dance halls. They appeared at jazz festivals and college auditoriums all over the world.

With very few exceptions, they played those concerts without women sitting in the horn and woodwind section chairs. Woody Herman hadn't hired a female horn player since World War II, when a shortage of available males put Billie Rogers in the trumpet section. In 1973 saxophonist Mary Fettig was the first female to play with Stan Kenton. The second and last female in Kenton's band, Lisa Hittle, played baritone saxophone in 1979. Janice Robinson played trombone in the Thad Jones/Mel Lewis Jazz Orchestra during roughly the same time that Mary Fettig played with Kenton. Trombonist Lolly Bienenfeld toured and recorded with that band in 1978. Although Janice Robinson was hired for a recording date with Buddy Rich, he wasn't aware he'd have a "chick" in the trombone section until he got to the session.[11] Ann

Patterson played lead alto, soprano sax, oboe, and piccolo in the innovative Don Ellis Orchestra. Don may have been enlightened, but the cameramen at their Montreux Jazz Festival concert were not. Instead of giving her on-screen time during one of her solos, the camera focused on a resting, all-male trumpet section. When Gerry Mulligan formed a concert big band in the late seventies, Laurie Frink played lead trumpet both on his world tours and for the Grammy-winning album *Walk on the Water*. For a short time, Gil Evans had both Janice Robinson and drummer Sue Evans in his traveling band. Again, a European cameraman tarnished that triumph by shooting an uncomfortably long shot focused on Sue Evans's breasts.[12] Besides this handful of women, no others had broken what author Don Heckman calls "the brass ceiling."[13]

Even though the traditional big band format was not welcoming to women, all-girl big bands were slow to form. Like its male counterpart, this late twentieth-century brand of all-female band was not interested in offering danceable music with commercial value. Careful attention to new arrangements that reflected a melting pot of musical influences—rock to soul to Latin to contemporary classical—meant finding women who could write as well as play. Horn and rhythm section players were recruited from music schools and late-night jams. Pink frilly dresses were forbidden.

As its name suggests, Maiden Voyage took off first. This West Coast band had morphed out of the Bonnie Janofsky-Roz Cron, then Ann Patterson, Big Band and, with WJF's help, gained national attention. In 1982 a fledgling form of the Kit McClure Band hit the scene in New York. The always affable Clark Terry formed an all-female big band to perform at the Wichita Jazz Festival in 1976, but the one-time concert served more as an exclamation point than a statement. It would be another decade before the formation of female concert big bands such as DIVA Jazz Orchestra, the Seattle Women's Jazz Orchestra, and Montclair

Women's Big Band. The unwieldy number of players to coordinate and the travel costs—aspects of the business that plague any bandleader—made smaller groups that much more attractive.

Without a doubt, WJF and her sister festivals aided in the proliferation of all-female small groups during this period. Unprecedented exposure to large audiences, national press coverage, and opportunities for networking and hearing new ideas made for fertile ground. All of this was enhanced by the fact that they were doing what they loved best. Kansas City was right in the center of this growing trend.

As evidenced by WJF lineups, all-female groups found March in Kansas City a nurturing oasis. Hometown favorite and jam session backbone, Airhart, gained national attention. The North Texas State band Yes M.A.A.M. showed a sense of humor as well as their proficiency. TNT groups Quintess, Mary Watkins Band, Maiden Voyage, Sojourner, Salamander, and ALIVE! had already made their marks. The first WJF Combo Contest winner, New York's Aerial, used their appearance in Kansas City as a springboard to the Newport Jazz Festival and beyond. Other all-female New York jazz groups included Melba Liston's self-named Melba Liston and Company (which included WJF alumni Dottie Dodgion, Carline Ray, and Janice Robinson), a salsa band called Latin Fever, and Jazz Sisters, with 1980 All-Star pianist Jill McManus, 1978 All-Star bassist Lynn Milano, and the very busy, 1978 All-Star trombonist Janice Robinson. Also in New York, singer Evelyn Blakey led a group called Celebration. In Los Angeles, a sextet called Satin Dolls played mainstream jazz. All of these groups played original material.

At Last

Picking up where the previous year left off, the 1982 TNT concert, now in the smaller, ornate Folly Theater in downtown, promoted all-female jazz by becoming international. For the second year the concert featured a Swedish group. Tintomara, named after a popular intersex character in Swedish literature, consisted of a quartet: Elise Einarsdotter on piano, Yvonne Riggebo on drums, Katarina Fritzen on flute, and the only male on stage that evening, Elise's husband Olle Steinholt on bass.[14] The original material this European-style progressive jazz band played was infused with rock, yet fresh as a spring fiord.

Representing Canada, bassist Rosemary Galloway and reed player Jane Fair returned for a second year, along with fellow Canadians pianist Jo Sarjeant and drummer Norma Thompson. Stacy Rowles, the only American in the group, rounded out the Swing Sisters. Ironically this Toronto group played not swing but Dixieland.[15]

Although all natives of the USA, the a cappella group Sweet Honey in the Rock displayed their African roots in sparse, primitive sounds combined with traditional gospel. Using the human voice as a primary musical instrument and infusing their songs with consciousness-raising messages, Evelyn Maria Harris, Ysaye Maria Barnwell, Yasmeen Bheti Williams, and Bernice Johnson Reagon held the audience spellbound. Their power left the audience believing.

Bougainvillea, the only straight-ahead jazz group of the evening and the 1982 Combo Contest Winner, started their set by showing off the improvisational prowess of tenor saxophonist Gwen Delbaugh, vibist Jeannette Muzima, and drummer Sharon Eldridge. This Boston-based group faltered in the minefield of "ensemble comping" during solos, resulting in an unintended haphazard feel, but bassist Maggi Rizzi and pianist Paula Gallitano held their ground, and Gwen Delbaugh's tunes held the crowd's interest.

But it was during the multiple jam sessions, now an enthusiastically expected portion of the weekend, that the cause of recognizing female jazz musicians rippled into new areas. Although name acts and emerging stars garnered most of the attention, the importance of the jam sessions cannot be overstated.

There was an expectation about jamming in Kansas City at any time, not just WJF weekend. Going back to the heyday of the 1930s, master musicians had passed down the secrets of improv to the novices. A loosely defined apprentice system kept Kansas City swing in everyone's musical vocabulary. Kansas City guitarist Rod Fleeman, who later toured with Karrin Allyson and Diane Schuur, experienced this early on. "I had a steady, after-hours gig when I was about eighteen, and all the older, revered players would come in after their gigs. Sitting next to those giants, listening and taking tips from them gave me a better education than I was getting in college."[16] This exchange of musical knowledge happened all over town. Calico bassist Joan Griffith recalls, "Kansas City was a great jam town in those days. Any happy hour gig was a jam session."[17]

"There were a lot of six-night-a-week gigs when I started out," explains another Kansas City native, guitarist Danny Embrey, who in 1982 was on the road with Sergio Mendez. "On those six-nighters we played the same tunes with the same people night after night, and we loved it when our friends would show up with their instruments to sit in. It kept the gig fresh and gave us a chance to try out new ideas."[18]

Two more jams were added to the 1982 lineup. Wednesday afternoon, Calico hosted a three-hour jam at the Signboard lounge in Crown Center. Simultaneously, as an encore to the previous year's TNT concert, ALIVE! played as the house band at a jam at Harling's Upstairs Bar and Grill.[19]

Hoping to expand on those playing opportunities, the Genesis Jam, this year held at Penn Valley Community College, again gave younger musicians a non-competitive, nurturing learning environment. With New York pianist Amy Duncan and her quartet leading the way, novice jazzers learned to "play solo choruses, trade fours, comp, and otherwise improve their improvisational skills."[20] Nowhere else could a high school jazz student sit in with professionals in an alcohol-free club setting and learn in that time-tested way.

The continued success of two simultaneous, eight-hour jam sessions attests to the popularity of this WJF offering. Both hosted by Crown Center, the jams dominated Saturday afternoon, evening, and night. The Jazzwomen Session, held in the International Cafe, again used Calico as the house band. Composed of WJF board member musicians—Joan Griffith, bass; Helen Marquette, drums; Lynn Riley, flute and alto sax; and Carol Comer, piano and vocals—the quartet was dedicated to creating a welcoming environment for women who were more comfortable playing with other women. "Supersinger" rhiannon, from the group ALIVE!, joined Calico as a special guest.[21]

"We had to call tunes everyone knew," remembers Lynn Riley. "There had to be common tunes. Most of them were straight ahead or blues, swing, not much contemporary or fusion. People coming to Kansas City to play in a jam session expected a certain amount of Kansas City swing to be included. It influenced our playing, consciously or unconsciously."[22]

Helen Marquette remembers, "It was glorious. I was mesmerized by what was going on. The sense of freedom to not be shy we had at those sessions showed that jazz transcends male/female labels. I just remember a lot of joy in playing."[23]

Dianne recalls how exhausted everyone was by the end of the session, especially rhythm section players. "The Women's session had few drummers and few bass players, so Calico's drummer and bass player played very long days. There were always lots of piano players and tons of singers, a respectable amount of saxophone players, and a few brass."[24]

Helen remembers the same thing. "Since it was an eight-hour gig, I really depended on there being drummers who wanted to sit in, and there were some, but not many."[25]

Carol says the singers represented all levels of experience. "Singers would come up and I'd ask them what key they wanted and they'd have no idea. They'd just sing, 'My funny valentine . . .' I could find it and play it in any key, but it wasn't fun. They'd stick to that one pitch. If it was the key of B, I'd try to talk them down to B flat, but no, 'My funny,' right there."[26]

In the Central Exchange of the Crown Center Shops, Mike Ning's quartet again hosted the mixed session. Along with special guest artists for this session, drummer Scotty Robinson, bassist Suzanne Vincenza, and Maiden Voyage reed player Carol Chaikin, the quartet anchored the session while scores of both male and female players waited their turns to play.[27]

These fertile sessions mixed seasoned players with the more inexperienced. Anything could happen, anyone could show up. Both 1982 All-Star drummer Debbie Katz and 1982 All-Star saxophonist Lisa Gordanier were "discovered" at these jam sessions.

"We had a sign-up sheet and a board member or two to man it," remembers Carol Comer. "We relied on people to be courteous and not take too many choruses, but some—and I'm talking guys mostly—would be so happy to be playing with players they would never play with otherwise, that it was hard to get them to stop. There were a couple who would still be up there playing if we hadn't called them off."[28]

"Most of the men who sat in were local," says Lynn, "but there were an awful lot of unfamiliar female faces, and I assumed they were from out of town."[29] A perusal of the 1982 sign-up list bears that out. Women from Alberta, Canada; San Antonio, Texas; and Indianapolis, Indiana, played alongside others from Milwaukee, Wisconsin; Topeka, Kansas; and Atlanta, Georgia.

Because the jam sessions were free, they generated a large audience. Crown Center loved having so many potential shoppers, many of them from out of town, in their enclosed shopping area. The jazz party atmosphere, the comfortable, relaxed setting, with plenty of eating and drinking options nearby, created civic goodwill toward what too many negatively referred to as a "Cow Town." Saturday at WJF testified to home-towners and out-of-towners alike that "Everything's Up to Date in Kansas City."

Close Enough for Love

"I didn't have any children," Marian McPartland once quipped, "but I had bassists and drummers."[30] Although it could be argued that mothering instincts will find a point of least resistance—Melba Liston as "Mamma," sewing on buttons and cutting hair for her Dizzy Gillespie bandmates, Mary Lou Williams always making sure musician friends had a hot meal and a warm bed when they came to New York—the elephant in the room wears a big sign that says "MOM."

The domestic life of a jazz musician, regardless of gender, is booby-trapped with challenges. Lonely extended periods on the road make it difficult to share experiences and household obligations. The unpredictability of long-term employment adds a particular stress. Being perpetually on-call means being perpetually unorganized and unreliable. Chaotic working and sleeping hours can defeat the best of intentions for compatibility. If there are children, all the problems can be exacerbated.

Musician couples aren't necessarily at an advantage. On the surface, their common tastes and interests, their shared friends would seem to give them a head start to long-term happiness. Sharing the level of communication music demands can facilitate a soul-satisfying expression of married love. But as with any couple working together everyday, nitty-gritty details and hassles can present countless opportunities for conflict.

Expectations can be unique. Carla Bley's first husband, Paul Bley, encouraged her to compose, "to keep the royalties in the family." Composing became her family job. "He'd come in and say, 'Well, I got a record date tomorrow and I need six hot ones.' I'd sit down and write six of them. I just functioned like that. Instead of cooking the dinner, that would be my job."[31]

Expectations can be violent. Mary Lou Williams told her friend Marsha Vick, "My husband would say, 'If you don't play, you're going to get a beating.' He used to take me around and he'd make me play with all of the top musicians. I think that each time he had to threaten to hit me. I was scared each time. 'Get up and play,' he said. I said, 'Oh no,' and I started crying. He said, 'You'd *better* play.' So I sat down and played with them."[32]

Expectations can be confusing. Drummer Dottie Dodgion was married twice. Husband number one, bass player Monty Budwig, thought it was "unladylike" for her to play the drums, but wanted her to sing. Husband number two, sax player Jerry Dodgion, wanted her to only play the drums and not sing.[33]

Dottie told author Linda Dahl, "I know several lady players who were really very, very good, but they didn't get support from their husbands and they gave it up. That would be competition—'Who do you love, me or the instrument?' Isn't that a shame? If they only realized that the happier a women is with herself, the happier she could be with him."[34] This is the flipside of the stereotypical arrangement of the women supporting the male musician. In an economic climate where jazz was no longer the most popular form of music, having a wife or "old lady" with a day gig was as essential as playing the best instrument possible. It works both ways.

In a *Down Beat* article from the sixties, Dottie spells out the formula for her successful marriage to Dodgion: mutual respect, understanding, concentrated effort, and genuine devotion. She cites Dodgion's support of her playing, his "constant strength and counsel" as key. As an example Dottie likes to tell the story of their first home in San Francisco and its 156 steps to the front door. "Jerry carried the drums up every step every night. Now that's love!"[35] But there are no givens in life. After twenty-seven years of marriage, the Dodgions decided to divorce to live and work in different cities.[36]

A sudden boost in the career of one spouse, especially if it's the wife, can spell trouble. Both husbands of Mary Lou Williams were ultimately overwhelmed by her genius. Although Marian McPartland married trumpeter Jimmy McPartland twice, her highly acclaimed career (and his drinking) drew them apart. Toshiko Akiyoshi's career eclipsed that of her first husband, alto saxophonist Charlie Mariano, as did the career of pianist Joanne Brackeen to saxophonist Charlie Brackeen.

As with the Dodgions, sometimes developing careers simply pulled couples apart. Carmen McRae was married to drummer Kenny Clarke and bassist Ike Isaacs, but their respective careers pulled them in different directions. Carla Bley's fifteen-year marriage to trumpeter Michael Mantler ended the same as her seven-year marriage to Paul Bley, because of irreconcilable musical differences. After ten years of a popular collaboration and not so successful marriage, Shirley Scott and Stanley Turrentine went their separate ways.

Pianist Jill McManus feels a lot of women "marry musicians and end up giving up their careers for their husbands. In fact, I don't know many women who are married and musicians. Most of us are functionally single."[37]

No one gets married with the expectation of divorce, and jazz musician families have all the same dreams of domestic bliss that others have. Children are desired and blessed. They also change the family dynamic from mezzo-piano to fortissimo. Joanne Brackeen stayed home with her four children when they were babies. When they reached school age and the oldest could look after the youngest, Joanne toured first with Art Blakey, then Joe Henderson, and later Stan Getz. With the help of husband Charles and babysitters, it was no different than any other mommy going on a business trip.[38] Pianist Barbara Carroll did the same. She stayed home with her daughter for her first ten years and effectively retired from playing during the 1960s.

Carol Kaye remembers that when she and her first husband broke up, she had the financial responsibility of supporting not only her children but her mother. Going on the road was out of the question, so she took as much studio work in Los Angeles as she could. The fact that movie, television, and recording studios wanted to hire her built her career and saved her family.[39]

Dottie Dodgion found herself in the same situation after she and Jerry divorced. She and daughter Debbie Budwig moved to Lake Tahoe, where she played not only for the love of playing but to support her daughter. When she and Monty Budwig had split up, she had worked three jobs at once: film cutter for Columbia, legal secretary, and singer three nights a week. She was never happy with this arrangement, and couldn't help feeling that she took better care of her daughter than any babysitter.

Carla Bley added her daughter Karen Mantler to the band early on. "She's just a stage baby. She's been in on it from the very beginning. She's been on most of my records. We really didn't have time to let her have a lonely childhood."[40]

Two of WJF 1982's artists became widows at early ages when their bandmate husbands died. Bobby Jaspar's fatal heart attack in 1963 came just seven years into his marriage with singer/pianist Blossom Dearie. Barbara Carroll and her bass player husband had been married only three years when he died, also of a heart attack, in 1957. Over fifty years later, there was still pain in Barbara Carroll's voice as she talked to *Fresh Air*'s Terry Gross about the devastation of becoming a widow when their life together had barely begun. Barbara had the added heartbreak of replacing her bass player. That audition process reopened the fresh wound. "It didn't take a long time to get back to work, but it took a long time to get over it."[41]

Some musician couples have beaten the odds. Cleo Laine and John Dankworth were married for fifty-two years, until Dankworth's death in 2010. Guitarist Mary Osborne and trumpeter Ralph Scaffidi matched that. Although it took three tries, Carla Bley has been happily partnered with bassist Steve Swallow for twenty-five years. Even the troublesome Flora Purim and Airto Moreira have been married for over half a century. Barbara Carroll married musician's agent Bert Block in 1960 and, until his death in 1986, lived quite happily.

Every woman who played at the WJF jam sessions had her own story. There were students and teachers looking for inspiration and a fresh perspective. There were young women looking for a break, damn the odds. There were housewives and secretaries and file clerks, nurses and real estate agents, all trying to recapture the thrill they once had playing jazz. Each of them had made a decision on some level at some point about her commitment to the art form and to her personal life. Each of them had to find her own peace with a balance of family and music.

I'm Hip

"When it was hip to be hep, I was hep," sang Blossom Dearie in a Wednesday night solo performance at The Folly Theater, which kicked off the fifth WJF, dubbed Jazzwomen '82. This "jazz pixie with a little-girl voice and pageboy haircut that camouflages a needling wit"[42] delighted the audience of 550—to the point that she did four encores. The added solo concert was yet another concession to fans of WJF who wanted a more intimate concert setting with just one artist. Blossom Margrete Dearie (sometimes her first and middle names were reversed; she said she didn't care which came first)[43] was the perfect match for this concert formula. Blossom, so named because her brother filled the house with spring flowers when she was born, preferred slower, hard-swinging tempos—"I can't play fast,"[44] she was known to say—that transformed tunes like "Surrey with the Fringe on Top," "Satin Doll," and "If I Were a Bell" into fresh, translucent versions of themselves. But her kittenish, wispy voice, with just a shimmering quiver of vibrato, shone brightest on the clever songs of Dave Frishberg and Bob Dorough. In "I'm Hip," a tune that pokes fun at non-players who consider themselves swingin' cats as long as they use the lingo and watch foreign films while wearing "shades," Blossom assures the audience that she's no square. In "My Attorney Bernie," Blossom attacks gullible attorney clients ready to sue and sign because Bernie knows how to pick wine and has Dodgers season tickets, all with perfect syncopation and diction, and just a hint of a sly smile. Blossom held the WJF audience in the palm of her hand when she introduced another of her Frishberg favorites "Peel Me a Grape," by saying it was her sexy song. "I only have one, but one is enough."[45]

Although she made lyrics sparkle, she only wrote the tunes. She told *Fresh Air* host Terry Gross that she learned or wrote the tunes at the piano first, rarely improvised, and purposely played the tunes the same way each time. She had trouble learning lyrics—"I hide them on the piano just in case I forget"—and liked lyrics that tell a story best because they were easier to remember. The audience was none the wiser.[46] Her collaboration with Johnny Mercer on "I'm Shadowing You" gave her her biggest hit.

Her outspoken lyrics calling J. Edgar Hoover a third wheel in the world of social protest spoke in direct contrast to her fragile voice. Blossom made her musical preferences clear, especially what she didn't like. She particularly loathed the music of Andrew Lloyd Webber.[47] Elevator and grocery store music bothered her because of its invasion and assumption that everyone would want to listen to the same music while they shopped or changed floors in a building. She felt it dulled the ears of listeners and made them too lazy to listen to live jazz.[48]

The most delicate of instruments, her ethereal voice needed special attention. Blossom told Terry Gross that she takes a voice lesson about once every ten years, but the teachers all tell her the same thing: she needs to breathe differently. Unwilling to risk changing her style, Blossom perfected her microphone technique and coddled her voice instead.[49] In the smoky night clubs of the fifties and sixties, she put it in her contract that patrons would refrain from smoking ten minutes before her set started and would not smoke as long as she was on the bandstand. She also wouldn't tolerate her mood being broken by waitresses serving drinks while she sang. She allowed no canned music between sets. She never hesitated to chide audience members for talking too loudly, so much so that Marian McPartland told her during a *Piano Jazz* segment that if people are too loud at Marian's gigs, she calls out, "Right now I'm going to do my impression of Blossom Dearie. Keep it quiet back there!"[50]

Blossom studied classical piano, but it was her unique voice that got her a job in the forties with Woody Herman's vocal group, the Blue Flames. From there she moved to Paris and formed The Blue Stars of France, an eight-piece vocal group that included composer Bob Dorough and Christine Legrand, Michel Legrand's sister. (When Ward Swingle later joined, this group became the Swingle Singers.) Michel Legrand's arrangement of George Shearing's "Lullaby of Birdland" for the octet became a popular hit in France. Before marrying Belgian flutist and saxophonist Bobby Jaspar, Blossom was singer Annie Ross's roommate, and it was in this fertile musical environment that her career blossomed.[51]

After meeting Norman Granz, owner of Verve Records, Blossom and Bobby moved to New York, where she made six albums in four years. Blossom was also in demand for commercials. In 1962 a very popular root beer ad led to *Blossom Dearie Sings Rootin' Songs*, "released as a premium item that could be ordered for one dollar and a proof of purchase." After Jaspar's death in 1963, Blossom recorded one album with a symphony orchestra, and although she went back to the "simplicity of her piano-based arrangements," critic Rickey Wright states that her rendition of "I'm Old Fashioned" "is so perfect for her that the song might as well have been retired after she recorded it."[52]

Like Ernestine Anderson, Blossom tried to stave off changing trends in popular music and jazz by traveling back and forth between New York and London. Her attempts to join the rock wave with tunes like "Feelin' Groovy" fell flat. She traded the smoky clubs for concert halls and gained a quirky cult that once again appreciated her quietly swinging, humorous songs. Working again with composer Bob Dorough, Blossom became familiar to a new generation without being known; her recognizable voice is heard in many of the songs in the popular 1970s children's educational series *Schoolhouse Rock*.[53]

Critic Kevin Whitehead commented in a 2003 review of the reissue of Blossom's 1961 album *My Gentleman Friend*—just months before her eightieth birthday—that "she sings as if she were from some land where people spoke by singing." It was as true then as when she was in her twenties.[54]

I Get a Kick Out of You

The blossom-strung path through WJF's fifth festival led to the annual Thursday night Student Big Band Invitational, featuring Helen Marquette's Indian Creek Junior High Jazz Band, the UMKC Jazz Band, back under the direction of John Leisenring, and the newcomer Mid-America All-Female Stage Band, directed by local teaching legend Leon Brady. For the younger crowd, Jackie Weissman and WJF board members presented Fun with Jazz for the second year, this time at Rockhurst College's Mabee Theater. As in previous years, the H&R Block $1,000 scholarship was awarded to an outstanding college student based on an audition tape. In memory of a recently deceased board member, John Lyman, a new high school student scholarship to be added in 1983 was mentioned in the festival program.[55]

Leonard Feather returned the next afternoon for his film and lecture series, promising to include clips never before shown in Kansas City. The clinics and workshops again covered all instruments and particularly emphasized the Business of Music, with five panelists, including for the first time, concert producer Ann Sneed.

The Sunday afternoon mood-changer this year was Naomi Woodspring presenting The Jazz Storyteller. This "itinerant storyteller," accompanied by pianist Amy Duncan, focused on "tales of jazz and jazzwomen."[56]

Regardless of the featured segment, WJF remained the gold standard for attention to fans and artists alike. "I've always been very proud about the Women's Jazz Festival," Marian McPartland told Terry Teachout the day before the 1982 WJF opened. "I can think of quite a few festivals where the atmosphere is simply miserable. The people are all so offhand, and they hardly seem to care about anything." She went on to say that everyone at WJF was "so nice and warm and friendly," and that's what made the difference.[57]

Dianne Gregg added, "Of course, our artists don't see us as just another gig. They're not treated as if it is just another gig. We're fans, you know. We're aware of the way jazz artists always wind up getting the short end of the stick, spending the night in some fleabag dump, and so we try to take care of them like the important people we think they are. And our artists give us 200 percent, too, because they know we care."[58]

A goal in 1978 became a reputation among musicians in 1982.

When L.A. pianist Joanne Grauer led the 1982 All-Stars at the Main Concert of WJF, she was in the middle of her career. As a teenager, her 1957 album *The Joanne Grauer Trio*, with bass player Buddy Clark and drummer Mel Lewis, marked the beginning of what promised to be a brilliant career. In his liner notes, Joe Quinn states, "Just what Joanne Grauer's future in music will be is pure speculation at this point in her career. For one of her years, she has made bold strides in attaining recognition for her talent."[59] He goes on to remind the listener, "The future of jazz as a fully developed art form is completely dependent on the zeal of youth and its ability to spark and sustain it for the benefit of other generations."[60] Looking ahead to 1982, Quinn would not have been disappointed. Besides playing in clubs throughout the Los Angeles area, Joanne was in demand as a piano coach for Hollywood stars with piano scenes. She worked with Barbra Streisand, Peter Bogdanovich, Audrey Hepburn, and Ellen Burstyn. It is Joanne's playing heard in the movies *Alice Doesn't Live Here Anymore*, *Lady Sings the Blues*, and *Forty Carats*.[61] Clint Eastwood called her "one of the best pianists in the world."[62] Her album with vocalist Lorraine Feather became a *Billboard* top pick in 1978. Lorraine's father, Leonard, said of Joanne, "All that is missing in a Joanne Grauer performance is a clearer sense of identity, which might well be achieved through the use of her considerable but seldom exposed talent as a composer."[63] WJF emcee Leonard Feather must have been pleased to hear Joanne's tunes showcased during the All-Stars' segment.

After her appearance at WJF, she continued to write, put out another jazz trio album, *Joanne Grauer*—this one heavily rock- and fusion-influenced—and accompanied singers as antithetical to one another as the Lennon Sisters and Michael Feinstein, Andy Williams and Juliet Prowse. She's heard in the movie *9½ Weeks*.

Regardless of the style, Ann Patterson, playing soprano saxophone for this set, felt right at home. Her big band, Maiden Voyage, so popular at the 1980 festival, had appeared on *The Tonight Show* and at the Playboy Jazz Festival and the Concord

Jazz Festival since her last time in Kansas City. With three music degrees and a two-year stint as lead alto in the Don Ellis Orchestra, Ann had established herself on the West Coast and was gaining a national reputation.

Ann went on to play countless gigs in the L.A. area, and Maiden Voyage gave scores of women the opportunity to play in a quality big band. But she made her biggest contribution to jazz through teaching. Frequently women approached her in public to say that a clinic she had done at their school or a concert with Don Ellis had inspired them to follow in her footsteps. But in 1982, Ann's influence on younger women had just started its second chorus. She was a welcome addition to the small group.

An academic background became the common denominator among the All-Stars. Debbie Katz, with a masters in percussion from Northwestern, had just returned from a Hong Kong tour with Paul Anka and had also performed with Sammy Davis Jr., Dionne Warwick, Johnny Mathis, and Henry Mancini. At the time of this concert, she was also the drummer for Maiden Voyage. She went on to teach at Lake Forest College and to play in the Lake Forest Symphony.[64]

Like Carol Kaye, bassist Valda Hammick, from Australia, had played professional guitar for ten years. After being inspired by bass lines she heard on Motown records—some of them Carol's—she switched to bass. Her guitar credentials included backing singers Carmen McRae, Tony Bennett, and Jack Jones. She toured for five years as a bass player with singer Lovelace Watkins. But it was in the realm of education that Valda had the most influence. Her electric bass instruction books have been standards in the field, as have Carol's.[65]

Another West Coast player, Lisa Gordanier completed the All-Stars' front line. Her fine flute and saxophone playing bellied the sound and rounded out the groove. After playing in Germany for two and a half years, Lisa was living in Seattle at the time of WJF.

In various large and small Seattle groups, Lisa accompanied name acts such as Johnny Mathis, Bob Hope, Ben Vereen, and Dionne Warwick.[66] She went on to spend many years as a popular Seattle player, particularly in the Seattle Women's Jazz Orchestra and the Jim Cutler Jazz Orchestra.[67]

The 1982 All-Stars represented different generations, different styles, different points in careers, even different continents. Except for Ann and Debbie, they hadn't played together before. Like all the All-Stars before them, they had a quick rundown of the tunes as their only rehearsal. But the WJF board trusted that this combination of players would satisfy the players and fans alike. As more and more women became confident and comfortable in a festival setting, and excellent but lesser known women jazz musicians surfaced, this segment of WJF became the voice of the future.

"I want a woman pianist who plays like a woman, with the warmth, sensitivity, feeling, perception and all the womanly virtues, plus a little masculine saltiness in humor, surprise and accent."[68] This 1959 quote by Marian McPartland described herself, as it did her good friend Barbara Carroll, who, as solo pianist, was the second act of the Main Concert. Contemporaries of each other, the two pianists' careers paralleled each other starting in the 1940s. While Marian entertained World War II troops in England, Barbara's trio toured camp shows for U.S. servicemen all along the east coast. Marian came to New York not long after Barbara had established herself in New York's vibrant club scene.[69]

During a *Piano Jazz* interview, Marian and Barbara reminisced about New York supper clubs. Both women played the Bemelmans Bar at the Carlyle Hotel for multiple decades. But in the early years, their gigs weren't always so classy. Discussing the Mermaid Room, they remembered that to get to the stage they had to crawl under the bar. "The stage revolved too," remembered Barbara. "It was slow, but just enough to make you sick to your stomach." She also remembered that opportunities for "chick" piano players were slim in the late forties and early fifties, so, happy to be playing, they put up with a lot.[70] As young, beautiful lady pianists, Marian and Barbara were also in demand socially, and that took them uptown into the elegant world of the wealthy. "In that wonderful era, there were swell-egent, elegant parties where music dictated the social scene. One of our favorite hosts was Sherman Fairchild, who had two golden Steinways in his apartment. Oh those golden Steinways,"[71] Barbara recalled wistfully.

That's not to say she didn't pay her dues. When Barbara first moved to New York, a male friend who played piano tried to send gigs her way. To avoid having her turned down he'd tell bandleaders that her name was Bobby Carroll. By the time she got to the gig, it was too late to find another piano player. During this time period—when men coming back from World War II were trying to re-establish themselves in the workplace, even in jazz clubs, and preferred their women in the kitchen—a woman player was automatically judged before she even played a note. She was inferior until proven otherwise. Along with other professional women, Barbara Carroll was part of a post-war wave of women fighting a home-front battle to defend the ground they had taken during the war. Nevertheless, her first important New York gig was at the Down Beat Club opposite Dizzy Gillespie.

This was the age of elegant supper club attire, and like the female patrons, Barbara dressed to the nines. She didn't shy away from bare shoulders and cleavage. She took the seen-as-well-as-heard attitude a step further by having her nose bobbed, a decision that didn't go unnoticed by *Down Beat* magazine. "Six months ago she was just a musicians' musician—and let's face it, looked like one. Today her handsome portrait has gazed down at a million passengers from posters in every Fifth Avenue bus."[72]

But in the postwar heyday of New York jazz clubs, the lady the jazz press dubbed "Barbara bebop"[73] quickly gained respect as a solid, modern jazz pianist. Billy Taylor stated, "Barbara could swing you right out of the room."[74] Marian admitted to a friend that, "I always felt somewhat inferior to her."[75] She later wrote in *Melody Maker* magazine that Barbara was a "warm, witty girl with a delicate Dresden china approach to jazz."[76] Mary Lou Williams, who played in the same clubs along New York's Fifty-Second Street during this time, had nothing but admiration for Barbara.[77]

Barbara came to jazz through classical piano. As a teenager she fell in love with the piano sounds of Nat King Cole, and although she studied at the New England Conservatory of Music, she applied those years of perfecting her technique to her developing jazz style.

That style has favored the Great American Songbook. "I play improvised music influenced by bebop. I'm not a jam session player, and I usually have my own groups."[78] She admits to stretching out more at concerts and festivals and preferring to work with only a bass player, sometimes adding a drummer. But her reading skills led her to jobs unique to most jazz players. An early trio that included then husband Joe Shulman spent a year on Broadway doing the Rodgers and Hammerstein musical *Me and Juliet*. A show within a show, Barbara played a rehearsal pianist.[79]

As a club pianist, it was perhaps inevitable she would begin singing at customers' request. "I was afraid to sing, not because then people would think of me as a singer, but because they would think I couldn't sing. I didn't think I had the voice. I didn't think I had the range. I do sing now and I love to sing, but I think of myself as a pianist who sings."[80]

At WJF '82 she presented the audience with a couple of her signature half-spoken vocals wrapped around standards like "Lullaby of the Leaves," the odd, but in her hands workable, juxtaposition of Irving Berlin's "I Love a Piano," and Chick Corea's "Spain," and a delicate but heartfelt presentation of "I Can't Get

Started." Regardless of how she saw herself, Barbara's performance left the audience charmed.

At Marian McPartland's eighty-fifth birthday gala at New York's Birdland, Barbara saluted Marian by singing the Stephen Sondheim song "Old Friends." The words rang as true for the two jazz piano giants in the twenty-first century as they had on New York's Fifty-Second Street in 1947: "Here's to us. / Who's like us? Damn few!"[81]

Guess Who I Saw Today

By limiting the Main Concert acts to three, Carol and Dianne hoped to avoid audience restlessness. With a shorter concert, listeners could savor every note. No one had the ability to captivate an audience more than this year's closing performer, Nancy Wilson. Terry Teachout reported that her singing was as exciting as ever with its "constant alternation of dynamic extremes and clipped phrasing." For once he was even disappointed that the concert ran short.[82]

There was never a time when Nancy Wilson was not a singer. At four she decided that's what she would do when she grew up. At fifteen she had her own television show in her hometown of Columbus, Ohio. When she met Cannonball Adderley, he suggested she move to New York City where her career would have a chance to take off. In 1959 that's what she did, obtaining Cannonball's manager John Levy and a record contract at Capitol Records in short order. Her debut single, "Guess Who I Saw Today," was an instant hit and became her signature tune. After two solo albums, *Like in Love* and *Something Wonderful*, Nancy was paired with George Shearing on *The Swingin's Mutual* in 1961 and *Nancy Wilson and Cannonball Adderley* in 1962. In a very short time, Nancy had secured footing in the toughest of careers.[83]

In his book *The Jazz Singers: The Ultimate Guide*, Scott Yanow profiles 521 jazz singers, then adds listings of a few hundred more.

Most have fame that is regional, and although Yanow's list is of singers, male and female, who have made contributions to the field of jazz from the early recordings to the first decade of the twenty-first century, there is no assumption that each made a living at it. The majority of names on the list are obscure. Even the female vocalists who became household names during the Big Band Era—Billie Holiday, Ella Fitzgerald, Sarah Vaughan, Peggy Lee, Carmen McRae—suffered professional and personal hardships that would break weaker spirits. Addictions, poor health due to living on the road for years, and exploitations by managers and club owners took away a large helping of the glamour associated with the profession. Most damning, many male musicians saw them as superfluous window dressing. *Swing* magazine blatantly stated in an October 1938 article, "Ask any ten bandleaders as to their pet headache . . . nine will answer 'girl vocalists.' . . . Yes, girl vocalists are a nuisance. Too many of them are beautiful, and can't sing."[84] Even for the ones who could sing, an obstacle course of prejudice remained.

America's pastimes have always been big business, and in the days when corporations sponsored radio shows in the same way arenas are sponsored today, big band names advertised everything from toothpaste to corn flakes. What better way to generate excitement—and sales—than to put a pretty girl in an eye-catching gown in front of the band, like a cheerleader. The sponsors didn't care if she sounded good or not. Linda Dahl explains, "As in the traditionally male-dominated games of basketball and football, the team took care of business—in this case, the musical business—while the vocal pom-pom girl stood supportively and decoratively on the sidelines. Her musical chores were usually limited to singing the thirty-two bars of the melody's refrain between the band's section arrangements and instrumental solos."[85]

Yet, it was as a girl singer that women jazz musicians had the most chance of getting work, an irony not wasted on the scores of female instrumentalists who weren't hired in big bands at all. In that cheerleader position out front, the girl singer was not intimidating to her bandmates. Male instrumentalists weren't threatened by possible competition. Some farsighted bandleaders even wrote arrangements using the female voice to the band's best advantage. Regardless of the hassles and heartaches, all the major singers of the era, of both genders, apprenticed as big band singers.

Any jazz singer putting a career together in the 1960s faced a shift in expectations. The potentially glorious days of the big band girl singer had gone the way of the zoot suit and cigarette girl. Since the mid-fifties, rock & roll had usurped jazz year by year as the popular music of the day, and torch singers were a dying breed. Because big bands were no longer profitable or practical, former "canaries" had to reinvent themselves or step back from the acts that had been so popular. Different rhythms, different tempos, different timbres of sound dictated what would sell. With the development of the electric amplifier, then the electric piano and bass, creative possibilities expanded at the expense of the intimate ballad at the piano bar. A younger, record-buying crowd reflecting a midcentury economy and culture now ruled.

Jazz singers tottered along a borderline of styles—pop, cabaret, r&b, even world music. Nancy Wilson's success as a song stylist—the term she prefers over singer—was built on the fact that she crossed that borderline deftly and elegantly, gathering an ever-widening audience along the way.

"I don't know anything about music, per se," Nancy told Marian McPartland during a *Piano Jazz* segment. "'Vocalese' is not in my vocabulary.[86] I've always just sung—never questioned it, just thanked God for it and did it." She went on to say she has sung all the "Baby, baby, baby" lines she'll ever sing, that she hates repetition in lyrics. She thinks of herself as a storyteller, so a lyric has to have a beginning, a middle, and an end. For that reason she is particularly fond of ballads. "I love ballads. I try to close my eyes and become aware of the story and put myself inside it."[87]

That story came in the form of "My Foolish Heart" in 1961, "Tell Me the Truth" in 1963, "(You Don't Know) How Glad I Am"—her most successful Billboard Hot 100 hit coming in at number eleven—in 1964, "The Best Is Yet to Come" and "I'll Only Miss Him When I Think of Him" in 1965, "Can't Take My Eyes Off of You" in 1969, and dozens more. From 1962 to 1970, Nancy recorded twenty-six albums, all of them on the Capitol label, all of them in the pop or r&b category, most of them in both. It wasn't until 1968 that she was involved in another jazz album, when she again worked with Cannonball Adderley on his live album, *In Person*.[88]

Nancy's song stylist offering to WJF's Jazzwomen '82 reflected the potpourri of styles she made famous. Along with John B. Williams on bass and Roy McCurdy on drums, she sang a Dinah Washington saloon song, a Donna Summer disco tune, a Ray Noble standard, and a whole hatful of Nancy Wilson golden oldies.

Festivals were a favorite of Nancy's. Because she was married to a Presbyterian minister, she had sworn off nightclubs and had consciously put family and home first, very aware that the music business could eat a person whole. "I saw so many wonderful women, great singers whose lives were a living hell," she told Marian McPartland. "What is it about this art of singing that puts addiction and abuse in their lives? I saw that and I didn't want it to happen to me."[89]

Critical praise, awards, and outstanding achievements characterize any point in Nancy Wilson's career. She won three Grammys. She received a star on the Hollywood Walk of Fame, an NAACP Image Award, an NEA Jazz Masters Fellowship award, and an Oprah Winfrey's Legends Award, to name a few. She received an honorary degree from the Berklee School of Music. She appeared on just about every late night talk show in the genre's existence and had her own variety show—which won an Emmy—in the 1967-68 season. As the voice of NPR's *Jazz*

Profiles, Nancy returned to jazz by sharing the stories of old and new tunes with the artists who brought them to life, many of them her friends, and came full circle.

Critics and audiences agreed that Nancy Wilson, ever cool, never harsh, was both singer and storyteller. That was all she ever wanted. Those were the qualities that brought Jazzwomen '82 to a satisfying end.

All Alone

And then a chink, just the tiniest crack of discontent. Three days after Jazzwomen '82, Carol and Dianne received a letter of resignation from a WJF board member. The letter cited conflicts with a video recording company's handling of the TNT concert, of which this board member was the producer. She felt the video crew took over control of where the instruments would be placed and what kind of lighting would be used. She called the crew's onstage presence an intrusion and said they upstaged the performers, not to mention her authority. When she voiced her concerns at a tech meeting about the possibility of this happening, she felt ignored.

Her displeasure didn't end there. She sent another letter to three other board members with a litany of complaints: not enough ticket outlets, questionable outside contracting decisions (there had been a problem with programs that year), a general lack of professionalism. She pointed to the "gypsy look" of WJF's offices in Carol Comer's basement.[90]

WJF had grown into a five-day festival in five years. Dozens of volunteers in almost as many capacities worked year-round to keep the necessary momentum. It was unrealistic to think that everyone would be content with everything. WJF had taken on a life of its own, a breathing engine that needed insatiable energy to survive. That engine's exhaust was starting to cloud the dream.

Chapter 7

The Sixth Year

March 23–27, 1983

"Imagine with yourself what an unsightly matter it were to see a woman play upon a tabour or drum, or blow in a flute or trumpet, or any like instrument; and this is because the boisterousness of them doth cover and take away that sweet mildness which setteth so forth every deed that a woman doth."

—Baldassare Castiglione
author, diplomat, philosopher, 1598

IN THE FALL OF 1982, DINO SANTANGELO, concert promoter and KOOL Jazz Festival spokesman, contacted Dianne Gregg, first by phone and then in a follow-up letter. The letter, copied to George Wein, stated, "Essentially, we are interested in working with you to change the name of the festival to include the KOOL Jazz Festival name, and to provide you with extensive marketing assistance. In addition to the marketing assistance, which we pay for in total, we would consider a grant to the Women's Jazz Festival."[1] Financial solvency was an attention-grabbing lure. The WJF board was always chasing its tail trying to get bills paid. Ticket sales covered only a portion of expenses. The Reagan years saw artery-severing cuts in arts grants. Carol had loaned WJF thousands of dollars of her own money to be paid back when grants came in, but as soon as one loan was paid off, it was necessary to take out another.[2]

Santangelo's letter goes on to point out that the proposed arrangement would be similar to one implemented in Chicago the year before. Kansas Citians were familiar with KOOL Festivals. Since the mid-seventies, this festival had played at Royals Stadium, as well as in other cities, but had been fusion- and soul-heavy. A conscious focus on getting back to a more acoustic festival made including WJF a logical move. A mini-version of the KOOL festival, KOOL Super Night, had played in Kansas City the same weekend as the 1980 WJF. The letter continues, "We will not even attempt to interfere with the artistic content of the festival. This being your sixth year, we do not propose coming in and telling you how to run the festival."[3] It was something to consider.

Twenty-six years of prestige and critical success along with organizational nightmares brought the Newport Jazz Festival to the same place as all music festivals. Funding was a constant challenge. By 1980, Brown & Williamson's corporate sponsorship put the festival on a firm financial footing and the Newport Jazz Festival became the KOOL Jazz Festival.[4] By name alone, KOOL lent itself nicely to advertising a jazz festival.

In an attempt to change its image, KOOL launched a massive advertising campaign featuring photographs of non-celebrity players holding their trumpets or trombones with the slogan "The only way to play it is KOOL." From a twenty-first century perspective, the idea of using people who make their livings by breathing correctly into an instrument to advertise cigarettes seems incongruent. That it was a very successful campaign for both the cigarette and the festival illustrates how much the culture has shifted in forty years.

Trombonist Dave Glenn, then with the Gerry Mulligan Orchestra, remembers the extent to which horn players were paired with KOOL cigarettes. "I made the call-backs for a photo shoot with KOOL. They wanted a white representative and a black representative for each wind instrument in the [male only] big band. Slide Hampton was the black trombone player. For about an hour, photographers took my picture as I played. In the end, Ed Neumeister got it. I didn't really care about having my picture on the side of buses and on billboards, but there was a big band made up of these guys that played a few promo gigs, and that would have been fun."[5] In the April 1983 issue of *Down Beat*, one of these ads takes up a full page. A "cool," bearded, white saxophone player, wearing a leather jacket, an open shirt, and large tinted glasses, plays. The copy says, "There's only one sensation this refreshing. Low tar KOOL Lights. The taste doesn't miss a beat."[6]

KOOL had advertised with a musician before. Nat King Cole, a three-pack-a-day KOOL smoker, maintained that the menthol cigarettes enhanced the tone of his smooth, rich, baritone voice. Cole died of lung cancer in 1965.[7]

The KOOL Jazz Festival also increased its fan base simply by putting on festivals in other cities. Atlanta, Chicago, St. Louis, Washington, D.C., and Cincinnati all hosted KOOL Jazz Festivals, some for the first time and others to shore up struggling hometown festivals. There were twenty-two KOOL jazz festivals in all. By 1983 it was the largest touring jazz showcase in the country.

Carol, Dianne, and the board didn't think about Santangelo's offer for very long before concluding that the risk of losing their autonomy, even if it meant financial help, was too high a price. They decided to pass.[8]

In the spring of 1983, Jonathan Poses of the *Kansas City Times* reported that, according to promoter George Wein, the KOOL Jazz Festival would present a concert in St. Louis, but not Kansas City. When asked why not Kansas City, with its rich jazz heritage and enthusiastic fans, George Wein responded that his festival had no desire to "override an already-existing festival." He told Poses,

"We did not want to go in and compete with the Women's Jazz Festival. That is an event I respect very much."[9]

Time and Time Again

WJF's financial concerns extended beyond paying concert bills. In 1983 the board received word that Ruth Kissane was suing them for punitive damages of $1 million. Ruth, the Los Angeles-based trumpet player and animator who broke her arm in 1980 falling off the big band risers during the tribute to the International Sweethearts of Rhythm, still didn't have full use of her right arm. At the top of her career as an animator when the accident happened, Ruth's inability to physically maintain the standard expected of her was disheartening. Anyone who has seen *A Charlie Brown Christmas* has seen Ruth's work. Her standing in the field of animation demanded her best. The suit against WJF and Crown Center stated:

> Plaintiff, Ruth Kissane, sustained severe, permanent, and progressive injuries to her right arm, elbow, wrist, and hand; plaintiff was caused to suffer a severe open dislocation of her right elbow and her right wrist was fractured and crushed; all of the bones, nerves, tendons, ligaments, muscles, veins, and arteries in plaintiff's right shoulder, arm, wrist, hand and fingers were severed, twisted, torn, bruised, contused, dislocated, fractured, crushed, and otherwise severely damaged, including but not limited to the ulnar nerve, median nerve, the brachial artery, and radius, resulting in a total loss of sensation, movement, and feeling in her right wrist, hand and fingers.[10]

The claims continued. According to the suit, Ruth suffered other "abrasions, contusions, scrapes, and cuts to her entire body," and "unsightly deterioration of muscles in her wrist, arm, and hand," causing headaches and lack of sleep. Most damning for an animator and musician, she allegedly had essentially lost the use of her right arm.

The news got worse. Ruth's lawyers stated, "All of the aforesaid acts of negligence, carelessness, and recklessness and conduct of defendants, and each of them, showed complete indifference to and were in gross and conscious disregard for the rights and safety of plaintiff and others." Cited was the fact that the risers were not equipped with "a guardrail, a chair rail, toe board, lip or other device to prevent persons and chairs positioned thereon from falling therefrom" and that, in violation of the Uniform Building Code, the top tier of the riser was "unenclosed and more than thirty inches above the floor." Also mentioned, "The legs of the chair were not equipped with rubber stops."[11]

Generally trumpet sections stand at the back of a big band. In this case, Maiden Voyage had chairs for the trumpet section, because they would not be playing during the presentation involving the International Sweethearts of Rhythm. The risers used were the standard concert risers used for countless other performances at Crown Center and other public concerts. Groups from Count Basie to school choirs had used similar risers without incident. The comments "complete indifference" and "gross and conscious disregard" were the most upsetting for Carol and Dianne and the board. On the NPR *Jazz Profile* original recording, Carol is very clearly heard announcing Ruth's injury and asking for assistance, then telling the audience that the ambulance had arrived and that Ruth was conscious and wanted the tribute concert to go on without her.[12] Carol and Dianne both relate that they later advised Ruth to file the insurance claim with WJF's insurance company, that it was the possibility of accidents like this that prompted WJF to get insurance in the first place. They expected all of Ruth's medical bills to be handled by their insurance.[13] Now, three years after the accident, a letter from their insurance company stated, "It is our duty to advise you that it is the position of this company that exemplary (punitive) damages are not covered by the above mentioned policy."[14] The insurance was set up to handle compensatory damages, medical expenses, and loss of income. Punitive damages suggest a desire to place blame and punish the defendants so that an injury such as Ruth's would not happen again.

That Crown Center Redevelopment Corporation, a subsidiary of Hallmark, is named on the petition as the primary plaintiff is telling. Perhaps more telling is the fact that in 1983 Kansas City prosecuting attorneys were up to their necks with lawsuits stemming from the Hyatt skywalk tragedy. In 1981 two skywalks across the lobby of the Hyatt Regency Hotel—across the street from Crown Center—fell during a tea dance. One hundred and fourteen people were killed and 216 more injured. Court dockets were backed up and cases unrelated to the Hyatt, like Ruth's, were still pending. Ruth's initial petition for damages could not be filed until the extent of her injuries was determined and resolved, and there was a five-year statute of limitations on injury claims. Her Kansas City-based lawyers—some who were also working on Hyatt injury cases—could afford to take their time and capitalize on the big-settlement climate in the city at that time.[15] WJF became inadvertently caught in the middle of a lawyer war.

The Beat Goes On

The sixth annual WJF, Jazzwomen '83, began on Wednesday, March 23, with the youngest and the oldest participants of the festival. For the third year, busloads of Head Start children attended Fun with Jazz, this year back at the Jewish Community Center's Danciger Auditorium, for a morning of exploring what it means to play and sing jazz. First by example, board members Milt Abel, Carol Comer, John Leisenring, Mike Ning, Scott Robinson, and Lynn Riley, along with Sauna Reif, showed how an ensemble works and then how solos are layered over the ensemble sound. Reinforcing what the musicians had done in previous years, the group encouraged children to scat-sing and experiment with rhythms. To an outsider, it may have sounded like a session of cacophonous fooling around, but the point was to expose new ears to new possibilities.[16]

At sixty-five, Marian McPartland was the oldest participant of Jazzwomen '83, but she was still exploring the art form she fell in love with as a teenager. A WJF board member since 1979, Marian hadn't officially participated as a musician since that year. (When she supplied filler music after Ruth Kissane fell, she did so as an audience member.) Her pairing with pianist Tommy Flanagan for Wednesday night's Folly Theater concert was inspired. Three years into her popular NPR radio show, *Piano Jazz*, Marian comfortably displayed a generous camaraderie with Flanagan, who had been one of her first guests on the show. Marian's natural rapport with musicians and audience members came from decades of trio work in New York clubs such as The Embers, The Hickory House, and Bemelmans Bar at the Hotel Carlyle, as well as the Café Carlyle. Although her cool, English manner made her playing look effortless, she saw it differently. "Swinging is like being on a tightrope or a roller coaster. It's like walking in space," she told *New Yorker* reviewer Whitney Balliett.[17] She also saw different keys in different colors—B flat in blue, D in daffodil yellow. Colorful or not, her evocative melodies sparked the imaginations of others, including Balliett. "Her sheer inventiveness is frightening. Her slow ballads suggest rain forests. The chords are massed and dark and overhanging, the harmonies thick and new and almost impenetrable." Marian couldn't completely explain the process. "The fingers and mind are welded together. It's hard to say what goes on in your head when you're swinging, when you're really improvising. But it's dangerous. You have to leave spaces in your playing."[18]

Called "The Jazz Poet" and "Gentleman of Jazz," Tommy Flanagan built his reputation playing with Sonny Rollins and John Coltrane. But it wasn't just tenor men who favored Flanagan. As Ella Fitzgerald's and later Tony Bennett's accompanist, he became a favorite of other musicians, but it was in a solo or trio setting that his stellar elegance shone. Leonard Feather felt that "Flanagan is the pianist most likely to be named a personal idol by other jazz pianists, whether they be swing veterans or avant-gardists."[19] In a *Jazz Profiles* segment, fellow pianist Roland Hanna attributes Flanagan's special mellowness of sound to the way he held his fingers. "Tommy had very long fingers, and he held them straighter than most pianists do. With his fingers that way, he could make phrases say things like a sentence."[20] In the same segment, others he worked with weighed in. Sonny Rollins talked about the role of a pianist playing with solo horns. "A pianist can play too much. It's a loud instrument, and it's very easy for it to cover up a horn solo. No one wants an obtrusive pianist."[21] Kenny Barron spoke of Flanagan's elegance and the "soft, thoughtful voice he brought to an ensemble."[22] But childhood friend and drummer Elvin Jones reminded *Jazz Profile* listeners that "he can raise as much hell as anyone else."[23] Their escapades on the road made for great anecdotes and even greater music.

It was that road work that took its toll on Flanagan's health, and in 1978, after a heart attack, he stopped working with Ella Fitzgerald. He then put together what *New York Times* reporter Ben Ratliff called a "democratic trio." With only a drummer and bass player, he "created arrangements lined with short improvisations, with one player's solo framed by concise phrases worked out between the other two musicians."[24]

Marian and Tommy, with two jet-black Bösendorfer pianos set on the Folly stage, created a sparkling evening of two-piano jazz. Together they played "Lady Bird," "Swingin' til the Girls Come Home," "Afternoon in Paris," and "A Child Is Born." A full-blown, old-fashioned cutting contest—fingers flying—ensued as the two took on "Donna Lee" and "All the Things You Are."

For a portion of the concert, each took a turn as soloist. Marian presented "a subtly harmonized, 'I'm Old Fashioned' and a bold version of 'I Hear a Rhapsody,' and her own 'Ambiance.'" Flanagan returned the favor with a wily interpretation of "Oh Lady Be Good" that he had worked out with Ella Fitzgerald. Besides other lesser known Great American Songbook tunes, Flanagan played his own "Minor Mishap."

But it was the improvised, unrehearsed duets, set between these segments, that most impressed listeners. This favorite of forms of Marian on *Piano Jazz* suited Flanagan. After decades of restrained accompaniment playing, he was ready to cut loose. It was difficult to tell who was having the most fun—pianists or audience.

Teach Me Tonight

Day two of Jazzwomen '83 was devoted, once again, to school jazz bands. Serving as house band for the sixth time, the UMKC Jazz Band featured three female students as soloists: Sauna Reif on trumpet, Angie Wellman on trombone, and Stephanie Cox on trombone. Not to be outdone, Ron McCurdy's KU Jazz Ensemble I featured Dianne Stettler[25] on trombone and Helen Marquette—no stranger to WJF audiences—on drums. Helen, who was working on her masters at KU, remembers, "When my junior high band played at WJF the year before, I really tried to impress on the kids what a great opportunity it was for them to be a part of this concert. Now here I was."[26]

Joining these two local college jazz bands, Alexandria's Ragtime Band, an all-female band from Texas Woman's University in Denton, Texas, won over the crowd with their eight-piece arrangements of ragtime, Dixieland, and other traditional jazz music. This enthusiastic group of women musicians was so excited about the opportunity to be a part of the WJF weekend that they, according to the band's director John Flohr, "drove all the way from Denton to appear gratis at tonight's concert."[27]

As students, they may not have had much choice about the money, but the fact remains that by 1983 playing in the school jazz band was as popular and common as taking a foreign language class. Mary Lou Williams' dream of having jazz taught in public schools was in full swing—and bebop. But it had been a long time coming.

Education has always been a part of jazz, going back to the first time King Oliver showed Louis Armstrong how best to buzz. In the beginning there was nothing formal or structured about discovering jazz, just one cat showing another what he'd come up with. Mentoring and a loose form of apprenticeship constituted the extent of jazz education in the early days. After school, neighborhood programs like the one Melba Liston attended existed only because of the dedication of an individual, not an educational system. Based on aural skills, students listened and repeated, an instrumental version of call and response, and all playing was based on improvisation. No written jazz music existed. Not a stagnant art form, like most endemic, aural and oral traditions, it quickly grew and evolved on its own.

In 1924 jazz came to school but only made it as far as the football field when the Southern Methodist University Band of Dallas played a Dixieland halftime show.[28] Interestingly enough, the game was played against North Texas State, for generations to come, the school most associated with collegiate jazz.

In the 1930s many colleges had informal dance bands that supplied music for student and faculty functions. Most of these were student inspired and led or, as in the case with the International Sweethearts of Rhythm, were formed to help raise funds for the rest of the school. Like garage bands a generation later, these bands, full of enthusiastic self-starters, wrote their own arrangements or copied name band arrangements by ear from recordings.[29] Making jazz almost a clandestine activity, many music schools would not allow jazz to be played in their practice rooms. Music educational journals reminded readers that jazz could have a degenerative effect on students. Barry Ulanov caught the fear of the times in 1948 when he remarked, "There is a danger of an entire generation growing up with the idea that jazz and the atom bomb are essentially the same natural phenomenon."[30]

Slowly jazz courses were added to fine arts programs. Leonard Feather's jazz history class began at the New School for Social Research in New York City in 1941.[31] In 1945 Lawrence Berk founded Schillinger House in Boston—nine years later to become Berklee School of Music—which offered classes but no degree until 1954, when a baccalaureate degree in jazz was added to its catalog.[32] By the end of the decade, pianist Teddy Wilson had been hired as an instructor at Juilliard.[33] All of this tacitly recognized a legitimacy of importance, but it wasn't until the late forties that jazz became an accredited major. North Texas State, already a renowned school for classical music majors, became the first school to offer a fully accredited college jazz degree in "Dance Band" and "Dance Band Arranging" in the fall of 1946.[34] Still, in academic and some cultural circles, jazz as a college major was suspect. Even at North Texas, the degree was added through the back door. In 2011 one member of that original class of jazz majors, trumpet player William Thomson (later a composer and dean of the Thornton School of Music), told Steve Wiest, then director of the famed North Texas One O'clock Lab Band, that the Dean had gone to the State College Board of Trustees in Austin to "request the initiation of a Dance Band at North Texas State College."[35] He reasoned that there were more jobs available for dance band players than symphony players in those immediate postwar years. "Several members of the Board were taken aback; they were devout Southern Baptists. One spoke up, 'We'll not have any dance band degree programs on our campuses.' Dean Bain was a helluva bright guy, to say the least. He responded, 'OK, let us call it a Laboratory Band Program.' And so it was passed with that lexical cleansing."[36] If there were dance band arranging classes, there had to be a dance band to play them.

Just months before the North Texas jazz classes started, a group of eighty high school students from Nassau County, New York, were given unexcused absences for attending a two-hour *Swing in Schooltime* clinic run by local music supervisor Glenn E. Brown. Brown, who taught traditional music classes in the area, also organized two swing bands after hours. According to a *Down Beat* article entitled "Klever Kids Kill Kats with Kapable Kombo," Brown thought it was important to give students a well-rounded approach to music, but his fellow music teachers disagreed. The *Down Beat* article stated, "Some individual teachers at the various schools, out of jealousy or horror, nixed the entire production, forcing the students to cut classes for the daytime rehearsal." The high school students were outraged, 1946-style. "Gee, at Hempstead High they won't even let us play a saxophone," one bemoaned. His buddy agreed. "Yeah, our schools are really square, like a box." Mr. Brown, who insisted that in this case playing hookey paid off, got the last word by telling *Down Beat* that swing was more difficult than classical music, telling of a student "who faked his parts with the symphony orchestra but had to learn to read when playing drums with the swing unit."[37]

Many jazz lovers felt the survival of the art form depended on the discipline and daily preparation found in an academic setting. In an October 1955 *Down Beat* article, bandleader Ralph Marterie made a farsighted connection. As one of the last commercially successful bandleaders, he traveled to many college campuses during the fifties and concluded, "The big bands of tomorrow are now being built on the campuses of our great colleges."[38] Drawing a parallel with baseball's farm club system, he explained, "Well, music has its farm system too—the schools where kids learn to blow their horns between sessions in a lab or lecture hall."[39] Convinced that the college students he heard "knew the score" and had a better sense of what their contemporaries wanted to hear, he felt a big band comeback was inevitable.[40] He also referred to all of the students as boys, because they were.

At the fiftieth annual Music Educators National Convention held in St. Louis in April 1956, jazz in the school was addressed for the first time. Attendee and presenter George Avakian reported in *Down Beat* that this "marked the first program in this long series of meetings of American educators that was devoted to a serious consideration of jazz as part of the study programs offered in music to the young people of America."[41]

Avakian, along with Father Norman O'Connor of Boston University, George Wein, and Dave Brubeck, stated the case for jazz. With Father O'Connor acting as moderator, Avakian explained to the gathering that "jazz always has been a part of the American cultural scene, adapting from and reflecting the changing cultural patterns of every period of American history since its earliest manifestations after the Civil War."[42] Brubeck, with the rapt attention of the younger delegates and the respect of the older ones, went to the piano for his demonstration. His point that the best course of study for any jazz musician is a thorough knowledge of basic music teaching along with a solid understanding of harmonic relationships was best served through his musical examples. Avakian told *Down Beat* readers that convention attendees responded positively, even the older guard whose skepticism had retarded the acceptance of educational jazz in the past. The elder statesmen of the conference "could have been flip or obviously polite about paying lip service to an unscrubbed but unavoidable stepchild. Instead they were genuinely interested, warm in their appreciation of our contribution [to] a better understanding of jazz and its future in the U.S. educational system."[43]

Maybe the elder statesmen of MENC were not flippant, but they also were not quick to act. Two years later, Billy Taylor and Stan Kenton were invited to address the same group on "the possibility of teaching jazz in an academic environment."[44] Changes in the music industry were not encouraging to young musicians, and the nation's music educators were still dragging their feet. As late as 1963, *Down Beat* writer and Notre Dame jazz educator, Father George Wiskirchen, found it necessary to inform readers of the difference between curricular and non-curricular jazz. In his article "Jazz on Campus," the sports analogy is again used: "A good analogy here would be the bickering, sloppiness, static level of a pick-up athletic game . . . as opposed to the well-trained, smoothly operated, always improving school-sponsored and coached team."[45] Wiskirchen concluded that each had its merits and dangers. "The curricular can become excessively educative and then will not attract the better, professional-quality college student musician. . . . In practice, more jazz often has been produced by the non-curricular program."[46]

Like a repeated, off-stage solo, other acclaimed voices joined the jazz education conversation. Leonard Feather felt that college musicians would guide the future of jazz. Rayburn Wright, trombonist and arranger for the United States Army Band and the Glenn Miller-Tex Beneke Orchestra, and long associated with the Eastman School of Music where he received a Bachelor of Music in trombone, felt that the need for conservatory-trained jazz musicians was obvious. While music schools strived to provide excellent training and playing opportunities in traditional music, they were graduating musicians into a professional world that included the recording and broadcast industry, theater playing, even contemporary symphony orchestra work without the benefit of a background in jazz theory and performance.

Bandleader Stan Kenton got tired of waiting on the academic community. No one worked harder to provide jazz education to interested high school students than Kenton. Believing that the future of jazz depended on current jazz masters mentoring younger students, he took it upon himself, with the help of North Texas's jazz leaders Gene Hall and Leon Breeden, to do just that. If high schools weren't providing students with jazz bands, he'd offer them opportunities in the summer. Starting in the summer of 1959, Kenton hosted weeklong jazz camps (later changed to clinics to make them sound more academic), first at Indiana University under the auspices of the National Stage Band Camp. The camps taught improvisational techniques, and jazz theory and arranging, with plenty of time for lots of big band playing. Not only did participants have a chance to hear the world renowned Stan Kenton Orchestra, they worked with performers, composers, and college jazz educators. Kenton explained he wanted his students to "take a bath in jazz."[47] Kenton band member and arranger Johnny Richards felt "Stan's most important contribution is his constant devotion to music and support of young talent."[48] Kenton Camps, and later Kenton Clinics, in various forms and in various cities, inspired thousands of jazz students from 1959 to 1979.[49] Camp alumni more than fulfilled Kenton's dream of perpetuating the art form. Among those who attended were Bob Curnow, Randy Brecker, Jim McNeely, David Sanborn, Lyle Mays, Pat Metheny, Jim Widner, Keith Jarrett, Peter Erskine, and first WJF saxophone All-Star, Mary Fettig.[50]

Because of the organization of The National Association of Jazz Educators—finally formed out of the MENC in 1968[51]—a standardized jazz curriculum, the advent of easy jazz charts written for school bands, and the accessible books of Jamey Aebersold, Jerry Coker, and David Baker, school jazz bands increased dramatically in the sixties. But with that came controversy.

Many of the older players, unschooled in the traditional sense, felt institutionalizing jazz and attaching a semester grade homogenized the art form. The spontaneity of a jam session or evolution of tunes created during a standing gig was lost in an environment dictated by set class time. Established techniques and vocabulary, both melodic and rhythmic, had evolved as jazz developed, and some were favored over others, making them standardized in a loose sense. But to these jazz elders, the building blocks of jazz were best learned by playing, not in a lecture hall. Others complained that educational emphasis gravitated to bebop—not much before and not much after. Educators countered with the fact that this rock & roll generation was coming back to jazz and rejuvenating it as well, that perfecting scales and chord progressions never hurt anyone. Just because students started with "Sonnymoon for Two" didn't mean they wouldn't progress, explore, and more than likely, set up their own jam sessions.

Finding a balance between the spontaneity of a jam session and the structure of the classroom is still a struggle in jazz education. But the fact that during the WJF years not everyone had access to open jam sessions made the copious jams available those weekends all the more inviting. The fact that women were welcomed and encouraged as nowhere else made them spectacular.

The yearly clinics spoke to the academic side but gave attendees a wide variety of topics and facilitators. Possibly they gave avid, non-musician fans[52] a better understanding of what they were hearing, or inspired a young, inexperienced player, or gave an unexpected boost to a seasoned player.

Clinic and Workshop topics at WJF '83 included, as before, guitar, percussion, and vocal, but new this year, Gene Aiken, of the University of Northern Colorado, talked about the relatively new vocal jazz ensemble movement.

Generating the most excitement of any clinician, David Baker brought a full spectrum of viewpoints to the lineup. Long associated with the University of Indiana, Baker's students included Randy and Michael Brecker, Peter Erskine, Jeff Hamilton, and

Chris Botti. Although only a few years his senior, Baker became mentor to the jazz education pioneer Jamey Aebersold. In 1973 Baker was nominated for a Pulitzer Prize and in 1979 for a Grammy. In 1981 he received the NAJE Hall of Fame Award. After his appearance at WJF, Baker was involved in arts and educational organizations including the National Council on the Arts, the American Symphony Orchestra League, the Jazz Advisory Panel to the Kennedy Center, and the Jazz/Folk/Ethnic Panel of the NEA. He was also president of the International Association for Jazz Education. One of the first to codify aural jazz for students, many of Baker's sixty books, including *Jazz Improvisation* and *Jazz Pedagogy*, still stand as seminal works. Besides over five hundred compositions, he has to his credit four hundred articles and sixty-five recordings. But to call David Baker an academic is to overlook his roots. Growing up in the Big Band era of the thirties and forties, he first worked as a trombone player in the Stan Kenton, Maynard Ferguson, Quincy Jones, and Lionel Hampton bands and in the combos of Wes Montgomery, Harold Land, and George Russell. After a jaw injury ended his trombone-playing career, he switched to cello and concentrated on writing and teaching. By all accounts a brilliant trombone player, with plenty of experience jamming and with a respect for the past, he was also a born teacher.[53] "He approached the subject of improvisation from a historical-cultural perspective," Nathan Davis says in Monika Herzig's book *David Baker: A Legacy in Music*:

> The students were first guided through a series of historical scenarios designed to provide a firm foundation for understanding the different jazz styles. Once the students appeared to intellectually embrace the historical importance of the period, David then began to lay out the theoretical principles associated with a particular style. Finally, only after the students seemed to be comfortable with the historical, cultural and theoretical aspects

> of the periods and styles did he introduce the principal patterns that form the language for a particular style.[54]

For WJF '83 attendees, spending an hour with David Baker and then moving to the eight-hour jam combined the best of what jazz education had to offer. By wanting to give all attendees what they felt they needed and allow them to bathe themselves in jazz—to evoke Stan Kenton—WJF had tied past and present jazz education components together.

Friday night's TNT concert began with a quintet of college-trained jazz musicians of the highest order. Joyspring, named 1983 Combo Contest winner from among forty-four entries, began at Eastman School of Music. Pianist Ellen Rowe, bass player Rick Shaw, vocalist Teri Koide, and trumpet player Dina Alexander were all members of the Eastman Jazz Lab Band, the Eastman Jazz Ensemble, or the Eastman Jazz Singers. Drummer Liz Vochecowicz had studied classical percussion but was at the time drummer for pianist Teddy Wilson of Benny Goodman fame.[55]

"We came together when Rayburn Wright, head of the jazz studies department at Eastman, told us about the competition. There weren't many women in the Eastman jazz program, so we thought a women's jazz festival sounded great," Ellen Rowe remembers. "When we won and were invited to play at the Festival, we rented a beat-up old station wagon and drove to Kansas City."[56]

Joyspring presented a mix of originals and standards. "I know we played 'Alone Together' and 'If You Could See Me Now,'"[57] recalls Ellen. As winner of the 1982 *Down Beat* award for Best Original Composition by a College Student, Ellen supplied much of the original material. In her review for *Sojourner*, Cathy Lee called Ellen's tunes "beautiful and memorable" and told her readers that it was a pleasure to hear songs showcased by "women whose contributions have not yet been adequately recognized by the greater jazz community."[58]

Eastman's training stood these young musicians in good stead. Trumpeter Dina Alexander, who received a bachelors, masters, and doctorate from Eastman, went on to a distinguished career as a jazz educator at Roberts Wesleyan College.[59] Bassist Rick Shaw played with Johnny Mathis and became the bass player for the Big Phat Band. Vocalist Teri Koide worked with the band Hiroshima and can be heard on the soundtracks of *Rocky Balboa*, *Catwoman*, and *Scream 3*, to name a few. Her onscreen credits include *The Princess Diaries 2*, *Norbit*, *Yes Man*, and *License to Wed*. In *Come See the Paradise*, Teri plays a Japanese American singer interned during World War II. She has also appeared on many television shows including *Boston Legal*, *Ally McBeal*, *The Big Bang Theory*, *ER*, and *Malcolm in the Middle*. Quite at home in the recording studio, Teri has rounded out her career with such projects as singing in a chamber piece with Linda Ronstadt scored for three vocals, harp, and glass harmonica.[60]

Kansas City audiences got only a taste of Ellen Rowe's talent. She composed ambidextrously from straight-ahead jazz to funk. Referred to as "that rare triple threat of pianist, composer-arranger, and teacher"[61] by the *Arizona Daily Star*, Ellen performed with such artists as Ingrid Jensen, John Clayton, Tom Harrell, and Kenny Wheeler. Groups such as the BBC Jazz Orchestra, the Berlin Radio Jazz Orchestra, the U.S. Navy Commodores, DIVA, and the Village Vanguard Orchestra have played her compositions all over the world. As Associate Professor of Jazz Piano, Chair of the Department of Jazz and Contemporary Improvisation, and Director of the Jazz Ensemble at the University of Michigan,[62] and as a much-in-demand clinician and academic jazz festival adjudicator, Ellen has helped ensure that the next generation is prepared to take jazz through this century.

Back for the third year, second at TNT, the San Francisco-based group ALIVE! delighted Kansas City fans and gathered more into its camp. Most impressed with singer rhiannon, Cathy Lee called her rendition of "Lazy Afternoon" "indescribably delicious."[63] She couldn't resist quoting fellow critic Teachout. "The dumbfounded *KC Star* critic said it '. . . literally shimmered with carnal knowledge' and you can believe him."[64]

Tea for Two

The remaining TNT artists, Sheila Jordan and Harvie Swartz (today known professionally as simply Harvie S.) generated the most curiosity. Appearing out of balance on the large Folly stage, the two looked like they were waiting for the rest of the band to show up—until they performed their first tune. Kirby Farrell of the *Daily Hampshire Gazette* and a big fan of the duo remarked, "Singing jazz tunes with only bass accompaniment is of course like playing violin while crossing Niagara Falls on a tightrope in the nude. Nothing's hidden, and there isn't much room for mistakes. The singer needs secure intonation. The bassist has to be a whole rhythm section."[65] Sheila and Harvie did not disappoint.

Also curious was Sheila's billing as Top *New* Talent. Her first album, *Portrait of Sheila*, released in 1962, earned her that year's "Talent Most Deserving Wider Recognition" spot in the *Down Beat* poll. Reviewer Don DeMichael called it a "better-than-good debut [album] for an out-of-the-ordinary vocalist,"[66] and although he felt she was a diamond in the rough, he recognized how deeply into her soul her musical expression went. "Most of all—and this is why Miss Jordan is a remarkable singer—she possesses rare sensitiveness, which gives her singing a poignancy that can be moving to the extreme."[67]

A disciple of Charlie Parker, who claimed Sheila had "million dollar ears," she moved to New York specifically to follow Parker and to learn all she could from him. As wife of Parker's pianist

Duke Jordan, Sheila lived in the epicenter of the bebop era. Her Manhattan loft was often the hangout for Dizzy Gillespie, Bud Powell, Thelonious Monk, Sonny Rollins, and anyone else who wanted to jam. She was in the right place at the right time with the right voice, but just as her career was poised to take off, her world changed. She and Duke divorced in 1962, and Sheila was left to raise their daughter by herself. She also developed a serious drinking and drug problem. Lacking the confidence to stick it out on her own as a full-time vocalist, and not wanting to compromise her vocal vision, she took a job as a secretary at an advertising agency in New York. She didn't mind working a day job when it allowed her to work only pure jazz gigs. She wanted to sing her way and that often was not the way the club owners wanted her to sing, even in jazz-oriented rooms. "It's much easier for me to do an office job than work the Playboy Club, where I know I'm gonna get fired. I've *been* to the Playboy Club, and I've *gotten* fired."[68]

By the early eighties, her daughter grown, her habit kicked, Sheila was ready to focus on music and to once again become a new talent. Having picked the challenging vocal/bass duo as her niche—her first bass player was Charles Mingus, then Steve Swallow, then Arild Andersen for her 1977 album, *Sheila*—she and Harvie Swartz put together some new arrangements, including Harvie's originals. The two had set up an empathetic musical intimacy while playing in the Steve Kuhn quartet together. Using her vacation time and long weekends, Sheila went on the road with Kuhn. "On tour, Harvie was the only one in the group who had his instrument in his hotel room."[69] Sheila explained that she always wanted to soak up more music, even after a gig. "My favorite way to sing is with the bass. In fact I think I might have been a bass player in a former life."[70] Her voice fit perfectly inside the space provided by the low, resonating, wood sound of the bass. Sheila and Harvie worked as a duo for fourteen years.

Her talent for finding excellent bass partners was apparent in Harvie Swartz. At the time of the 1983 WJF, besides his work with Steve Kuhn, Harvie had performed with Dexter Gordon and Stan Getz. Over his career, his prodigious gig history included work with John Scofield, Kenny Barron, Gil Evans, Arturo Sandoval, Chick Corea, and Michael Brecker, as well as Jane Ira Bloom, Virginia Meyhew, Jay Clayton, Maria Schneider, Ingrid Jensen, and Emily Remler. *New York Post* writer Richard Sudhalter concluded that Harvie's playing in the duo is as "a virtuoso of uncommon sensitivity and responsiveness."[71]

Together Sheila and Harvie created what Cathy Lee called "expected sensitive interaction between two highly imaginative musicians."[72] Kirby Farrell told his readers that Harvie "showed what a bassist with seven fingers on each hand can do at high speeds," and by using double and triple-stops as well as runs, "he was able to make the bass line so tuneful and complementary that the music seemed full." All this led to a "personal rather than packaged" performance without "aggression or hype."[73] W. Patrick Hinely of *Jazz Forum* remarked that Sheila seldom took a tune where the listener expected it to go and that her singing "constantly surprises, somehow managing to be on both sides of the line between happy and sad."[74] In the liner notes for one of the several albums Sheila and Harvie did together, Kirk Silsbee concludes, "She often interprets standard material, but never in a standard way."[75]

Harvie was as pleased with WJF as the board was with him. "The organizers did things right. I have only good memories. I can't come up with a negative, and believe me, I would if there was something I didn't like. Most festivals aren't run as well. I was treated with respect."[76] His only complaint was with the press. "We were early enough in our association that good strong press could have really been a boost. *Down Beat* didn't even mention us."[77]

There is strong doubt that *Down Beat* reviewer Tom McDermott was even there. His June 1983 review of WJF is riddled with mistakes. He mentions the "President of Women's Jazz Festival, Dianne *Greer*." Perhaps working from an early press release, he gives credit to Emily Remler for being the All-Star guitarist when she was not. He credits the big band Maiden Voyage as having a spot on the TNT concert when in fact only leader Ann Patterson attended the festival as house reeds player at the Mixed Session of the Jumbo Jam. And, as Harvie noted, the Sheila Jordan-Harvie Swartz Duo is missing from the review.[78]

Straight No Chaser

Giving Kansas City audiences something completely new, the University of Northern Colorado Vocal Jazz Ensemble I kicked off the Main Concert Sunday night. Representing a relatively new but increasingly popular addition to the jazz family, this twenty-voice choir plus rhythm section, led by Director of Jazz Studies Gene Aitken, had already won three *Down Beat* awards.[79] Evoking groups like Manhattan Transfer and Singers Unlimited, the UNC Vocal Jazz Ensemble used dense, close harmonies, scat singing, and vocalese to present a variety of tunes.

Incorporating instrumental jazz into academic programs had proved difficult. Vocal jazz had an even tougher time. Traditional vocal teachers and department heads, insisting that type of singing damaged young vocal cords, resisted adding vocal jazz to their catalogs. Aiken tells how one group got the attention of educators. "The start came when the Axidental II, a University of Washington group, tried to get invited to Yakima to sing for the Washington Music Educators, around 1963, and were refused. So we drove to Yakima and found out where the band/choral directors were hanging out and went in the bar and started singing jazz with eight voices from Rod Eichenburger's select UW Choir. The place went crazy. Vocal jazz was born."[80]

Aitken explained the appeal of vocal jazz to Amy Duncan in an interview for her *Christian Science Monitor* article. "When you're singing a phrase it has to be the most beautiful thing in the world. That beauty is communicated to the audience."[81] Aitken felt people could relate to song lyrics, which made the presentation of the music more relative. But in vocal jazz, there's much more going on than simply singing a song. "The essence of vocal jazz is improvisation," Aitken continued. "One good example would be to take a show tune, and then add an element of improvisation and extended chords—a lot more color to the chords. In vocal jazz, you take the time to zero in more on the lyrics, accentuate the phrasing, and fluctuate the tempo. Many times it helps a vocal jazz soloist if he can visualize himself as a saxophone or trumpet player."[82]

That afternoon, in the Imperial Ballroom of the Radisson Muehlebach Hotel, the Sunday afternoon offering had featured two local college groups to introduce the concept of vocal jazz ensemble. The University of Kansas Jazz Choir, led by Ron McCurdy, and the UMKC Conservatory Jazz Singers, under the direction of Marvin Beach, affirmed that "the human voice can duplicate any band instrument perfectly."[83]

Fans (and no doubt parents) were enthusiastic at both the afternoon and the evening performances. Critics seemed a bit put off. *Sojourner's* Cathy Lee called the UNC group "okay." She, perhaps unrealistically, expected a Lambert/Hendricks/Ross type of sound. But the fact that UNC's group was made up of twenty voices, rather than three, made the possibility of an up-tempo, bopping, syncopated cascade of words unlikely. She identified the selections as pop/funk and took exception to the number of male soloists.[84]

Terry Teachout thought the ensemble was well rehearsed, but felt that they lacked a full, blended sound. The group sang "It's Sand Man"—by no stretch considered a pop tune—but Teachout was not impressed. "There is something un-nerving about hearing Count Basie's 'It's Sand Man' sung by twenty vocalists in head voice."[85] He did, however, enjoy a rendition of the Singers Unlimited tune "One More Time, Chick Corea" and acknowledged that the crowd displayed an acceptance keener than his. No mention of the UNC Vocal Jazz Ensemble I was made in Tom McDermott's *Down Beat* piece.[86]

Amy Duncan had appeared at previous WJFs in multiple capacities: as a jam session participant at one and as a jam session leader at another, as a clinician on The Business of Music, and as a reporter for the *Christian Science Monitor*. But, as pianist for the 1983 WJF All-Stars, she now had a chance to show the audience what she loved best. Amy's perspective as both a journalist and musician gave her an inside view. As a journalist she observed, "There's a feeling that the festival is running out of steam."[87] And the only thing that would help that would be to have a "big headliner"[88] of the caliber of Ella Fitzgerald or Sarah Vaughan. As she saw it, WJF wasn't changing with the shifting landscape for women in jazz. She cited the fact that the Jazzwomen Jam—for women only—was practically empty, while the Mixed Session participants spread out into the hallway and endured long waits until they could play. Amy felt those early years of women only wanting to play with women were waning. Plus the cold, hard fact was there just weren't enough women bass players and drummers to keep an eight-hour jam going. In addition, the militant feminist protesters of the first year were gone. Carol and Dianne had always said they wanted to make the "women" part of the jazz festival obsolete, and Amy felt they needed to be moving more in that direction.[89]

She had ruffled feathers the year before as a panelist in the Business of Music clinic when she suggested that women could make their own opportunities as long as they played as well as men. In her autobiography, *Getting Down to Brass Tacks*, Amy says, "I frankly got tired of hearing them whine about how they couldn't get a gig or a record deal because they weren't men. The truth of the matter was that most of them just didn't play as well as their male colleagues."[90]

As objective and pithy as her journalistic remarks were, as the All-Stars pianist and leader, Amy couldn't have been happier. She had handpicked this group from around the country to represent the best in young jazz talent. Except during WJF jam sessions over the years, she had never played with any of them before. From New York City, twenty-year-old saxophonist Carol Chaikin already had an impressive list of credentials. She had played with Roger Calloway, Freddie Hubbard, and Marian McPartland. She was Bobby Vinton's lead alto at the MGM in Las Vegas. Besides fronting her own quartet, she recorded with Maiden Voyage and Mary Watkins. In the summer of 1982, she was the improvisation teacher at the Aspen Music Festival. Amy referred to Carol as a "hot bebop"[91] saxophonist, and critic Cathy Lee reported that she "tore it up as usual."[92]

Referred to as a "super-wonder of the music world," fifty-four-year-old veteran musician Nadine Jansen came from Arizona. Difficult to classify, Nadine played trumpet and flugelhorn with the All-Stars but had as her specialty the ability to play trumpet with her right hand and piano with her left and, in Amy's words, "amazingly made it not seem like a gimmick."[93] She also sang.

Nadine thought of herself as a vaudevillian entertainer. At eighteen, in the late forties, she played with Horace Heidt and His Musical Knights and in live groups that performed between double features in the movie theaters. She played for Rosemary Clooney when Rosemary still did an act with her sister Betty. She shared the spotlight with Skitch Henderson and Tony Pastor. She also appeared with Kai Winding, Paul Horn, and Charlie Parker. Cathy Lee concluded, "Nadine Jansen's simultaneous solo on trumpet and piano sounds like it would be outrageous, but worked fine musically."[94]

As the drummer for ALIVE!, Barbara Borden had already charmed WJF audiences with her glowing smile and enthusiasm. Cathy Lee put it simply: "Barbara Borden should be taking her place among the heavies any minute now."[95]

Hometown girl Carole Brown was no stranger to WJF either. She received the Friends of Jazz scholarship in 1979 and had been house bassist at jam sessions. Growing up in a musical family—both of her parents played violin in the Kansas City Philharmonic and later the Kansas City Symphony—Carole was always surrounded by classical music but came to jazz on her own. Moving to New York City in 1980, she played with Ed Shaughnessy, Red Rodney, Gary Foster, and Harry "Sweets" Edison. She performed at both the Nice and Montreux Jazz Festivals. At the time of the 1983 WJF, she was playing with the New York groups String Fever and the Kit McClure Band.[96] In Cathy Lee's words, "Carole Brown made that job [as bassist] look effortless, which it emphatically is not."[97]

"I did something a little different in that I let each woman have her own feature spot,"[98] Amy remembers. In other years, pianist-composers who worked for a unity of sound had led the All-Stars. Amy had a different vision. "I featured each of these women on a number of her choice, and then, for our finale, I wrote an updated, boppish arrangement of the old Rodgers and Hammerstein show tune from *Oklahoma!* 'Everything's Up to Date in Kansas City' with a free jazz, 'organized chaos' section in the middle that Leonard Feather described in his review in *Jazz Times* as a 'riotous impression of Sun Ra.' We got a standing ovation."[99]

More Than You Know

There was one more All-Star who had played the year before in that capacity and hadn't expected to appear in 1983. Brandy Herbert (aka Brandy Anthony) had agreed, with little notice, to fill in for scheduled All-Star guitarist Emily Remler. In the festival program and in press the day of the concert, it was reported that Emily Remler's father had become ill, leading to Emily's last-minute cancellation. Those who knew her suspected another reason. Emily's substance abuse problem was an open secret. It would end her life in 1990, when she was just thirty-two.

"I can't help but think that there's something in the business that will do that to you," Nancy Wilson had said to Marian McPartland. "Because all of these women [who were downed by substance abuse] weren't weak. What is there that puts that in their lives?"[100]

The reasons are cultural and personal, obvious and subtle, and as varied as they are common. Easy access set the scene. After World War II, the Mafia reopened supply markets from the Far East and Turkey. Heroin became readily available on the streets of New York about the same time that the revolutionary, anti-establishment, modern jazz called bebop hit the clubs. Of course drugs have always been accessible to those who are driven to find them, but the list of successful jazz musicians of the fifties and sixties who lost careers, loves, and lives to drugs is legendary. At the top of the list, on thrones, are Billie Holiday and Charlie Parker. The fact that these idols of the era embraced heroin habits has been used as an excuse for others who wanted to achieve Billie's and Parker's level of musicianship. That's too simple. Singer Sheila Jordan, who struggled with alcoholism, revered Parker and his playing, but she told her biographer Ellen Johnson, "When I was around Bird, he never influenced me in any way to use drugs. If anything, I think he was proud of the fact that I didn't take anything."[101] Billie Holiday also didn't encourage others to enter drug hell. In her biography, *Lady Sings the Blues*, she says, "If you think dope is for kicks, you're out of your mind. There are more kicks to be had in a good case of paralytic polio or by living in an iron lung. All dope can do for you is kill you—and it can kill people you love right along with you."[102]

Yet a whole litany of other reasons explains the lure. The act of playing music in front of a live audience is a type of high in itself. The supercharged energy that comes from the communication among like-minded musicians who love playing with each other is difficult to duplicate offstage. It's also difficult to tear away from when the performance is over. If that performance is far from home, away from family and a supportive, loving environment, the need to fill the psychological hole can be overpowering. Varying degrees of stage fright, perhaps difficult for the audience to imagine but nevertheless real, can cripple the inherent creativity that is so critical for an improvising musician. Getting used to having "a taste" to take the edge off quickly modulates from casual use to a drug habit. Sometimes it's the fear of audience disapproval or not being good enough to please oneself and other players. Often feeling like outsiders from the normal flow of humanity, jazz musicians aren't always comfortable with their blend of inner and outer selves. Emily Remler not so jokingly told friends, "I may look like a nice Jewish girl from New Jersey, but inside I'm a 50-year-old, heavyset black man with a big thumb, like Wes Montgomery."[103]

Add to all that the prejudice against female jazz musicians and the pressure of others' expectations and you're left with quite a cocktail. Although highly respected as a player, Emily still was hassled by the "girl issue." W. Royal Stokes reports in his book *The Jazz Scene*, "Emily was especially annoyed at a prominent critic who had objected (in print) to her habit of intermittently holding the guitar pick in her mouth whenever she switched to bare-finger playing. The critic confessed that he preferred to look away whenever she was doing this, to which Emily testily replied, 'Good! I wish he'd look away the whole time and picture me as John Coltrane!'"[104]

Sometimes club owners set musicians up for failure. Sheila Jordan remembers a gig in the early days of her career where she was expected to mix with the customers on breaks. The idea was for band members to encourage customers to spend more money by buying drinks for the band. Sheila explained to the club owner that she had grown up seeing her mother drunk every day and that she herself had started drinking at a young age only to stop when her daughter was born. She hated the idea of possibly ending up like her mother and was afraid of the temptation to drink. The club owner told her to let the customers buy her a drink, and then have a chaser of water to spit the drink back into when no one was looking. Sheila tried this for a while but, "I remember one night there was a couple in the club who loved my singing. They bought me a Cherry Herring and I spit it back into the water chaser and they caught me. I was embarrassed, so I told them it was an accident and then drank the Cherry Herring. That immediately set off the phenomenon of craving for alcohol. So that's what got me started again."[105]

There was a strong socialization element to drinking and drug use. As in all types of social situations where pressure to get high is present, musicians succumbed to the promise of an altered—and in the musician's case—creative state. Sheila explained, "Everybody thought they were going to be able to play or sing better if they got high, especially with heroin. Of course that wasn't true and Bird tried to tell them. He tried to tell Duke [Jordan] too and fortunately I never got involved with heroin, it was mostly booze and later cocaine."[106]

Because of Sheila's day job, she only drank on the weekends, but when that got out of control, she finally realized she was an alcoholic, and she stopped drinking. That's when she started using cocaine. "I switched seats on the Titanic [*sic*],"[107] she said. It was a "spiritual awakening," in the form of a heavenly voice that told her to take care of her musical gift or it would be taken away, that finally turned her to the help she needed to stay clean.[108]

"The trouble with drugging is that at first it's all laughs." Anita O'Day explains in her autobiography, *High Times, Hard Times*, how quickly the fun changes. A jealous master, the drug demands full attention in exchange for the promise of nirvana, which only leads to a sinister possession. Yet the one possessed always thinks they're street smart enough to handle it. "I never knew a junkie who didn't initially feel that way."[109]

Like Sheila Jordan, WJF Headliner Anita O'Day had an unhappy, unstable childhood and never knew quite where she belonged. The bands she sang with became like family. After a couple of drug busts for marijuana (one in Kansas City), she felt the press put a heavier junkie mantle on her than she deserved, but as she was fond of saying, "If you have the name, you might as well play the game."[110]

Her long-time drummer and best friend, John Poole, didn't drink and seemed to have his life together, so when Anita found out he was a heroin user, she begged him to let her try it. At first John refused and tried to dissuade her from even considering using, but Anita persistently hounded him until he gave in. John reasoned that if Anita was determined to use, he'd rather be the one to control how much she got than leave her to her own devices. For years he administered the dosage and inserted the needle. When he was out of town without her for a gig once in 1966, Anita gave herself the drug. With the thought that if a little is good, more will be better, she gave herself an extra zing. Almost immediately a heavenly feeling of well-being spread throughout her body. "I thought, "This is the most! Pow!' And after that—nothing."[111] A friend found her and rushed her to the hospital in time.

All of these women lived for music at the exclusion of all else, as their artistry proves. All made outstanding contributions to jazz. Yet their demons controlled them in ways music never could.

Musicians don't have exclusive rights to these problems, but the pressures endemic to constantly striving to be at the top of your playing ability without distractions and not care about critics and critical fans, or money for that matter, can quickly take its toll. Nancy Wilson was right. It can be something in the business.

Thanks for the Boogie Ride

When Anita O'Day began singing professionally, the first thing she did was change her last name from Colton to O'Day. She reasoned that because "oday" was pig latin for "dough," it would help her make some.

Anita O'Day's sense of humor and innate resilience made her the consummate survivor. The attention she got winning walk-athons and dance-a-thons spurred her into a singing career while still a teenager. "I was a 'personality singer' for years before the big band days," she told Amy Duncan for a *Christian Science Monitor* article. "They called me that because I smile when I sing. They're gonna throw tomatoes, you smile and they don't throw 'em. So that was what I was."[112]

For a short time, she was the girl singer in the Woody Herman band, for a longer time in Stan Kenton's (although she said that band was too straight for her—on their breaks, they read), and for five years she was song stylist—her term—for Gene Krupa's Big Band. While with Krupa, Anita often sang with trumpet player Roy Eldridge, especially on hard-swinging tunes like "Let Me off Uptown." Although Eldridge was miffed that Anita upstaged him, their appearance together onstage was groundbreaking. At a time when even troops fought fascism with forced segregation, their easy, jiving style was bold and potentially dangerous.

Not interested in convention—and because of that, some bandleaders—Anita had some disappointing auditions. One was with Benny Goodman. "When my turn came, I handed this nothing song they'd assigned me to the audition pianist. He played the intro and I took off. I paid my respects to the melody to make sure I was keeping in touch with my listeners, then I began to play around with the chord structure and the beat, returning to a bit of melody in the end. Benny jumped up, obviously annoyed. 'What was that? You didn't sing the melody.' 'I don't sing the melody on songs like this one,' I informed him. 'Everybody already knows the melody.'"[113] That was the end of the audition.

Anita heard the tunes as a series of chords and, like a horn player, used those to individualize her solos as well as the melody. "You listen to the chords. When I'm gonna learn a song, I learn the chords, and then I learn the song as a poem . . . like without music. Now the game that I play is to put the poem of the story into the chords and make a picture. And that's jazz—oh, yeah! I took ideas from out of nowhere, from imagination—I guess."[114] That style, and her slightly husky tone quality, made her the most popular swing singer of the forties. The jitterbugging teenagers loved her, but staid critics steeped in the mellow sounds of crooners didn't. "Anita O'Day should clear her throat,"[115] grumbled Barry Ulanov.

Norman Granz, who, it was said, built his record label, Verve, on junkies, took a chance on Anita to the advantage of everyone. Through it all, Anita built a reputation on never doing a tune the same way twice, because she didn't feel it was worthwhile doing something that had already been done. At live gigs she frequently ended by telling the audience that they shouldn't expect to hear her sing a tune like that ever again.

Despite her drug detours and band changes, Anita always stayed close to the music. "The music is all I have. Period. It's all I know. I don't know how to do anything, because that's all I ever did. And I was very happy with that. That was my life—one track."[116]

Never one to embrace the girl-singer-canary-window-dressing image of the chick in front of the band, however, Anita believed in a professional presence and a memorable look. If she hadn't been a jazz icon before, her Newport Jazz Festival performance in 1958 alone would have assured it. Dressed in a straight, tight-fitting, black sleeveless dress, she wore a black "cartwheel" hat trimmed with white feathers, and short white gloves. Her set started in the middle of the afternoon—teatime—and she wanted a look to complement that. She sang nine tunes that afternoon, but when she and John Poole launched into "Tea for Two" at more than double the usual speed, the crowd, somewhat apathetic up to that point with the late afternoon drags, went wild. "I was high as a kite," Anita remembers, meaning it in both senses of the phrase.[117]

Harvie Swartz, who played bass with Anita at the 1983 WJF, remembers another clothing issue. "I didn't have a sports coat. I never wore one with Sheila [Jordan], just a shirt and tie, so I didn't have a jacket with me. So Anita asked me where my sports coat was, and when I told her I didn't have one, she said, 'Listen kid, when you play with a broad over fifty, you wear a sports coat.'"[118]

"Anita traveled with John Poole, who was also her manager at that time, but she always used pick-up musicians on the road," Harvie adds. "I had played for her a few times in New York, so when she heard that I would be in Kansas City playing with Sheila, she hired me."[119] Saxophonist Roger Neumann and Kansas City's own, pianist Paul Smith, completed the group.

Because of Anita's reputation for unpredictability as well as high professionalism, Paul remembers he didn't know quite what to expect. "I had always liked Anita's voice and admired her musicianship. I saw her on TV a couple of months before the festival, and she did a tune with the piano player doing the line with her. That was the first time I called Carol and Dianne and suggested they get someone else. I think they had to bring me in from the ledge a time or two after that."[120]

At the afternoon rehearsal before the concert, Paul told Harvie he was apprehensive about holding his own. "He was a big help in easing my terror. He said not to worry because Roger Neuman would cover all those unison lines with Anita. But then Roger's flight was late and he missed the rehearsal."[121]

The concert went smoothly. Roger arrived and, as Harvie promised, filled in the lines that had concerned Paul. Everything was charted and Anita didn't introduce any surprises. "She couldn't have been more gracious. She was absolutely cool," Paul says. "At one point I was to give her a cue note or something like that, and I forgot. I remember she made a joke out of it and everybody (including me) laughed."[122] Familiar tunes like "Emily," "Wave," and "In a Mellotone" also helped ease the fear of the unknown, but in Anita's hands, those tunes became a brand new entity. Terry Teachout told his readers, "Anita O'Day is in a class by herself." He also reported, "Paul Smith played as if he's been working with the singer since the beginning of time."[123]

Kansas City Mayor Richard Berkley gave Anita the key to the city, a gesture to temper her 1954 visit, which had ended with a police run-in, but "the show-biz veteran treated him like just another autograph hound."[124]

After the final song was played, after the applause had died down, after all the artists were paid and the lights turned off, Carol and Dianne just wanted to crash. They always had a hotel suite, now at the Radisson Muehlebach (a switch since an obscenities-painted-on-the-ceiling incident in a musician's guest room at Crown Center), and although it was open to concert artists who needed a central place to regroup, they just wanted to put their feet up and sleep. The weeks leading up to the festival were exhausting. Making sure performers actually made it to Kansas City, that they were met at the airport and settled into their hotel rooms with everything they requested, that the lighting and sound people were all on board with no communication glitches, that the tickets were sold and accounted for, that grants and contributions were all entered into their proper columns and banked, that jam session rooms were secured and staffed, that the student bands were settled and chaperoned, that all transportation arrangements were secure, that the press was pacified, all meant Carol and Dianne, and most of the board and volunteers, were running on empty.

Carol and Dianne approached their suite with the fervent hope that no one was there. That this was the sixth time they had finished WJF made the post-festival let down no less draining. But their rest would have to wait. They opened the door onto a room full of fans and musicians paying court to Anita O'Day, who sat on one of the beds like a queen.[125]

Chapter 8

Every Time We Say Goodbye

THE HEADLINE HURT. Those involved knew it was coming, but the reality of seeing it in print left everyone with sick hearts. "Women's Jazz Festival Is Canceled for 1984." Just ten days before Christmas, the *Kansas City Star* announcement was no present. "Next year will be the first time in seven years that the annual event, which some jazz leaders say has drawn international attention to Kansas City and had been a model for festivals elsewhere, will not be held."[1] After months of debate and upheaval, the WJF board had come to the sad conclusion that the fiscally responsible thing to do was to cancel the 1984 festival and concentrate on reorganizing for 1985.

The months directly following each WJF were always a financially tenuous time. Final bills for one festival had to be reconciled at the same time that the following year's commitments were planned. The only way to guarantee that there would be enough money to cover everything in that post-festival deluge of bills was for Carol to float the organization a loan until the NEA grant came in June. It had always seemed like a logical fix to Carol, and she was happy to do it as long as she got her money back.[2]

The 1983 WJF hadn't brought in as much revenue as hoped. Although Nancy Wilson was the only real headliner, she performed the entire second half of the Main Concert, making her appearance more expensive than two lesser known acts would have been. The audience of two thousand was down in numbers from the Main Concert of previous years. Grants and corporate contributions had kept apace of projections, but the individual donor list was disturbingly short.

This became the main topic of discussion at the April 1983 board meeting. The idea of hiring a paid staff with professional expertise was raised and rejected. The idea of collaboration with the KOOL Jazz Festival, again, passed through the room and promptly exited. Even with a more aggressive campaign for individual donations and a plethora of fundraising ideas, just how was WJF going to stay afloat?

Volunteer burnout was also an issue. WJF required a yearlong time commitment that ballooned in February and March. By November 1983 longtime board members, citing heavy loads of personal and professional obligations, resigned. As a strictly volunteer organization, everyone who worked on WJF did so because of their passionate belief in what they were accomplishing. With no less passion, but with considerably less energy, even some of the original board members—Mike Ning, Milt Abel, and John Leisenring—resigned. Marian McPartland also bowed out. Of the original eighteen directors, only two, Marie Spearing and Ben Seagraves, remained. There had always been a lot of board members in order to spread the work around and because if someone wanted to help, Carol and Dianne didn't feel they could tell them no. By 1981 the number of board members had swelled to thirty-three with an additional six officers, creating a too-many-cooks situation with potential communication issues. Although united by common goals, longtime board members, new board members, and musician board members didn't always have common visions of how to achieve those goals. It was time to step back, take a deep breath, and regroup. Many of those who resigned made clear they still supported WJF and would volunteer during festival weekends, but they needed a break from the year-long commitment.[3]

Although the Ruth Kissane lawsuit had been settled without financial harm to WJF, it had left everyone emotionally drained, especially Carol and Dianne. For the first time, they considered that they too needed to be less involved. "The weeks leading up to the festival each year were ten-to twelve-hour days," Carol says. "My kids were in high school during these years. February and March were a big disruption in their lives because the Women's Jazz Festival World Headquarters was in our basement. My poor kids. They put up with a lot."[4] When the election of officers for the coming year—1984 and WJF Seven—took place in May, Carol and Dianne decided not to run. A WJF newsletter sent to board members reported, "In the interest of their careers, Carol and Dianne are no longer able to work full-time for the WJF." The newsletter goes on to say, "Their contributions to women in jazz is certainly significant if not awesome, and they should be applauded for a job well done." Stating that the pair intended to remain on the board, the newsletter concludes, "Their efforts will be concentrated on the March festival, and they will be doing the booking and coordination for the festival."[5] The position of executive director was eliminated, and Julie Hanson, a neurology nurse at Menorah Hospital and a board member for just one year, was elected president.

Dianne explains, "We hand-picked Julie to be president. We groomed her to take over. She was at the headquarters a lot, and we showed her everything. We were more than willing to give up our officers jobs, but we still wanted to be on the board."[6]

With a new set of officers in place, the board went about its business of planning the 1984 WJF. But changes in management led to gaps in communication, and one of these gaps led to an unmendable breech. Carol gives this account: "Everything I loaned WJF was on the books. We always had the treasurer come over, and it was always understood that we had nothing to do with the books. So Julie took over, the NEA grant came in, and I asked for my reimbursement. Julie just said, 'What?' There was a big brouhaha over that."[7] New board officers claimed they knew nothing about the long-standing arrangements Carol had set up to help the cash flow problem as they waited for NEA funds. The total loaned over a period of seven years approached $16,000, but each year's loan, always paid off promptly, was not much more than $2,000. "I'm telling you, that broke my heart, that just broke my heart. That anyone associated with the festival would think that I was trying to take money, when I was just trying to fill in that time gap, was too much to take."[8]

By late autumn, it was obvious that money was a bigger problem than usual. At the November board meeting, members filled out a ballot: "I vote *for* or *against* the following resolution. Be it resolved that no festival be held in 1984 and that major efforts be directed toward funding a festival in 1985." Twenty board members, including Carol and Dianne, voted to not have a festival in 1984 and six voted to have it. Three abstained; two abstainers—John Leisenring and Ron Brown—took the opportunity to resign from the board.[9]

Ginney Coleman, a local jazz radio personality, wrote on the bottom of her ballot, "I think the group made a good decision considering the circumstances."[10] Another who voted against the 1984 festival, Troy Garrison wrote, "A good general knows when to retreat."[11] M. Carol Smith, the newly elected treasurer, who voted to have the 1984 festival, added this to the bottom of her ballot: "Need additional budgeting information before making informed decision."[12] Jane Flynn, director of the Kansas City Landmark Commission and WJF's new corresponding secretary, who was the third member to abstain, left this cryptic and inflammatory note on her ballot: "I refuse to vote as I am not sufficiently satisfied with the reasons given to cancel, and I firmly believe that the 'hidden agenda' needs to be put on the table. To flippantly cancel is vastly unjust to those who have supported WJF. This includes not only contributors but the many thousands who have paid their money to attend."[13]

Shortly after this vote and the decision to cancel 1984's WJF, Jane Flynn and a few other board members approached Carol and Dianne. "It was an ambush," Carol says sadly even now. "They told us, 'It's time to give your baby up.'"[14]

"We were starting to make transitions, and to do so with responsibility and a future vision," Dianne recalls. "But a few on the board felt we wouldn't be able to let go, that we wouldn't be able to keep our hands off, so we really didn't have the chance to change our direction of commitment to WJF. Even though we were fine with our greatly reduced responsibilities, the few thought it might be easier for the organization if we weren't even there."[15]

"So we said, 'We wish you well,' and left,"[16] Carol adds.

"But we weren't happy about it. That was painful," Dianne goes on. "For seven years we had lived the festival. It was tremendously hard work, but it was a tremendous amount of fun, too. We still laugh when we think about our musician friends playing basketball: our baby-drummer Scotty Robinson, at eleven, playing with the big boys; Steve Cardenas, not much older, shooting mid-court baskets, both of them going on to become very successful and respected musicians on the east coast; our great friends Milt Abel and Mike Ning hugging the bench, but looking great in a pair of shorts. They were on the board with us, giving their all, through 1983. Johnny Lyman played that game, too. His death was such a tragedy, and we hated thinking we wouldn't be able to see to it that his scholarship went on. Major events happened in our lives during that time, and we had shared them with our WJF friends."[17]

"We were at Crown Center with ALIVE! when President Reagan was shot." Carol adds and remembers another time that the members of ALIVE! came to her house for a pot roast dinner. "We watched the Academy Awards together. That might have been the same year we talked one of the Swedish groups into eating barbeque for the first time. We'd had such fun with Urszula Dudziak and Michal Urbaniak. They were so proud that they had saved us money on transportation and kept saying, 'Supersaver,' in their broken English. Even at our very first board meeting, we entered laughing because we shared a space with the North American UFO Organization."[18]

Dianne recounts the priceless experiences they had with fans, performers, press, students. When Terry Teachout moved to New York City and a job at *Harper's Magazine*, he wrote a note to Carol and Dianne. "Quite the nicest thing about being jazz critic of the *Kansas City Star* has been my association with you two."[19] They would always be proud of the fact they re-united the International Sweethearts of Rhythm and brought Melba Liston out of retirement. Coming full circle, they both agree that, above it all, getting to know Marian McPartland and Leonard Feather had been one of the joys of their lives. To have all of that abruptly stop felt like an amputation.

Dianne concludes, "So many of the board members who would have supported us staying on the board had already resigned. It wouldn't have served any purpose for us to fight the decision, and after all, we didn't want to compromise the future of WJF. It was so hurtful and sad, because although we were ready to step back, we weren't ready to step away."[20]

In his December 15 *Kansas City Star* article announcing the cancellation of the 1984 festival, Robert C. Trussell told his readers that although continued efforts to raise money for a festival in 1985 were underway, there was no hope for the upcoming year. He went on to quote Mike White, then co-chairman of the

Kansas City Jazz Commission and former WJF board member. "It's too important an event to let it die. It's really put Kansas City on the map. It's the first one like it in the world, and being first and oldest, it ought to continue."[21] But a general press release drafted by the new WJF board officers made it official. "The Board felt that projected funding was not enough to protect the organization from a substantial deficit that could not be quickly and easily recovered. Significant restructuring on all levels of the organization is taking place."[22] As if prolonging the goodbye, a December 29 editorial in the *Star* mentioned that a $9,000 budget deficit (what would still exist after everything from 1983, including Carol, was paid and the NEA grant applied) had ultimately ground the entire production to a halt. "That might appear to be a relatively small amount but it is huge indeed if it cannot be raised." The editorial's headline spoke for the Kansas City jazz community and those who had come to love the WJF week in March: "We'll All Miss the Lost Jazz Festival."[23]

At the January 14, 1984, WJF Board meeting, new president Julie Hanson reported that she had been contacted by a representative from Hallmark who indicated "that Hallmark may have been willing to fund the $9,000 projected to be necessary to put on the limited 1984 festival." It was too late. The Board decided to view this as a vote of confidence and continue to work toward a festival in 1985.[24]

I've Got You under My Skin

With renewed vigor and commitment, the Board set out to prove WJF '85 a worthy successor. To signify a fresh start, a new logo—Mike Ning, the resident graphic designer and artist who had designed the original logo, had resigned from the board—headed all correspondence and adorned the newly designed WJF program. Using a grant from the Hall Family Foundation to do so, board members worked with the Center for Management Assistance Inc., a non-profit management assistance organization, in hopes of defining underlying WJF goals and strategies. A hired consultant compiled an extensive list of strengths and weaknesses, both internal and external. Labeled as internal strengths, two of the twelve listed show the direction the new board wished to move: "no expectation that board members or volunteers must be jazz experts" and "willingness to operate organization as a business." With far more weaknesses listed, both internal and external, there was plenty of room for improvement: "lack of good fund raising strategies," "lack of carefully thought out advertising and promotion campaign," "no long-range planning, always operating in a crisis mentality," and " no formal community relations plan" were some of the perceived deficiencies.[25]

Again the idea of a paid staff surfaced. "We've got to show that we're building and growing each year," Julie told William Hollan of the *Kansas City Times*. She hoped a pared down board of directors and a rented office space would project the image of "a more professional, formal organization."[26]

Despite changes behind the scenes, WJF '85 events were familiar. Scheduled in the same order as previous WJFs, the festival began with Fun with Jazz, the only WJF activity that had taken place in 1984. This year four high school students from Paseo Academy, along with Milt Abel, demonstrated their instruments and taught the basics of ad-libbing to the gathering of 470 Head Start children.[27]

Although the $1,000 WJF scholarship—previously sponsored by H & R Block—had been awarded in January of 1984 during a Friends of Jazz concert, the winner was again announced to WJF audiences in 1985. Canadian pianist and vocalist Diana Krall, who was attending Berklee College of Music at the time, reported that she would use her scholarship money to study with Los Angeles pianist Alan Broadbent.[28] Her subsequent fifteen million worldwide album sales and her five Grammys attest to money well spent, and to yet another way that WJF touched the future of jazz.

Continuing the educational theme, the High School/College Big Band Invitational Concert, held at the recently opened downtown luxury hotel Vista International, featured the UMKC jazz band, now under the direction of Mike Parkinson, the Sumner Academy jazz band, and the Raytown South High School jazz band. Rosetta Reitz, the jazz historian who had collected early recordings of women jazz musicians for her record label, Rosetta Records, acted as emcee and facilitated the jazz film portion of the weekend since Leonard Feather had not been asked back.

In a letter to Feather, board members explained that, in the hopes of receiving a larger NEA grant, they were trying to get away from repeated talent and were looking for new faces to front WJF events. To that end they would not ask him to emcee the 1985 WJF. The next paragraph asks that he recommend "talent we should consider," and if asked, that he put in a good word for them with NEA. He is also informed that, although "things became pretty emotional and ugly last winter," the new board had "straightened things out administratively," and they were on the right track.[29]

Despite the board's reported desire to find new talent, Amy Duncan again led a portion of the Super Jam with her pick of New York and Los Angeles musicians. Jean Fineberg, who in 1981 had been the reeds All-Star, co-led the TNT Combo Contest winner, Deuce, with trumpeter Ellen Seeling. The first performer of the Main Concert, Judy Roberts, had also been an All-Star in 1981. Closing out the main concert, Toshiko Akiyoshi returned to Kansas City with a trio. Amy had kept up a correspondence with WJF and enthusiastically voiced her desire to help out in any way,[30] and WJF's established relationship with Judy and Toshiko trumped the more difficult process of contracting new talent.

The TNT Concert, held at the Folly Theater, across the street from the Vista International, with ticket prices ranging from $6.50 to $15.00, presented what the *Kansas City Star* reviewer Robert C. Trussell called a "mixed bag of sophisticated piano stylings, Latin-infused fusion and full-throttled blues."[31] Deuce led the evening off with their exciting blend of high-energy rock, blues, salsa, funk, and jazz—a musical portrait of the group's New York home base. As winner of the Combo Contest in 1984, Deuce was contracted a year in advance. The group consisted of co-leaders Jean Fineberg and Ellen Seeling, along with Julie Homi on piano, Marvin Horne on guitar, Frank Gravis on bass, Nydia "Liberty" Mata on percussion, and Kim Plainfield on drums. Playing all original material, Deuce collectively raised the heart rate and adrenaline levels of everyone in the audience, in no small part because of Mata who played a collection of percussion instruments in a manner that was as much fun to watch as to hear. In her review for *Sojourners*, Cathy Lee attributed the tight ensemble sound to the fact that Ellen, Jean, and Nydia had met a decade before and had honed their Latin chops in an all-woman salsa orchestra called Latin Fever. With pyrotechnic-like facility, Jean and Ellen whirled all these musical elements of their experience together. Their performance was well worth the year-and-a-half wait.

Joyce Collins, a seasoned Los Angeles pianist and vocalist—by no stretch a *new* talent—along with bass player Andy Simpkins, performed a mix of originals, ballads, and works by Mary Lou Williams, Marian McPartland, Bud Powell, and Lil Hardin. As warm-up act for the live studio audiences of both *The Mary Tyler Moore Show* and *The Bob Newhart Show*, Joyce knew how to please a crowd. Simpkins's work as Sarah Vaughan's bass player and his long associations with George Shearing, Carmen McRae, and Joe Williams provided a solid foundation for anything Joyce had in mind. "Her unpretentious vocal style and sophisticated piano work"[32] served as the palate-cleansing act between two energy-infused bands.

Taking to heart emcee Rosetta Reitz's comment that "blues is to jazz what yeast is to bread—without it, it's flat,"[33] hometown girl Ida McBeth settled into the double-entendre blues of Julia Lee with "You Can Have My Husband but Don't Mess with My Man." Whistles and whoops from the crowd accompanied her, as did pianist Rich Hill, bassist Forest Stewart, guitarist Monte Musa, and drummer Sam Johnson. But Ida was about more than the blues, as her Kansas City fans knew. With her deep and velvety sound, she took control of jazz tunes as varied as "Perdito" and "It Don't Mean a Thing," then segued into a sophisticated Roberta Flack cover. Cathy Lee, enthusiastically impressed, concluded, "The only mystery surrounding Ida McBeth is why she isn't already famous—she can do it all."[34] But despite this outstanding concert, all the enthusiasm and excitement couldn't make up for the feeble attendance number of 500.

As before, the Saturday workshops were entertaining and insightful for listeners, yet informative for musicians. Held at the new showplace hotel, Vista International, the workshops preceded the Genesis Jam hosted by former Calico bass player Joan Griffith. Amy Duncan and friends led the Super Jam at 6:00 and were followed by guitarist/leader Steve Cardenas, drummer Scott Robinson, bassist Forest Stewart, and pianist Paul Smith, who took over at 9:00. Because the jams were still free to the public, they received the largest attendance and created the most problems. As in years before, there were complaints that the wait to play was too long and individual jammers played too many choruses. On paper, the Vista ballrooms, all named for Kansas City jazz legends, promised to be ideal jam locations. The idea was that the Genesis Jam, set up in the Andy Kirk ballroom, would host novices as in years past. Following them in the Count Basie ballroom, a Super Jam would go on until one in the morning. The two ballrooms were close to each other with a common spillover space. It was in this spot that planning and reality differed. The swelling crowds of musicians, all anticipating a chance to jam—the Super Jam combined multiple former jams into one—congregated in the same area, creating a super bottleneck. Even during the Genesis Jam, beginners tended to be pushed out by more experienced players who happened to get there early. Cathy Lee, there as a pianist as well as a journalist remarked, "The experienced jam leaders were only too happy to perform for the crowd, but we beginners cowered, too intimidated to get up and make mistakes."[35] In spite of problems, over one hundred musicians, some from as far away as Wisconsin, Atlanta, New Mexico, and Boston, sat in, and more than 1,200 fans crowded into the ballroom.

Sunday afternoon's unusual offering brought a new dimension to jazz performance. Feminist sign artist Susan Freundlich, a staff interpreter and sign language coach for the Tony Award-winning Broadway play *Children of a Lesser God*, presented Sign Jazz/Sign Dance. Using recorded music for the first half of the concert, Susan reached out to both the hearing impaired and the general public to form a type of visual music. Framed against a black cloth backdrop, she used her hands and fingers, as well as kinetic dance moves, to create "a kind of lip-sync, which combines American Sign Language, mime, and dance to interpret folk, rock, and children's songs as well as express some controversial themes."[36] Those themes included a protest song against the killing of South African anti-apartheid activist Steven Biko and a mimed poem concerning "Jewish opposition to the slaughter of Arab people in Israel." Some irate audience members objected to material that they felt was anti-American and asked for their money back—all two dollars of it. In the second half of the program, Susan worked with a jazz quintet led by violinist and vocalist Betty MacDonald, who had also helped at the Genesis Jam. Pianist Amy Duncan, drummer Andrea Carol, and bassist Jennifer Condos joined her. Over two hundred people attended this ground-breaking performance in the Vista International's Count Basie Ballroom. After overlooking the oddness of the performance, they concluded it was indeed possible to sign jazz.

Moving back into the realm of traditional jazz, the Main Concert—with ticket prices the same as TNT, $6.50 to $15.00—began with the Judy Robert's Trio. As she had in 1981, Judy charmed the audience—of only 800—with her polished blend of styles. Her set included a little bit of everything with humorous bits sprinkled between tunes. Bassist Jim Cox and drummer David Derge rounded out the trio. With technical brilliance, they played tunes by Leon and Mary Russell and Horace Silver. Judy scatted her way through Fats Waller's "Honeysuckle Rose" and Annie Ross's "Twisted." To the satisfaction of hometown listeners and discerning out-of-towners, the trio included tunes by Kansas City favorite Russ Long. But it was Judy's humor that set up a rapport with the audience and anchored the set.

Evoking the Andrew Sisters, the Hi-Lows, or the Pied Pipers, the next group, Rare Silk, gave the audience a carefully choreographed floor show, as well as a complex, if somewhat anachronistic, display of harmonies. This group from Boulder, Colorado, consisted of vocalists Gaile Gillaspie, Marylynn Gillaspie, Barbara Reeves, and Todd Buffa, along with keyboardist Eric Gunnison, bassist Kip Kuepper, and drummer Michael Berry. They kept the genre fresh with tunes like "Spain," "Red Clay," "You Know It's Wrong," and an original, "American Eyes." The set began in a fever and crescendoed to a frenzy. Together since 1978, this group performed at the 1980 Playboy Jazz Festival with Benny Goodman and at the Wichita Jazz Festival in 1984, in addition to winning two Grammy awards for their 1983 album, *New Weave*. Rare Silk "stormed the stage like a Las Vegas dust devil."[37]

In a much more subdued mood (partly due to the fact that she had broken her left thumb that afternoon), Toshiko Akiyoshi took the stage for the last act. Leaving her big band at home, Toshiko took the opportunity to show what she could do in a trio setting. Accompanied by Jay Anderson on bass and Jeff Hirshfield on drums, the trio provided a pleasing change of pace. Robert C. Trussell remarked that Toshiko "provided an impressive performance that emphasized her physical strength, agility and versatility."[38] Choosing to play her original tunes, the highlight of the set was her tribute to her earlier mentor, Bud Powell. Despite her injury, Toshiko never backed away from her improvisational power or left the ensemble unbalanced.

The musical symmetry of Toshiko Akiyoshi closing out the 1985 WJF, as she had for the first WJF in 1978, would not become apparent for a few months, but as her final chord faded into the Folly Theater rafters, so did the music of the Kansas City Women's Jazz Festival.

Let's Call the Whole Thing Off

"Women Vote to End Popular Jazz Festival," the headline simply stated. "This takes an awful lot of our personal time and effort that we felt we just couldn't donate,"[39]acting WJF president Mary Hodges told Tim O'Connor of the *Kansas City Times* on December 16, 1985. After the 1985 festival, Julie Hanson had resigned, confident that she left WJF solvent, but also aware that she had nothing left to give.

Although the vote was, according to Mary Hodges, unanimous, board member Jeff Charney, who also served as vice chairman of the Kansas City Jazz Commission, told Robert C. Trussell in a *Kansas City Star* article later that day, "I argued for it because I don't like to see this quit. I just don't want to see the Women's Jazz Festival die."[40] He went on to say that he didn't see why WJF couldn't go on in another, less-grand form, but that he realized "the people on the board want to quit. They're tired."[41]

Not being veteran musicians, or people who had the connections, understood the artist's needs, and frequently had their days free, and thus the job flexibility needed to attend to the cascade of responsibilities, most board members, as volunteers, felt they were drowning in details. By 1985 there was only one musician left on the board. Other board members had jobs at Western Union, Southwestern Bell Telephone, insurance companies, and advertising firms. They were financial planners and medical librarians and social workers. No one had time to personally visit each corporate donor. No one had the expertise, or the willingness to learn the skills, to deal with grants, agents, the precarious schedules of artists, sound and lighting companies, piano providers and tuners, hotel managers, scholarship and combo auditions, performer selections, and venue negotiations.

In a press release dated January 5, entitled "Women's Jazz Festival for 1986 Is Cancelled," that fact is addressed. "Due to the growth of the organization, there was need for a paid staff person to coordinate and augment volunteer efforts, and funds for such a position were not available."[42] But on the flip side, with a newly hired paid administrator, without shared WJF experiences, the organization would have lost its heart. For all but the last eighteen months of WJF history, Carol Comer and Dianne Gregg, partly because of their flexible schedules, had acted in all capacities. Their devotion and full-time commitment to the health of their festival baby had made it all possible. Their love for what they were doing and the love they inspired in others created the forward momentum. In their absence, the energy needed to maintain what they had started could not be regained.

The press release reflected the board's conclusion that the original goal had been achieved and that they were justified in aborting further efforts to produce more festivals. "The organization's mission—to create a market and performance platform of national stature for female jazz performers, and to promote jazz in general—has been accomplished through seven festivals. The decision was made by the board with the recognition that the organization is financially solvent, has been successful, and is leaving a legacy of performance milestones."[43]

That the legacy was secure was undisputable. Both female and male musicians had benefitted in ways not dreamed of a decade earlier, and attitudes toward women's aptitudes for and performance of jazz had changed as a result of exposure to excellent veteran players, up-and-comers, and students. The need for recognition and equality still existed in the jazz world, but WJF, as the first of its kind, had sounded the call and led the charge into a new time.

In a letter to Julie Hansen dated January 27, 1986, Mary Hodges tells Julie she had just returned from the NAJE Convention and that the year's topics had been Women in Jazz and Jazz and the Media. "I came away with the impression that for seven festivals, for seven years, we really meant something to women in music. We did something right and we did it consistently."[44]

To further the cause, the WJF board voted to donate any remaining funds to the UMKC Conservatory of Music. Scholarships for female instrumental and vocal students who wanted to study jazz would be awarded each school year until the money ran out. After all WJF debts were paid, the scholarships added up to $4,000.

Leonard Feather, the only former WJF participant interviewed for Trussell's December 16 article, commented that he was disappointed but not surprised. "They never had the financial support that they needed so it was really difficult to find the really big attractions."[45] Although WJF had brought exceptionally talented female performers, the famous and the not-so-famous, to Kansas City, the queens—Ella Fitzgerald and Sarah Vaughan—had eluded them. Even in this last year, negotiations with Rosemary Clooney had seemed very hopeful until they came to the final financial arrangements. The WJF board had decided that was a fight they could never win. The baby had stopped running.

Epilogue

MARCH IS STILL WOMEN IN JAZZ MONTH IN KANSAS CITY. The American Jazz Museum—the only museum of its kind in the world—designates March, in sync with Women's History Month, as a time to focus on female jazz musicians. In 2015 a series of concerts and special events held at the Gem Theater and The Blue Room jazz club, both under the direction of the Museum, in Kansas City's historic 18th and Vine district,[1] began with a screening of Judy Chaikin's film, *Girls in the Band.* This 2011 documentary traces the history of female participation in jazz from early exploitations as ludicrous as saxophone-playing-while-roller-skating Siamese twins to composer and bandleader Maria Schneider's exasperation over persistent gender issues. When asked by a journalist, "What's it like to be a female composer," Maria responds, "What's it like to be a male journalist?"[2]

The Gem audience of approximately seventy-five mostly middle-aged women and college students groaned appropriately at the stories and photos of limb-swallowing, cotton candy-inspired, pink gowns that served as band uniforms. They nodded with recognition when the women on the screen explained why they picked the instruments they did: Viola Smith played drums by default, because her seven sisters had picked everything else; Clora Bryant picked trumpet after her father put her on his shoulders to see a dance band; Helen Woods, of the International Sweethearts of Rhythm, liked the way the trombone slide went up and down; and Jessie Bailey, of the Ina Ray Hutton band, was first drawn to the trombone because she liked Tommy Dorsey and she wanted to join her high school's marching band so she could get into the football games for free.[3]

A segment on the International Sweethearts of Rhythm is central to the film. With WJF's *Jazz Alive* audio recordings of the 1980 reunion for voiceovers, newspaper headlines and publicity stills tell their story. Interviews with surviving members point out how the music changed their lives and how the fight against prejudice drew them closer. When saxophonist Roz Cron tells stories about the dangers they faced as a racially mixed (not to mention all-girl) band, a rumble of emotional response could be heard from the audience.[4]

Girls in the Band recognizes Carol Comer and Dianne Gregg as women's jazz festival pioneers. Their dedication and commitment to creating opportunities for women in jazz is portrayed as the opening chord of a continuing opus. Photos of the first year's performers play across the screen as Carol and Dianne talk about how WJF came about. Marian McPartland is heard explaining how important their vision became to the future of all jazz. Various artists tell of the joy they experienced jamming with other women at WJF and how the solidarity of that opportunity gave them confidence.[5]

Present at the screening, Carol and Dianne whispered to each other and pointed at the screen as the images of old friends flashed before them. This was not the first time the pair had seen the film, but it was the first time they had seen it with an audience, and the response of others touched them.

Neither woman has rested on her WJF experience. Carol continues to perform around Kansas City as both a singer and piano player. Generally thought of as a musician's musician, her reputation has never wavered. Countless young women and men have discovered the joy of playing jazz through Carol's clinics, workshops, residencies, and school performances. Carol's commitment to jazz education, paired with WJF, leaves a lasting legacy.[6]

As Senior Arts Partners Coordinator at Young Audiences in Kansas City, Dianne has tirelessly promoted arts education of all kinds, but jazz education still has a hold of her heart. Dianne has worked at Young Audiences for most of the time since WJF. Her behind-the-scenes expertise has proven to be an invaluable asset and has assured the success of this arts provider. New York's Cobi Narita has nothing over Dianne. She organizes camps for school-aged children that range in topic from musical theater to visual arts to garage band to improv. She sets up voice lessons, guitar lessons, and ballet lessons. She oversees in-school performances, classroom workshops, and school assemblies. But of everything on her agenda over the years, her favorite endeavor was setting up a jazz quintet to tour schools. Dianne's tireless commitment to arts education—in an era when it is all too often overlooked—has left the community richer.[7]

Girls in the Band concludes with a female reconstruction of the famous 1958 *A Great Day in Harlem* photo. In the original, the only women pictured are singer Maxine Sullivan on one side and Marian McPartland and Mary Lou Williams standing together, chatting like old friends, on the other side. In the 2011 version only three men—Billy Taylor, Bob Cranshaw, and Stanley Kay—join the tiers of women.

A shot of Marian McPartland in a wheelchair, fondly gazing over the assembly, shows how happy she is to be a part of this picture day. Pride plays around the corners of her smile. She nurtured and promoted so many of the younger players, and their success is evidenced by their attendance at the photo shoot. Marian created the day and its photo as much as anyone, and the genesis of that was in no small part created by the Kansas City Women's Jazz Festival.[8]

Following the screening, the conversation continued with a panel discussion led by local vocalist Millie Edwards as moderator,

New York drummer and co-founder of the all-girl band DIVA, Sherrie Maricle, and director of the Friends University Big Band and a Kenton band alumnus, Lisa Hittle. Lisa's excellent college band, which played as a warm-up act before the film, brought the issues addressed in *Girls in the Band* to the present. The band swung genderlessly. Not only did they display total command of the music, they clearly enjoyed playing with each other and had a tightness that can only come from shared experiences, musical and otherwise. A former baritone saxophone player for Stan Kenton, Lisa has directed Jazz Studies at this small, formerly Quaker school in Wichita, Kansas, for twenty-six years. Under her direction, the band has gone to Europe twice, attended jazz festivals throughout the country, and had the honor of being the only U.S. college band invited to attend the Havana Jazz Festival in Cuba.

Lisa's obvious rapport with her students and their attention to her direction made it clear they consider the gender of their instructor immaterial. She makes the experience of playing in a mixed-gender (and mixed-ethnicity) ensemble all about the music. Her solo trombone player said it succinctly. "It's about the sound, not who's producing that sound."[9] This echoed Carline Ray's comment in the film. "You put a bunch of musicians behind a curtain and who's going to tell me who's the male. You can't do that. The music is the thing."[10]

Although a greater percentage of bandleaders and audience members are now more enlightened than in 1978, and there has been undeniable movement toward equality in jazz, that the panel's conversation was not considered anachronistic suggests that the playing field is still not level. Sherrie Maricle, a successful New York drummer with over twenty years of big band leadership to her credit, had a portmanteau of stories, many of them disheartening. She told of a female lead trumpet player friend of hers who was asked by an impertinent young man during a panel discussion to name the kind of lipstick she used. (Her friend responded, "The kind that allows me to play double high C.") Sherrie also told of a recent phone call from a prominent New York booker asking her to recommend women who played "boy instruments."[11] That these stories were peppered among happier ones of gender-blindness made them no less depressing. After almost a century of women playing jazz and nearly forty years since the first Women's Jazz Festival, the subject should be moot.

For Lisa Hittle it is. "I can honestly say that I've never felt discriminated against because I'm a woman, either as a player or as a jazz educator. I know it happens. I sympathize with women who have gone through that, but it hasn't happened to me."[12] Lisa felt none of the pressure from the press that Mary Fettig experienced playing with the Kenton band. "Mary Fettig was the first woman to play with Stan Kenton and I know the press was relentless about making a big deal of it. I was the only other female instrumentalist to play with Stan, but by the time I came along, having a female bari sax player wasn't considered newsworthy."[13]

Lisa frequently talks to women jazz musicians at collegiate jazz festivals and jazz educator conventions. She has an artist-in-residence program at her school that allows musicians to work with her students for a week. Many of these artists are women. "I know I'm not the only one who sees more equality in jazz. A large percentage of these women feel momentum is in our favor, and they are comfortable in their careers without worrying about men keeping them from doing anything they want musically."[14]

It isn't always the musical community that debates the gender issue in jazz. An academic psychological study presented as a paper at a recent jazz educator convention in Dallas left Lisa fuming. "The lecture was on why there aren't more girls in high school and college jazz bands. I was curious about the answer to that question that a non-musician would come up with. The upshot of the argument was that teachers fail to recognize that girls learn differently, and they aren't catering to the girls, that teachers need to treat girls differently because they are fragile. That goes totally against everything I've stood for as a teacher. It seemed like a giant step in backwards thinking."[15]

Yet, there is clear evidence of progress. For any proponent of female equality in jazz, Wayne Shorter's eightieth birthday gig in 2014 felt like a resolved chord. Sidewomen, rather than sidemen, consisted of Geri Allen on piano, Esperanza Spalding on bass, and Terri Lynn Carrington on drums.[16] This gig may have only been an accent in the otherwise slow but consistent tempo of acceptance, but for anyone who has fought for women in jazz—Carol and Dianne included—it symbolized victory.

While many individual woman performers are leading successful, respected careers in jazz and have assimilated into the still male-dominated art form, the issue of jazz festivals devoted to women still carries a defensive element that can turn contentious. Carol and Dianne have said from the beginning that their dearest hope was that women's jazz festivals would become obsolete because women would be heard as equals. Others would rather play with women and leave the possibility of male dominance out altogether. The evidence shows that all-woman musical events are as popular as ever. Whether these festivals are still popular because women like playing together or because they feel unwelcome elsewhere is debatable. The question has as many answers as there are individual musicians.

Palm Springs and Seattle have had recent Women's Jazz Festivals. In Washington D.C., the Washington Women in Jazz Festival "creates equitable performance opportunities for women while uplifting the image of the jazz community and drawing in dynamic new audiences."[17] Created in 2011 by Amy K. Bormet, the annual event is held in March, like the Kansas City Jazz Museum's, to coincide with Women's History Month. Carline Ray's daughter, singer Catherine Russell, along with

Lakecia Benjamin, have organized a Women's Jazz Festival at the Schomburg Center for Research in Black Culture in New York City.[18] Cobi Narita, still dedicated to jazz at ninety, hosts regularly scheduled New York City jam sessions, although these are not officially festivals. All-Stars of the 1982 festival, Jean Fineberg and Ellen Seeling, who as members of Deuce played at WJF in 1985, run a Women's Jazz and Blues Camp each March. They are joined by other members of their Montclair Women's Big Band under the auspices of the Jazzschool Community Music School in Berkeley, California.[19] The Lady Got Chops festival, now in its eleventh year in New York City, was the brainchild of bassist Kim Clarke. A former member of Kit McClure's band, Kim was inspired to spotlight instrumentalists. "In particular, we wanted to address the anonymity issue, as it refers to women (primarily instrumentalists) in music, as well as provide a platform for those who have never met to enjoy an evening of performing together outside of their comfort zones."[20] All of these events aim not only to increase awareness but to expose audiences to the rich and varied offerings women continue to bring to the art form of jazz. They are also unapologetic about the exclusion of men.

The grandmother of all post-WJF festivals, the Mary Lou Williams Jazz Festival, held at the Kennedy Center in Washington, D.C., is currently celebrating its twentieth year. Founded by jazz pianist and educator Billy Taylor to honor Mary Lou's legacy as not only player, but composer, bandleader, and educator, the festival has given scores of woman jazz performers opportunities not offered anywhere else. Many in the women's jazz musician community have seen this festival as a jazz world oasis. Now under the leadership of Jason Moran, the festival is blanketed in controversy because of the addition of male performers. A spokesman states, "The emphasis on women was too limiting and might at this cultural moment have the unintended negative effect of raising the question of it performers: is she a great musician, or a great female musician?"[21] Although the 2015 lineup included a variety of women instrumentalists and singers, the inclusion of male performers offends women jazz festivals purists. Others see the change as a victory for genderless jazz. The Kennedy Center's Director of Jazz, Kevin Struthers, says, "We're not going to diminish the opportunities for women to perform here. I hope the impact will be a fulfillment of Billy's vision that we don't need to designate these wonderful women by gender. Talent is talent is talent."[22]

Many of the women who performed at WJF have spent the past thirty-plus years sharing those talents with audiences and students alike. Joanne Brackeen is now a Berklee professor. Mary Fettig teaches at the San Francisco Conservatory of Music and gives clinics throughout the western states. Ellen Rowe is professor and chair of the Jazz and Contemporary Improvisation Department at the University of Michigan. Carol Kaye has authored a collection of bass instruction books. Carla Bley still tours with Steve Swallow, and although their brand of jazz is more sophisticated than in the past, it still gives convention the raspberry. Dianne Reeves, winner of the 2015 Grammy for Best Jazz Vocal Album, tours extensively throughout the world. Sheila Jordan and Dottie Dodgion, now both in their late eighties, are still actively involved performers.

All have experienced slights and hostility during their long careers, but have silenced critics with their music. Their examples serve as lessons.

After an hour of questions and comments for the panel, the evening came to an end. All the panelists had agreed that education and exposure are key and that they keep the struggle moving forward. As people rose to leave, a gaggle of fans gathered around Carol and Dianne, underlining the point made earlier in the evening that they were still considered Grand Dames of the cause. WJF had sounded the call, and Carol and Dianne had given the downbeat.

As they turned to go, Lisa Hittle, surrounded by her own fans, slowly made her way from the stage and called out to Carol and Dianne. "I just wanted you to know, I've always wanted to tell you how much your festival meant to me,"[23] she said as she got their attention. "In '82 I went to the festival by myself, and it changed my life. I didn't know anyone, didn't have a place to stay or much money, but I met so many wonderful people that weekend. I wasn't going to stay for the Main Concert, but I did, and it became one of those concert experiences that stays with you."[24] Lisa went on to say that, although she had already played with Stan Kenton's band by then, she didn't know who that year's headliner, Nancy Wilson, was. "I was star struck. I couldn't tell you who her sidemen were. It was all Nancy as far as I was concerned: her appearance, the way she delivered a lyric, her stage presence, the whole package."[25] The fact that Lisa ended up at the after party with people she had met that weekend made it possible for her to have a closer look at the star. "I was standing by some double doors, and in came Nancy, drop-dead gorgeous in a mink stole, with a guy on either side of her. There I was in my jeans and T-shirt. It was such an astounding experience. I almost dropped my beer."[26]

Waiting for their teacher, the Friends University students gathering at the back of the hall enthusiastically chatted about the stories they had heard and about how lucky they were to be sharing this music. How many of them would cause that ripple of acceptance to widen? That these students, mirroring others throughout the country, don't think in terms of girl instruments and boy instruments goes a long ways toward solving the problem. In their time in the history of jazz, they hear the sound first, then see the face. That's how they were taught.

Walking out with Carol and Dianne, Lisa continued talking about her WJF experience. "You know, what I remember the most was how supportive everyone was at the jams and clinics. Everyone just wanted to play, and that created a real joyous atmosphere. Ann Patterson and I had a conversation about saxophone neck strap placement. She was so gracious and helpful. It was all positive, it really changed things, and that's stayed with me. I've always wanted to thank you, so it's about time."[27]

Notes

Chapter One: Crazy Little Women

1. Dianne Gregg and Carol Comer interviews with the author, March 3, 2011 and July 30, 2012.
2. Ibid.
3. Ibid.
4. Tommy Ruskin interview with author, June 25, 2013.
5. Paul Smith interview with author, June 26, 2013.
6. Julie Turner Ruskin interview with author, June 25, 2013.
7. Shifra Stein, "KC Jazz: Is It All Past Glory?" *Kansas City Star*, March 4, 1979, 1-G.
8. Rod Fleeman interview with author, July 5, 2013.
9. Ibid.
10. Sally Placksin, *American Women in Jazz* (USA: Wideview Books, 1982), 274.
11. Greg Whitfield interview with author, June 11, 2013.
12. Helen Marquette interview with author September 21, 2013.
13. Brooks Wright interview with author, June 26, 2013.
14. Greg Whitfield interview with author, June 11, 2013.
15. Dianne Gregg interview with author, March 3, 2011.
16. Leonard Feather, "Girls in Jazz: East Saw West; Twain Met," *Down Beat*, July 13, 1951, 13.
17. Dianne Gregg and Carol Comer interview with author, March 3, 2011, July 30, 2012.
18. Paul De Barros, *Shall We Play That One Together? The Life and Art of Jazz Piano Legend Marian McPartland* (New York: St. Martin's Press, 2012), 283.
19. "Down Beat in Review," *Down Beat*, July 15, 1976, quote from letter dated February 1938, 15.
20. *Down Beat*, quote from letter dated April 1938, 15.
21. Interview with Roz Cron, *The Girls in the Band*, directed by Judy Chaikin, DVD, 2012.
22. Ibid.
23. "Down Beat in Review," *Down Beat*, July 15, 1976, quote from letter dated April 1938, 15.
24. "Mrs. Cugat Can't See Gals as Tooters: Kills Glamour," *Down Beat*, May 4, 1951, 13.

25. Mike Metheny interview with author, June 27, 2013.
26. Dianne Gregg interview with author, July 30, 2012.
27. Carol Comer interview with author, July 30, 2012.
28. Paul Smith interview with author, July 1, 2013.

Chapter Two: The First Year, March 18–19, 1978.

1. Carol Comer interview with author, July 30, 2013.
2. Dianne Gregg interview with author, July 30, 2013.
3. Carol Comer interview with author, March 3, 2012.
4. Dianne Gregg interview with author, July 30, 2013.
5. Carol Comer interview with author, March 3, 2013.
6. WJF board meeting minutes, June 12, 1977, Mike Ning collection.
7. Dianne Gregg interview with author, July 30, 2012.
8. WJF board meeting minutes June 12, 1977, Mike Ning collection.
9. "The Parks Will Resound," *Kansas City Times*, June 17, 1973, E-1.
10. Mike Ning interview with author, July 26, 2012.
11. Ibid.
12. Dianne Gregg interview with author, July 30, 2013.
13. WJF board meeting minutes, July 10, 1977, Mike Ning collection.
14. Dianne Gregg interview with author, July 30, 2013.
15. WJF board meeting minutes, July 10, 1977, Mike Ning collection.
16. Carol Comer interview with author, July 30, 2012.
17. Dianne Gregg interview with author, July 30, 2013.
18. Carol Comer interview with author, July 30, 2012.
19. WJF board meeting minutes, July 10, 1977, Mike Ning collection.
20. Steve Paul, "Women's Jazz Festival a Major Event," *Kansas City Star*, July 17, 1977, 1-E.
21. Carol Comer interview with author, March 3, 2012.
22. Mike Ning interview with author, July 26, 2012.
23. Shifra Stein, "Musicians Pick Up Basketballs for Good Cause," *Kansas City Star*, November 17, 1977, 17.
24. Dale Weddle, my cousin, and I had many discussions about the differences between classical and jazz musicians, and their physical approach to playing. He died in 1991.
25. Jeanne A.Fox, "Musicians Finish on Low Note in Benefit Basketball Game," *Kansas City Times*, November 21, 1977, E-1.
26. Dianne Gregg interview with author, July 30, 2013.
27. Carol Comer interview with author, July 30, 2013.
28. WJF board meeting minutes, January 29, 1978, Mike Ning collection.
29. Carol Comer interview with author, April 22, 2010.
30. WJF board meeting minutes, October 17, 1977, Mike Ning collection.
31. Dianne Gregg interview with author, July 30, 2013.

32. Mike White interview with author, July 22, 2013.
33. Dianne Gregg interview with author, July 30, 2013.
34. Mike White interview with author, July 22, 2013.
35. Dianne Gregg interview with author, July 30, 2013.
36. Carol Comer interview with author, July 30, 2013.
37. Dianne Gregg interview with author, July 30, 2013.
38. 1978 WJF program booklet, 3.
39. WJF board meeting minutes, February 26, 1978, Mike Ning collection.
40. Dianne Gregg interview with author, July 30, 2012.
41. John Leisenring interview with author, August 25, 2014.
42. Jane Ira Bloom interview with author, September 5, 2012.
43. Leonard Feather, "Ladies Invitation," *Melody Maker*, April 15, 1978, 59.
44. Ibid.
45. Ibid.
46. Elizabeth York post on KC Women's Jazz Festival Memories Facebook page, August 23, 2013.
47. Shifra Stein, "First Festival for Women Jazz Artists a Big-Time Event," *Kansas City Star*, March 23, 1978, 8.
48. Linda Dahl, *Morning Glory* (Berkeley: University of California Press, 1999), 310.
49. 1978 WJF program booklet, 14.
50. WJF board meeting minutes March 7, 1978, Mike Ning collection.
51. Copy of information packet given to Father Karels, Mike Ning collection.
52. Leonard Feather, "Everything Up to Date in Kansas City," *Los Angeles Times*, March 21, 1978, 14.
53. Gerald Jordan, "A Spiritual Message," *Kansas City Star*, March 20, 1978, 7-C.
54. Leonard Feather, "Ladies Invitation," 59.
55. Chuck Berg, "Caught! International Premiere of Women's Jazz Festival," *Down Beat*, August 10, 1978.
56. Joe Waz, "Annual Women's Jazz Festival—Kansas City," *International Jazz Federation*, Warsaw, Poland, April 1978, 55.
57. Feather, "Everything Up to Date in Kansas City," 15.
58. Shifra Stein, "Festival Proves Jazz Prowess of Women," *Kansas City Times*, March 17, 1978, 8C.
59. Cache International T.V., Betty Carter, You Tube.
60. Feather, "Everything Up to Date in Kansas City," 14.
61. Feather, "Ladies Invitation," 59.
62. John S. Wilson, "Concert Ends Women's Jazz Festival," *New York Times*, March 21, 1978.
63. Feather, "Ladies Invitation," 59.
64. Ibid.
65. Although Mary was married to saxophonist Kim Park at the time of the festival, the marriage was short-lived. Mary will be referred to as Mary Fettig hereafter.

66. Mary Fettig interview with author, November 25, 2012.
67. Dottie Dodgion interview with author, August 19, 2013.
68. Feather, "Everything Up to Date in Kansas City," March 21, 1978.
69. Chuck Berg, "Caught! International Premiere of Women's Jazz Festival," *Down Beat*, August 10, 1978.
70. Joe Waz, "Annual Women's Jazz Festival—Kansas City," *International Jazz Federation*, Warsaw, Poland, April 1978, 55.
71. Leonard Feather, "Everything Up to Date in Kansas City," 14.
72. Jim Carlton, "Mary Osborne: Charlie's Angel," *Vintage Guitar Magazine*, December 5, 2012, 1.
73. Linda Dahl, *Stormy Weather: The Music and Lives of a Century of Jazzwomen* (New York: Limelight Editions, 1984), 219.
74. Ibid.
75. Dottie Dodgion interview with author, August 19, 2013.
76. Ibid.
77. Ibid.
78. Linda Dahl, *Stormy Weather*, 219.
79. Paul De Barros, *Shall We Play That One Together?*, 209.
80. Dottie Dodgion interview with author, August 19, 2013.
81. Ibid.
82. Carol Sloane, "A Drum Is a Woman: The Swinging Dottie Dodgion," *Down Beat*, March 20, 1969, 17.
83. Mary Fettig interview with author, November 25, 2012.
84. Janice Robinson interview with author, September 2, 2015.
85. Mary Fettig interview with author, August 31, 2015.
86. Mary Fettig interview with author, November 17, 2012.
87. Mary Fettig interview with author, August 31, 2015.
88. Mary Fettig interview with author, November 25, 2012.
89. Mary Fettig interview with author, August 31, 2015.
90. Sally Placksin, *American Women in Jazz*, 287.
91. Janice Robinson interview with author, September 2, 2015.
92. Ibid.
93. Sally Placksin, *American Women in Jazz*, 287.
94. Mary Fettig interview with author, November 25, 2012. There were two other firsts while Mary was in the band. The other alto player, John Park's stepson, Kim, played tenor, making them the first father and son members of the Kenton band. Mary and Kim were also the first Kenton band married couple.
95. Mary Fettig interview with author, August 31, 2015.
96. Mary Fettig on *What's My Line*, August 23, 1973; Janice Robinson and Marian McPartland on *What's My Line*, 1973; Dottie Dodgion on *What's My Line*, April 16, 1961. Found at *www.tv.com/shows/what's-my-line*, retrieved March 13, 2015.

97. Janice Robinson interview with author, September 2, 2015.
98. Sally Placksin, *American Women in Jazz*, 288.
99. Ibid.
100. Mary Fettig interview with author, November 25, 2012.
101. Ibid.
102. Ibid.
103. Sally Placksin, *American Women in Jazz*, 292.
104. John C. Wilson, "Concert Ends Women's Jazz Festival," *New York Times*, March 21, 1978.
105. Ibid.
106. Steve Paul, "Music: The Bond That Counts," *Kansas City Star*, March 19, 1978, 12-B.
107. Leonard Feather, "Ladies Invitation," 67.
108. Shifra Stein, "Women's Festival a Labor of Love," *Kansas City Star*, March 20, 1978, 7-C.
109. Mary Fettig interview with author, November 17, 2012.
110. Leonard Feather, "Ladies Invitation," 67.
111. Mary Fettig interview with author, November 25, 2012.
112. Linda Dahl, *Morning Glory, A Biography of Mary Lou Williams* (Berkeley: University of California Press, 1999), 349.
113. Leonard Feather, "Ladies Invitation," 59.
114. Linda Dahl, *Morning Glory*, 71.
115. Sylvia Bell interview with author, July 26, 2013.
116. Leonard Feather, "Ladies Invitation," 59.
117. Linda Dahl, *Morning Glory*, 350.
118. Linda Dahl, *Morning Glory*, 181.
119. Linda Dahl, *Morning Glory*, 325.
120. Linda Dahl, *Morning Glory*, 279.
121. Ibid.
122. Marian McPartland, "Mary Lou Williams: Into the Sun," *Down Beat*, August 27, 1964, 16.
123. Ibid.
124. Paul De Barros, *Shall We Play That One Together?*, 297-298.
125. Linda Dahl, *Morning Glory*, 349.
126. Steve Paul, "Innovation, Energy Guide Jazz Performers," *Kansas City Star*, March 20, 1978, 7.
127. Leonard Feather, "Everything Up to Date in Kansas City," 14.
128. John C. Wilson, "Concerts Ends Women's Jazz Festival," *New York Times*, March 21, 1978.
129. Steve Paul, "Innovation, Energy Guide Jazz Performers,"*Kansas City Star*, March 20, 1978, 7.
130. Leonard Feather, "Toshiko Akiyoshi: The Leader of the Band," *Ms.*, November 1978, 35.

131. Peter Rothbart, "Toshiko Akiyoshi: Arranging on a Steady Ascent," *Down Beat*, August 1980, 14.
132. Dianne Gregg interview with author, July 30, 2012.
133. Leonard Feather, "Ladies Invitation," 67.
134. Ibid.
135. Chuck Berg, "Caught! International Premiere Women's Jazz Festival," *Down Beat*, August 10, 1978.
136. Steve Paul, "Innovation, Energy Guide Jazz Performers," *Kansas City Star*, March 20, 1978, 7.
137. Chuck Berg, "Caught! International Premiere Women's Jazz Festival."
138. Carol Comer interview with author, April 22, 2010.
139. Leonard Feather, "Everything Up to Date in Kansas City," 15.
140. Carol Comer interview with author, July 30, 2013.

Chapter Three: The Second Year, March 23–25, 1979

1. Lois Gordan and Alan Gordan, *American Chronicle* (New York: Atheneum, 1987), 588.
2. WJF board meeting minutes, May 7, 1978, Mike Ning collection.
3. Shifra Stein, "Drummer to Provide K.C. Beat to Jazz Olympics," *Kansas City Times*, June 1, 1979. 1-C.
4. Shifra Stein, "Jazz Greats Open Olympics," *Kansas City Times*, June 2, 1979, 8-C.
5. Shifra Stein, "Promoter of Jazz Olympics Paid for Missing the Beat," *Kansas City Times*, June 8, 1979, 1-C.
6. Ibid.
7. Ibid.
8. Ibid.
9. Dianne Gregg interview with author, April 22, 2010.
10. Ibid.
11. Sally Placksin, *American Women in Jazz*, 179.
12. Linda Dahl, *Stormy Weather*, 253.
13. *Melba Liston: Bones of an Arranger*, NPR Documentary, July 9, 2008, *http://www.npr.org/2008/07/09/92349036/melba-liston-bones-of-an-arranger* retrieved January 17, 2014.
14. Ibid.
15. Ibid.
16. Ibid.
17. Sally Placksin, *American Women in Jazz*, 181.
18. Ibid.
19. Melba Liston–Randy Weston, African Rhythms, *www.randyweston.info/randy-weston-sidemen-pages/melba-liston.html* retrieved January 9, 2014.

20. Susan Fleet Archives, *Women Who Dared: Melba Liston*, *http://archives.susanfleet.com/documents/melba_liston.html* retrieved January 9, 2014.
21. Linda Dahl, *Stormy Weather*, 256.
22. *Melba Liston: Bones of an Arranger*, NPR Documentary, July 9, 2008, *http://www.npr.org/2008/07/09/92349036/melba-liston-bones-of-an-arranger* retrieved January 17, 2014.
23. Linda Dahl, *Stormy Weather*, 258.
24. 1979 Women's Jazz Festival program booklet, 13-22.
25. Linda Dahl, *Stormy Weather*, 188.
26. Leslie Gourse, *Madame Jazz: Contemporary Women Instrumentalists* (New York: Oxford University Press, 1995), 60-61.
27. Ibid.
28. Constance Valis Hill, Cobi Narita website *http://www.cobinarita.com/aboutcobi.html* 2. retrieved June 8, 2014.
29. Cobi Narita, *The Jazz Catalyst: Universal Jazz Coalition Salutes Women in Jazz*, souvenir book, June 26-29, 1978, 1.
30. Ibid.
31. Leslie Gourse, *Madame Jazz*, 62-63.
32. Janice Robinson interview with author, August 25, 2014.
33. Constance Valis Hill, *Cobi Narita website http://www.cobinarita.com/aboutcobi.html* 2, retrieved June 8, 2014.
34. Leslie Gourse, *Madame Jazz*, 62.
35. Leonard Feather, "Second Annual Women's Jazz Festival," *Down Beat*, June 7, 1979, 36.
36. Shifra Stein, "Aerial Sounds Fly to Tempo of Its Choice," *Kansas City Star*, March 22, 1979, 8.
37. In 1950, at the age of twenty-four, Irv Kratka started the Music Minus One music production and recording company.
38. Undated letter from Nina Sheldon to Carol Comer, Carol Comer collection.
39. Shifra Stein, "Aerial Sounds Fly to Tempo of Its Choice," 8.
40. 1979 Women's Jazz Festival program booklet, 18.
41. Leonard Feather, "Second Annual Women's Jazz Festival," 36.
42. Linda Dahl, *Stormy Weather*, 172.
43. Audio recording of concert, loaned to the author by Carol Comer and Dianne Gregg, April 22, 2010.
44. Shifra Stein, "Aerial Sounds Fly to Tempo of Its Choice," 8.
45. Nina Sheldon interview with author, February 9, 2013.
46. Ibid.
47. Undated letter from Nina Sheldon to Carol Comer, Carol Comer collection.
48. Shifra Stein, "Women Dispel Jazz Myth," *Kansas City Star*, March 26, 1979, 12.
49. Audio recording of 1979 concerts, loaned to author by Carol Comer and Dianne Gregg, April 22, 2010.

50. Shifra Stein, "Women Dispel Jazz Myth."
51. Linda Dahl, *Stormy Weather*, 183.
52. 1979 Women's Jazz Festival program booklet, 19.
53. Audio recording of 1979 concerts, loaned to author by Carol Comer and Dianne Gregg, April 22, 2010.
54. Carol Comer interview with author, March 3, 2012.
55. Ibid.
56. Audio recording of 1979 concerts, loaned to author by Carol Comer and Dianne Gregg, April 22, 2010.
57. Diane Lewis, "Jazzing It Up," *Wichita Eagle and Beacon*, April 1, 1979. 2C.
58. Leonard Feather, "Second Annual Women's Jazz Festival," 37.
59. Audio recording of 1979 concerts, loaned to author by Carol Comer and Dianne Gregg April 22, 2010.
60. Jane Ira Bloom interview with author, September 9, 2012.
61. WJF board meeting minutes, "Final Tally on Artist Ballot," April 1978, Mike Ning collection.
62. Jane Ira Bloom interview with author, September 9, 2012.
63. 1979 Women's Jazz Festival, program booklet, 20.
64. Ibid.
65. Jane Ira Bloom interview with author, September 9, 2012.
66. Ibid.
67. WJF board meeting minutes, "Final Tally on Artist Ballot," April 1978, Mike Ning collection.
68. 1979 Women's Jazz Festival program booklet, 20.
69. Ibid.
70. Leslie Gourse, *Madame Jazz*, 130.
71. Ibid.
72. Ibid.
73. Monnette Sudler interview with author, January 28, 2014.
74. WJF board meeting minutes, "Final Tally on Artist Ballot," April 1978.
75. Monnette Sudler interview with author, January 28, 2014.
76. Ibid.
77. 1979 Women's Jazz Festival program booklet, 21.
78. Monnette Sudler interview with author, January 28, 2014.
79. Linda Dahl, *Stormy Weather*, 176.
80. Shifra Stein, "Women Dispel Jazz Myth," *Kansas City Star*, March 26, 1979, 12.
81. Suzanne Cloud, "Monnette Sudler: Daring to Dream," All About Jazz website, *http://www.allaboutjazz.com/php/article.php?id=45585* October 8, 2013, retrieved January 23, 2014.
82. 1979 Women's Jazz Festival program booklet, 21.
83. Carol Kaye email to author, "Some Guitar Hits I Did," September 8, 2015.
84. Carol Kaye email to author, "Working For Quincy Jones," September 8, 2015.

85. Carol Kaye interview with author, February 4, 2014. Although Carol is listed as a member of the "wrecking crew" in multiple books and a recent movie by that name, she finds the term offensive and false. She is adamant about the fact that the number of jazz musicians who recorded pop hits in the 1960s were always and respectfully called "studio musicians" and hired independently, not as a band. Carol says at no time in over a decade of almost daily studio work did she hear any other studio musician say that the jazz musicians hired to play pop recordings were "going to wreck the business," as alleged elsewhere.
86. Ibid.
87. Carol Kaye email to author, "Some Movie Scores I've Recorded," September 8, 2015.
88. Carol Kaye email to author, September 8, 2015.
89. Leonard Feather, *Encyclopedia of Jazz in the Seventies* (New York: Horizon Press, 1976), 210.
90. Dianne Gregg interview with author, July 30, 2012.
91. WJF board meeting minutes, "Final Tally on Artist Ballot," April 1978, Mike Ning collection.
92. 1979 Women's Jazz Festival program booklet, 13, 21.
93. Dianne Gregg interview with author, July 30, 2012.
94. Carol Kaye interview with author, February 4, 2014.
95. Ibid.
96. Dianne Gregg interview with author, July 30, 2012.
97. Carol Kaye interview with author, February 4, 2014.
98. Dianne Gregg interview with author, July 30, 2012.
99. Audio recording of concert, loaned to author by Carol Comer and Dianne Gregg, April 22, 2010.
100. Leonard Feather, "Second Annual Women's Jazz Festival," 37.
101. Ibid.
102. Ibid.
103. Dianne Gregg interview with author, July 30, 2012.
104. Carol Kaye interview with author, February 4, 2014.
105. Shifra Stein, "Women Jazz It Up At Clinics," *Kansas City Star*, March 25, 1979, 2B.
106. Carol Comer interview with author, July 30, 2013.
107. Audio recording of 1979 concerts, loaned to author by Carol Comer and Dianne Gregg, April 22, 2010.
108. Leonard Feather, "Second Annual Women's Jazz Festival," 37.
109. Audio recording of 1979 concerts, loaned to author by Carol Comer and Dianne Gregg, April 22, 2010.
110. Nelson George, "Pianist for a New Era," *Down Beat*, July 1980, 22.
111. Nelson George, "Pianist for a New Era," 23.

112. Ibid.
113. Linda Dahl, *Stormy Weather*, 171.
114. Nelson George, "Pianist for a New Era," 23.
115. Leslie Gourse, *Madame Jazz*, 178.
116. Nelson George, "Pianist for a New Era," 23.

Chapter Four: The Third Year, March 20–23, 1980

1. WJF board meeting minutes, April 1, 1979, Mike Ning collection.
2. Robert P. Laurence, "Mixed Notes in Women's Jazz," *San Diego Union*, April 1, 1979, E-1.
3. WJF board meeting minutes, April 1, 1979, Mike Ning collection.
4. WJF board meeting minutes, May 6, 1979, Mike Ning collection.
5. WJF board meeting minutes, April 1, 1979, Mike Ning collection.
6. Carol Comer and Dianne Gregg interview with author, March 3, 2012.
7. WJF board meeting minutes, May 6, 1979, Mike Ning collection.
8. WJF board meeting minutes, July 15, 1979, Mike Ning collection.
9. Ibid.
10. Dianne Gregg interview with author, July 30, 2013.
11. Ibid.
12. Ibid.
13. D. Antoinette Handy, *The International Sweethearts of Rhythm: The Ladies Jazz Band from Piney Woods Country Life School* (Lanham, MD: The Scarecrow Press, 1998), 90.
14. Women and Jazz: International Sweethearts of Rhythm, YouTube, *www.youtube.com/watch/v=_Cjmg8Jepvw* Uploaded by Smithsonian, April 10, 2011, retrieved July 15, 2013.
15. Audio recording of 1980 WJF Tribute to the International Sweethearts of Rhythm, March 23, 1980, loaned to author by Carol Comer and Dianne Gregg, April 22, 2010.
16. D. Antoinette Handy, *The International Sweethearts of Rhythm*, 131.
17. "Girls' Band Flees Dixie after Tiff with School," *Afro American*, April 26, 1941, 13.
18. Audio recording of 1980 WJF Tribute to the International Sweethearts of Rhythm, March 23, 1980, loaned to author by Carol Comer and Dianne Gregg, April 22, 2010.
19. D. Antoinette Handy, *The International Sweethearts of Rhythm*, 21.
20. Women and Jazz: International Sweethearts of Rhythm, YouTube, *www.youtube.com/watch/v+_Cjmg8Jepvw* Uploaded by Smithsonian, April 10, 2011. retrieved July 15, 2013.
21. D. Antoinette Handy, *The International Sweethearts of Rhythm*, 158.
22. Women and Jazz: International Sweethearts of Rhythm, YouTube, *www.youtube.com/watch/v+_Cjmg8Jepvw* Uploaded by Smithsonian, April 10, 2011. retrieved July 15, 2013.

23. Audio recording of 1980 WJF Tribute to the International Sweethearts of Rhythm.
24. Women and Jazz: International Sweethearts of Rhythm, YouTube, *www.youtube.com/watch/v=_Cjmg8Jepvw* Uploaded by Smithsonian, April 10, 2011, retrieved July 15, 2013.
25. D. Antoinette Handy, *The International Sweethearts of Rhythm*, 161.
26. "Girls' Band Flees Dixie after Tiff with School," 13.
27. Ibid.
28. Audio recording of 1980 WJF Tribute to the International Sweethearts of Rhythm.
29. Ibid.
30. Ibid.
31. Ibid.
32. WJF board meeting minutes, February 10, 1980.
33. Ibid.
34. Ibid.
35. 1980 Women's Jazz Festival program booklet, 10.
36. Terry Teachout, "Women's TNT Jazz Show Is Dynamite," *Kansas City Star*, March 23, 1980, 4-B.
37. TAG Blog, "A Portrait of Five Women: Ruth Kissane," *http://animatorionguildblog.blogspot.com/2006/09/portrait-of-five-women* retrieved August 1, 2013.
38. Terry Teachout, "Women's TNT Jazz Show Is Dynamite," 4-B.
39. Ibid.
40. 1980 Women's Jazz Festival program booklet, 24.
41. Ibid.
42. Christine Minderovic, "Contemporary Black Biography," *Encyclopedia.com*, 2005, *www.encyclopedia.com/topic/Diane_Reeves.aspx* retrieved March 27, 2014.
43. Ibid.
44. Leonard Feather, "Women's Jazz Festival," *Down Beat*, July 1980, 57.
45. Ibid.
46. Paul Hohl, "Women Blow in Kansas City," *Billboard*, April 5, 1980, 69.
47. Terry Teachout, "Women's TNT Jazz Show Is Dynamite," 4-B.
48. Leonard Feather, "Women's Jazz Festival," 57.
49. Paul Smith interview with author, August 17, 2014.
50. Terry Teachout, "Women's TNT Jazz Show Is Dynamite," 4-B.
51. 1980 Women's Jazz Festival program booklet, 11.
52. Mary Watkins, liner notes to *Something Moving*, Olivia Records, Oakland, California, 1978.
53. Terry Teachout, "Women's TNT Jazz Show Is Dynamite," 4-B.
54. Leonard Feather, "Women's Jazz Festival," 57.
55. Paul Hohl, "Women Blow in Kansas City," 69.
56. Audio recording of TNT Concert, March 21, 1980, loaned to author by Carol Comer and Dianne Gregg, April 22, 2010.

57. James Liska, "Maiden Voyage," *Down Beat*, November 1981, 53.
58. Audio recording of TNT Concert, March 21, 1980, loaned to author by Carol Comer and Dianne Gregg, April 22, 2010.
59. Linda Dahl, *Stormy Weather*, 266.
60. James Liska, "Maiden Voyage," 53.
61. Ibid.
62. 1980 Women's Jazz Festival program booklet, 6.
63. Ibid.
64. Paul Hohl, "Women Blow in Kansas City," 69.
65. 1980 Women's Jazz Festival program booklet, 6.
66. 1980 Women's Jazz Festival program booklet, 7.
67. 1980 Women's Jazz Festival program booklet, 8.
68. Ibid.
69. 1980 Women's Jazz Festival program booklet, 13.
70. 1980 Women's Jazz Festival program booklet, 14.
71. Audio recording of Tribute to the International Sweethearts of Rhythm, March 23, 1980, loaned to author by Carol Comer and Dianne Gregg, April 22, 2010.
72. Ibid.
73. D. Antoinette Handy, *The International Sweethearts of Rhythm*, 7.
74. Audio recording of Tribute to the International Sweethearts of Rhythm.
75. Ibid.
76. Ibid.
77. Ibid.
78. Ibid.
79. Ibid.
80. Ibid.
81. Leonard Feather, "Women's Jazz Festival," 58.
82. Carol Comer interview with author, July 30, 2012.
83. Audio recording of Tribute to the International Sweethearts of Rhythm.
84. President Jimmy Carter letter to Women's Jazz Festival, March 6, 1980, Carol Comer and Dianne Gregg collection.
85. Paul Hohl, "Women Blow in Kansas City," 69.
86. WJF board meeting minutes, August 19, 1979, Mike Ning collection.
87. 1980 Women's Jazz Festival program booklet, 20.
88. Grant Jackson, *Piano Jazz: Stacy Rowles*, March 8, 2013, *www.npr.org/2010/03/05/.../stacy-rowles-remembered-on-piano-jazz*, retrieved April 20, 2014.
89. Keith Thursby, "Stacy Rowles Dies at 54: Jazz Trumpet and Flugelhorn Player," *Los Angeles Times*, November 8, 2009, *http://www.latimes.com/local/obituaries/la-me-stacy-rowles-2009n* retireved April 21, 2014.
90. Ben Ratliff, "Stacy Rowles, Jazz Musician, Is Dead at 54," *New York Times*, November 8, 2009, *http://www.nytimes.com/2009/11/07/arts/music/07rowles.htm* retrieved April 21, 2014.

91. Ibid.
92. Leslie, Gourse, *Madame Jazz* (New York: Oxford University Press, 1995), 110.
93. Chris Bosley, audio recording of *Jazz Alive* interview with Carla Bley, loaned to author by Carol Comer and Dianne Gregg, April 22, 2010.
94. Leonard Feather, "Women's Jazz Festival," 57.
95. Chris Bosley, audio recording of *Jazz Alive* interview with Carla Bley, loaned to author by Carol Comer and Dianne Gregg, April 22, 2010.
96. Leonard Feather, "Women's Jazz Festival," 57.
97. Chris Bosley, audio recording of *Jazz Alive* interview with Carla Bley, loaned to author by Carol Comer and Diane Gregg, April 22, 2010.
98. Ibid.
99. Maureen Paton, "Bley Time," *Melody Maker*, September 10, 1977, Linda Dahl, *Stormy Weather*, 206.
100. Linda Dahl, *Stormy Weather*, 206.
101. Linda Dahl, *Stormy Weather*, 207.
102. 1980 Women's Jazz Festival program booklet, 19.
103. Terry Teachout, "All That Jazz Simply Amazing," *Kansas City Star*, March 24, 1980, 15.
104. Audio recording on Main Concert 1980 Women's Jazz Festival, March 23, 1980, loaned to author by Carol Comer and Dianne Gregg, April 22, 2010.
105. Marian McPartland *Piano Jazz*, NPR, Carla Bley and Steve Swallow interview originally recorded August 15, 1995, originally broadcast February 24, 1996, *www.npr.org/2011/08/12/.../carla-bley-and-steve-swallow-on-piano-jazz* retrieved April 13, 2013.
106. Ibid.
107. Ibid.
108. Leonard Feather, "Women's Jazz Festival," 57.
109. Nina Sheldon interview with author, February 9, 2013.
110. Terry Teachout, "All That Jazz Simply Amazing," 15.
111. Nelson George, "Pianist for a New Era," *Down Beat*, July 1980, 59.
112. Ibid.
113. Ibid.
114. Ibid.
115. Ibid.
116. Nelson George, "Pianist for a New Era," 23.
117. Ibid.
118. 1980 Women's Jazz Festival program booklet, 22.
119. Ibid.
120. Audio recording of Main Concert 1980 Women's Jazz Festival, March 23, 1980, loaned to author by Carol Comer and Dianne Gregg, April 22, 2010.
121. Leonard Feather, "Women's Jazz Festival," 58.

Chapter Five: The Fourth Year, March 25–29, 1981

1. Dianne Gregg and Carol Comer interview with author, March 26, 2015.
2. Terry Teachout, "A More than Worthy Successor," *Kansas City Star*, March 30, 1981, 6B.
3. 1981 Women's Jazz Festival program booklet, 17.
4. Carol Comer interview with author, March 26, 2015.
5. *Florapurim.com/stories.htm*, *Stories to Tell*, retrieved October 10, 2014.
6. Ibid.
7. Diana later married Krishna Booker, who is bassist Walter Booker's son, Wayne Shorter's nephew, and Herbie Hancock's godson.
8. Edward Bunker, with Flora Purim, *Freedom Song* (New York: Berkley Books, 1982), 99.
9. Terry Teachout, "New Jazz Groups Get a Chance to Shine," *Kansas City Star*, March 29, 1981, 41A
10. Letty Cottin Pogrebin, "Reagan Accused of Being 'Anti-woman'," *Kansas City Times*, March 27, 1981, 3A.
11. Marian McPartland, *Women In Jazz*, DVD YouTube
12. Ibid.
13. Terry Teachout, "New Jazz Groups Get a Chance to Shine," 41A.
14. Amy Duncan, "ALIVE!—Five Women with a Special Brand of Music," *Christian Science Monitor*, November 9, 1981.
15. Ibid.
16. Ibid.
17. Jean Fineberg interview with author, December 8, 2012.
18. 1981 Women's Jazz Festival program booklet, 20.
19. 1981 Women's Jazz Festival program booklet, 21.
20. 1981 Women's Jazz Festival program booklet, 20.
21. Peter Blecha, "Ernestine Anderson, Jazz Singer," HistoryLink.org, History Link Essay 8520, March 7, 2008, 1, retrieved October 10, 2014.
22. Walter Royal Stokes, *The Jazz Scene: An Informal History From New Orleans to 1990* (New York: Oxford University Press, 1991), 159.
23. "Emotional Brass," *Time*, August 4, 1958, 34.
24. Richard S. Ginell, "Ernestine Anderson Artist Biography," *Allmusic.com*, 1, retrieved October 10, 2014.
25. "Emotional Brass," 34.
26. Peter Blecha, "Ernestine Anderson, Jazz Singer," HistoryLink.org, History Link Essay 8520, March 7, 2008, 4, retrieved October 10, 2014.
27. Peter Blecha, "Ernestine Anderson, Jazz Singer," 6, retrieved October 10, 2014.
28. Brian Lanker, *I Dreamed a World: Portraits of Black Women Who Changed America* (New York: Stewart Tabori & Chang, 1989), 48.

29. Andrew Gilbert, "Ernestine Anderson: A Strong Second Act," *Jazz Times*, May 2009, *jazztimes.com/articles/24596-ernestine-anderson-a-strong-second-act*, retrieved May 16, 2015.
30. Peter Blecha, "Ernestine Anderson, Jazz Singer," 4, retrieved October 10, 2014.
31. Marian McPartland, *Piano Jazz*, NPR, June 13, 1992.
32. Tom Wilson, *Hip Twist*, LP, Prestige 7226, 1961.
33. Marian McPartland, *Piano Jazz*, NPR, June 13, 1992.
34. Jazz Night in America, The Legacy of the Jazz Organ in Philadelphia, NPR, April 22, 2015.
35. *Wikipedia*, Hammond organ, *https://en.wikipedia.org/wiki/Hammond_organ*, retrieved June 2, 2015.
36. Linda Dahl, *Stormy Weather*, 77.
37. Ibid.
38. Harry Duncan, *Shirley Scott Memorial Album*, CD, Prestige Records, Berkeley, California, PRCD-11027-2, 2003.
39. Dianne Gregg interview with author, March 26, 2015.
40. Carol Comer interview with author, March 26, 2015.
41. Dianne Gregg interview with author, March 26, 2015.
42. Carol Comer interview with author, March 26, 2015.
43. Dianne Gregg and Carol Comer interview with author, March 26, 2015.
44. Carol Comer interview with author, March 26, 2015.
45. Dianne Gregg interview with author, March 26, 2015.
46. Terry Teachout, "A More than Worthy Successor," 6B.
47. Dianne Gregg interview with author, March 26, 2015.
48. Carol Comer interview with author, March 26, 2015.
49. Dianne Gregg interview with author, March 26, 2015.
50. Ibid.

Chapter Six: The Fifth Year, March 24–28, 1982

1. John S. Wilson, "Mary Lou Williams Obituary," *New York Times*, May 30, 1981.
2. Ibid.
3. Linda Dahl, *Stormy Weather*, 63.
4. Linda Dahl, *Morning Glory*, 44.
5. Whitney Balliett, "Profile: Out Here Again," *New Yorker*, May 2 1964, 52.
6. Marian McPartland, "Mary Lou Williams: Into the Sun," *Down Beat*, August 27, 1964, 16.
7. Marian McPartland, *Piano Jazz*, NPR, taped October 8, 1978, broadcast in 1979.
8. Paul De Barros, *Shall We Play That One Together?*, 309.
9. Ibid.

10. Marian McPartland, "Mary Lou Williams: Into the Sun," 16.
11. Janice Robinson interview with author, August 25, 2014.
12. Gil Evans Orchestra, *Jazz Jamboree 1976*, TVP Kultura, YouTube 7 minutes 48 seconds to 7 minutes 54 seconds.
13. Don Heckman, "Film: *The Girls in the Band*," *The International Review of Music*, November 15, 2013, *http://iron.wordpress.com/tag/annpatterson/*
14. 1982 Women's Jazz Festival program booklet, 15.
15. Ibid.
16. Rod Fleeman interview with author, October 13, 2014.
17. Joan Griffith interview with author, September 29, 2012.
18. Danny Embrey interview with author, October 6, 2014.
19. 1982 Women's Jazz Festival program booklet, 6.
20. 1982 Women's Jazz Festival program booklet, 12.
21. 1982 Women's Jazz Festival program booklet, 17.
22. Lynn Riley interview with author, November 9, 2012.
23. Helen Marquette interview with author, September 21, 2013.
24. Dianne Gregg interview with author, April 11, 2011.
25. Helen Marquette interview with author, September 21, 2013.
26. Carol Comer interview with author, April 11, 2011.
27. 1982 Women's Jazz Festival program booklet, 17.
28. Carol Comer interview with author, July 30, 2013.
29. Lynn Riley interview with author, November 9, 2012.
30. Leslie Gourse, *Madame Jazz*, 206.
31. Linda Dahl, *Stormy Weather*, 219.
32. Linda Dahl, *Morning Glory*, 47.
33. Dottie Dodgion interview with author, August 19, 2013.
34. Linda Dahl, *Stormy Weather*, 219.
35. Carol Sloane, "A Drum Is a Woman: The Swinging Dottie Dodgion," *Down Beat*, March 20, 1969, 17.
36. Dottie Dodgion interview with author, August 19, 2013.
37. Leslie Gourse, *Madame Jazz*, 25.
38. Leslie Gourse, *Madame Jazz*, 204.
39. Carol Kaye interview with author, February 2, 2014, February 4, 2014.
40. Linda Dahl, *Stormy Weather*, 204.
41. *Fresh Air: Barbara Carroll*, NPR, December 12, 2012.
42. Stephen Holden, *New York Times*, online obituary, February 8, 2009, *http://www.nytimes.com/2009/02/09/arts/music/09dear.html?_r=0* retrieved June 10, 2015.
43. Marian McPartland, *Piano Jazz, Blossom Dearie*, NPR, recorded in 1985, rebroadcast October 30, 2009.
44. Ibid.
45. Terry Teachout, "Perfection Personified," *Kansas City Star*, March 25, 1982, 3B.

46. Terry Gross, *Fresh Air*, NPR, recorded March 31, 1998, rebroadcast November 28, 2003.
47. Stephen Holden, online obituary.
48. Marian McPartland, *Piano Jazz, Blossom Dearie*, NPR, recorded in 1985, rebroadcast October 30, 2009.
49. Terry Gross, *Fresh Air*, NPR, recorded March 31, 1998, rebroadcast November 28, 2003.
50. Marian McPartland, *Piano Jazz, Blossom Dearie*, NPR, recorded in 1985, rebroadcast October 30, 2009.
51. Adrian Jack, *The Guardian: Blossom Dearie*, online obituary, February 8, 2009, *http://www.theguardian.com/music/2009/feb/09/obituary-blossom-dearie* retrieved June 11, 2015.
52. Ibid.
53. Ibid.
54. Kevin Whitehead, *Review of My Gentleman Friend*, NPR, November 28, 2003.
55. 1982 Women's Jazz Festival program booklet, 5, 11, 28.
56. 1982 Women's Jazz Festival program booklet, 18.
57. Terry Teachout, "The Beat Goes on for Women in Tune at Jazz Festival," *Kansas City Star*, March 23, 1982, 1B.
58. Dianne Gregg interview with author, April 11, 2011.
59. Joe Quinn, *The Joanne Grauer Trio*, liner notes, 1957.
60. Ibid.
61. 1982 Women's Jazz Festival program booklet, 20.
62. *World Renowned Pianist Joanne Grauer*, website reviews (Clint Eastwood) *www.neweb4u.com/grauer/inaex.html* retrieved May 8, 2015.
63. Leonard Feather, "Pianist Grauer's Intimate Style," *Los Angeles Times*, June 20, 1989, *articles.latimes.com>collections* retrieved May 8, 2015.
64. 1982 Women's Jazz Festival program booklet, 20.
65. Ibid.
66. Ibid.
67. Liner notes to Jim Cutler and Seattle Women's Jazz albums *The Jim Cutler Jazz Orchestra, In Progress*, Pony Boy Records, 2006.
68. Linda Dahl, *Stormy Weather*, 75.
69. Ibid.
70. Marian McPartland, *Piano Jazz: Barbara Carroll*, NPR, March 12, 2009.
71. Ibid.
72. L.E.N., "Cuter Carroll Culling Classier Customers; Capitol Contract?," *Down Beat*, July 2, 1952, 8.
73. Paul De Barros, *Shall We Play That One Together?*, 135.
74. Ibid.
75. Ibid.

76. Paul De Barros, *Shall We Play That One Together?*, 194.
77. Linda Dahl, *Morning Glory*, 326.
78. Arnold Jay Smith, *OctoJAZZarian Profile: Barbara Carroll*, website *http://www.jazz.com/features-and-interviews/2009/2/15/the-octojazz* retrieved June 22, 2015.
79. Ibid.
80. Terry Gross, *Fresh Air: Barbara Carroll*, NPR, December 23, 1990.
81. Paul De Barros, *Shall We Play That One Together?*, 398.
82. Terry Teachout, *Kansas City Star*, untitled, March 29, 1982, 6B.
83. *All About Jazz: Nancy Wilson*, *http://musicians.allaboutjazz.com/nancywilson* retrieved June 24, 2015.
84. Linda Dahl, *Stormy Weather*, 121.
85. Linda Dahl, *Stormy Weather*, 122.
86. Vocalese is written lyrics to a jazz solo.
87. Marian McPartland, *Piano Jazz: Nancy Wilson*, NPR, recorded August 3, 1993, broadcast January 15, 1994.
88. *Wikipedia: Nancy Wilson*, last modified June 9, 2015, 2, 9, *http://en.wikipedia.org/wiki/Nancy_Wilson* retrieved June 24, 2015.
89. Marian McPartland, *Piano Jazz: Nancy Wilson*, NPR, recorded August 3, 1993, broadcast January 15, 1994.
90. Dory DeAngelo letter to Carol Comer and Dianne Gregg, March 31, 1982, Folder number 13, Women's Jazz Festival (KC 314) State Historical Society of Missouri Research Center-Kansas City (hereafter SHSMO-KC).

Chapter Seven: The Sixth Year, March 23–27, 1983

1. Dino Santangelo letter to Dianne Gregg, October 20, 1982, Folder number 18, Women's Jazz Festival (KC314) SHSMO-KC.
2. Carol Comer interview with author, July 30, 2012.
3. Dino Santangelo letter to Dianne Gregg, October 20, 1982, Folder number 18, Women's Jazz Festival (KC314) SHSMO-KC.
4. Ferguson and Marsalis, *Newport Jazz in New York*, "KOOL Jazz Festival History," *http://www.boogie/com/Newport.Jazz16.html* retrieved June 29, 2015.
5. David Glenn interview with author, July 11, 2015.
6. *Down Beat*, April 1983 advertisement for KOOL cigarettes, 1982 B&W T Co., 7.
7. *Wikipedia, Kool cigarettes*, additional notes Nat King Cole, *http://en.wikipedia.org/wiki/KOOL_(cigarette)* retrieved June 29, 2015.
8. Carol Comer and Dianne Gregg interview with author, July 30, 2012.
9. Jonathan Poses, "KOOL Jazz Festival to Skip Kansas City," *Kansas City Times* (no date or page given), copy found in Folder number 59, Women's Jazz Festival (KC314) SHSMO-KC.

10. Petition for Damages, Circuit Court of Jackson County, Missouri, Case: CV81-22501, Ruth Kissane vs. Crown Center Redevelopment Corporation and Women Jazz Festival, Folder number 19, Women's Jazz Festival (KC314) SHSMO-KC.
11. Ibid.
12. Audio recording of 1980 WJF Tribute to the International Sweethearts of Rhythm, March 23, 1980, loaned to author by Carol Comer and Dianne Gregg, April 22, 2010.
13. Carol Comer and Dianne Gregg interview with author, July 30, 2012.
14. Letter to Women's Jazz Festival from Fidelity and Guaranty Life Insurance Company, April 5, 1984, Folder 22, Women's Jazz Festival (KC314) SHSMO-KC.
15. Attorney John Cusick interview with author, July 30, 2015.
16. 1983 Women's Jazz Festival program booklet, 6.
17. Whitney Balliett, "Profiles: 'The Key of D is Daffodil Yellow,'" *New Yorker*, January 20, 1973, 43.
18. Ibid.
19. Leonard Feather, "Stop and Bop with Tommy Flanagan," *Los Angeles Times*, January 26, 1992.
20. *Jazz Profiles*, NPR, "Tommy Flanagan: Poet of Piano," July 16, 2008, *www.npr.prg/2008/07/16/92568276/tommy-flanagan-poet-of-piano* retrieved July 2, 2015.
21. Ibid.
22. Ibid.
23. Ibid.
24. Ben Ratliff, "Tommy Flanagan, Elegant Jazz Pianist, Is Dead at 71," *New York Times*, November 19, 2001, *http:/www.nytimes.com/2001/11/19/arts/tommy-flanagan-elegant-jazz* retrieved July 2, 2015.
25. 1983 Women's Jazz Festival program booklet, 11.
26. Helen Marquette interview with author, September 21, 2013.
27. 1983 Women's Jazz Festival program booklet, 11.
28. Wikipedia, "Timeline of Jazz Education," last modified June 30, 2015, *https://en.wikipedia.org/wiki/timeline_of_jazz_education* retrieved July 3, 2015.
29. My father, Bill Glenn, participated as drummer, pianist, singer, and ultimately leader in such a band while he attended Carleton College in Northfield, Minnesota in the late thirties. Although not a music major, Dad's tuition was reduced each semester for playing in this dance band that performed not only for student dances but for administration social functions.
30. John S. Wilson, "Stan Kenton, Band Leader, Dies; Was Center of Jazz Controversies," *New York Times on the Web*, August 27, 1979, *http://www.nytimes.com/learning/general/onthisday/bday/0219.html* retrieved July 6, 2015.

31. University of Idaho Library, Leonard Feather Collection, *www.ijc.uidaho.edu/feather_leonard/author.html* retrieved August 9, 2015.
32. Berklee College of Music, A Brief History, *https://www.berklee.edu/about/brief-history* retrieved July 6, 2015.
33. Barry Kernfeld, ed., "Teddy Wilson," *The New Grove Dictionary of Jazz* (New York: St. Martin's Press, 1988), 1302.
34. David Joyner and John Murphy, *The History of Jazz at North Texas*, Division of Jazz Studies website last updated June 3, 2015, *https://www.jazz.unt.edu/history* retrieved July 6, 2015.
35. Ibid.
36. Ibid.
37. G.O.T., "Swing in Schooltime Pays Off, Klever Kids Kill Kats with Kapable Kombo," *Down Beat*, July 1, 1946, 13.
38. Ralph Marterie, "Tomorrow's Bands in School of Today," *Down Beat*, October 5, 1955, 13.
39. Ibid.
40. Ibid.
41. George Avakian, "Music Educators Take a Long, Close Look at Jazz," *Down Beat*, June 13, 1956, 14.
42. Ibid.
43. Ibid.
44. Terry Vosbein, "Artistry in Jazz Education: Jazz Camps," *http://www.vosbein.com/lagniappe/words/jazz_education_article/* retrieved July 6, 2015.
45. George Wiskirchen, C.S.C., "Jazz on Campus," *Down Beat*, May 23, 1963, 39.
46. Ibid.
47. Terry Vosbein, "Artistry in Jazz Education," *http://www.vosbein.com/lagniappe/words/jazz_education_article/* retrieved July 6, 2015.
48. Leonard Feather, *International Musician*, 1961; stankenton.org/ "The Creative World of Stan Kenton," (Noel Wedder's page), retrieved July 6, 2015.
49. Not everyone was a Kenton fan. Leonard Feather, who didn't care for Kenton's experimental, progressive jazz/big band sound, called him, "Kent Stand'em."
50. *Wikipedia*, "Stan Kenton Band Clinics," *https://en.m.wikipedia.org/wiki/Stan_Kenton_Band_Clinics* retrieved July 6, 2015.
51. *Wikipedia*, "Timeline of Jazz Education," *https://en.wikipedia.org/wiki/Timeline_of_jazz_education* retrieved July 3, 2015.
52. These are called "alligators" in the jive language of the big band era.
53. Monika Herzig, *David Baker: A Legacy in Music* (Bloomington: University of Indiana Press, 2011), 62.
54. Ibid.
55. 1983 Women's Jazz Festival program booklet, 24.

56. Ellen Rowe interview with author, December 4, 2012.
57. Ibid.
58. Cathy Lee, "Jazzing It Up in KC," *Sojourner*, May 1983, 15.
59. Roberts Wesleyan College: Dina Alexander, *http://www.roberts.edu/faculty staff/dina-alexander-aspx* retrieved July 15, 2015.
60. Teri Koide, *Profile*, *www.terikoide.com/* retrieved July 15, 2015.
61. Ellen Rowe, "Biography," www.ellenrowe.com, retrieved July 15, 2015.
62. 1983 Women's Jazz Festival program booklet, 24.
63. Cathy Lee, "Jazzing It Up in KC," 15.
64. Ibid.
65. Kirby Farrell, "Classy Duo Makes Real Music," *Daily Hampshire Gazette*, June 22,1982.
66. Don DeMichael, "Record Review: Sheila Jordan, *Portrait of Sheila*," *Down Beat*, March 14, 1963, 30.
67. Ibid.
68. Robert Palmer, "Sheila Jordan: The Music Stays Pure," *Rolling Stone*, July 23, 1981, 47.
69. Kirk Silsbee, liner notes to *Yesterdays*, Highnote Records, Inc., HCD 7234, 2012.
70. Ellen Johnson, *Jazz Child: A Portrait of Sheila Jordan* (Lanham, MD: Rowman and Littlefield, 2014), 113.
71. Richard Sudhalter, "Jordan: The Thrill Is Here," *New York Post*, May 19, 1981.
72. Cathy Lee, "Jazzing It Up In KC," *Sojourner*, May 1983, 15.
73. Kirby Farrell, "Classy Duo Make Real Music," June 22, 1982.
74. W. Patrick Hinely, "Sheila's Song of Joy," *Jazz Forum*, March 1982 (no page number given), Folder number 81, Women's Jazz Festival (KC314) SHSMO-KC.
75. Kirk Silsbee, liner notes to *Yesterdays*, Highnote Records, Inc. HCD 7234, 2012.
76. Harvie S. interview with author, February 7, 2013.
77. Ibid.
78. Tom McDermott, "Women's Fest Turns Six," *Down Beat*, June 1983, 12.
79. 1983, Women's Jazz Festival program booklet, 20.
80. Gene Aiken interview with author, August 27, 2015.
81. Amy Duncan, "Groundbreaker for Vocal Jazz," *Christian Science Monitor*, August 12, 1982, 18,19.
82. Ibid.
83. 1983 Women's Jazz Festival program booklet, 18.
84. Cathy Lee, "Jazzing It Up in Kansas City," *Sojourners*, May 1983, 15.
85. Terry Teachout, "Jazz Singer Anita O'Day Is in a Class by Herself," *Kansas City Star*, March 28, 1983, 6B.
86. Tom McDermott, "Women's Festival Turns Six," 12.

87. Amy Duncan, "Big Names Needed—But Where Do You Find Them?," *Christian Science Monitor,* April 18, 1983.
88. Ibid.
89. Ibid.
90. Amy Duncan, *Getting Down to Brass Tacks* (USA: Amy Duncan, 2012), 230.
91. Amy Duncan interview with author, September 12, 2012.
92. Cathy Lee, "Jazzing It Up in Kansas City," 15.
93. Amy Duncan interview with author, September 12, 2012.
94. Cathy Lee, "Jazzing It Up in Kansas City," 15.
95. Ibid.
96. 1983 Women's Jazz Festival program booklet, 21.
97. Cathy Lee, "Jazzing It Up in Kansas City," 15.
98. Amy Duncan, *Getting Down to Brass Tacks*, 201.
99. Ibid.
100. Marian McPartland, *Piano Jazz: Nancy Wilson*, NPR, recorded August 3, 1993, broadcast on January 15, 1994.
101. Ellen Johnson, *Jazz Child: A Portrait of Sheila Jordan* (Lanham, MD: Rowman & Littlefield, 2014), 142.
102. "In Memory of Billie," *Down Beat,* July 21, 1960, 16.
103. Tzvi Gluckin, "Forgotten Heroes: Emily Remler," *Premier Guitar*, posted July 29, 2014, *http://www.premierguitar.com/articles/21113-forgotten-heros-emily* retrieved July 13, 2015.
104. W. Royal Stokes, *The Jazz Scene* (New York: Oxford University Press, 1991), 216.
105. Ellen Johnson, *Jazz Child*, 142.
106. Ibid.
107. Ellen Johnson, *Jazz Child*, 144.
108. Ibid.
109. Anita O'Day with George Eells, *High Times Hard Times* (New York: Limelight Editions, 1981), 272-273.
110. Robbie Cavolina and Ian McCrudden, *Anita O'Day: The Life of a Jazz Singer*, DVD, Elan Entertainment, AOD Productions, 2012.
111. Anita O'Day with George Eells, *High Times Hard Times*, 13.
112. Amy Duncan, "Anita O'Day Can Still Command a Band—And an Audience," *Christian Science Monitor,* June 20, 1989.
113. Anita O'Day with George Eells, *High Times Hard Times*, 77.
114. Amy Duncan, "Better-Than-Ever Comeback for Anita O'Day," *Christian Science Monitor,* July 3, 1989.
115. Anita O'Day with George Eells, *High Times Hard Times*, 104.
116. Amy Duncan, "Better-Than-Ever Comeback for Anita O'Day."
117. Robbie Cavolina and Ian McCrudden, *Anita O'Day: The Life of a Jazz Singer*, DVD, Elan Entertainment, AOD Productions, 2012.

118. Harvie S. interview with author, February 7, 2013.
119. Ibid.
120. Paul Smith interview with author, July 16, 2015.
121. Ibid.
122. Ibid.
123. Terry Teachout, "Jazz Singer Anita O'Day Is in a Class by Herself," *Kansas City Star*, March 28, 1983.
124. Cathy Lee, "Jazzing It Up in Kansas City," May 1983, 15.
125. Carol Comer and Dianne Gregg interview with author, July 30, 2012.

Chapter Eight: Every Time We Say Goodbye

1. Robert Trussell, "Women's Jazz Festival Is Cancelled for 1984," *Kansas City Star*, December 15, 1983.
2. Carol Comer interview with author, July 30, 2013.
3. WJF board meeting minutes, February 26, 1984, Folder number 8, Women's Jazz Festival (KC314) SHSMO-KC.
4. Carol Comer interview with author, July 30, 2013.
5. Julie Hanson letter to WJF board members, December 1983, Folder number 17, Women's Jazz Festival (KC314) SHSMO-KC.
6. Dianne Gregg interview with author, July 30, 2013.
7. Carol Comer interview with author, July 30, 2013.
8. Ibid.
9. WJF board meeting minutes, November 26, 1983, Folder number 7, Women's Jazz Festival (KC 314) SHSMO-KC.
10. Ibid.
11. Ibid.
12. Ibid.
13. Ibid.
14. Carol Comer interview with author, July 30, 2013.
15. Dianne Gregg interview with author, July 30, 2013.
16. Carol Comer interview with author, July 30, 2013.
17. Dianne Gregg interview with author, July 30, 2013.
18. Carol Comer interview with author, July 30, 2013.
19. Terry Teachout note to Carol Comer and Dianne Gregg, March 1983, Folder number 18, Women's Jazz Festival (KC314) SHSMO-KC. Teachout later became the drama critic for the *Wall Street Journal* and has written biographies of H.L. Mencken, George Balanchine, and Louis Armstrong.
20. Dianne Gregg interview with author, July 30, 2013.
21. Robert Trussell, "Women's Jazz Festival Is Canceled for 1984."
22. Press release, "Women's Jazz Festival Postponed for a Year," January 1984, Folder number 53, Women's Jazz Festival (KC314) SHSMO-KC.

23. Editors, "We'll All Miss the Lost Jazz Festival," *Kansas City Star*, December 29, 1983.
24. WJF board meeting minutes, January 14, 1984, Folder number 8, Women's Jazz Festival (KC314) SHSMO-KC.
25. Center for Management Assistance, summary of planning meeting, May 17, 1984, Folder number 4, Women's Jazz Festival (KC314) SHSMO-KC.
26. William Hollan, "Women's Jazz Event to Resurface in '85; Money Being Raised," *Kansas City Times*, September 22, 1984.
27. Around Kansas City, "Jazz Fest Includes Events for Young People," *Kansas City Times*, March 21, 1985, B-2.
28. Diana Krall, letter to Julie Hanson, October 1984, Folder number 18, Women's Jazz Festival (KC314) SHSMO-KC.
29. Unsigned letter to Leonard Feather, July 2, 1984, Folder number 15, Women's Jazz Festival (KC314) SHSMO-KC.
30. Amy Duncan letter to Julie Hanson, October 19, 1984, Folder number 18, Women's Jazz festival (KC314) SHSMO-KC.
31. Robert Trussell, "TNT Blows up a Storm in Women's Jazz Event," *Kansas City Star*, March 24, 1985, 54A.
32. Ibid.
33. Ibid.
34. Cathy Lee, "K.C. Women's Jazz Festival 1985: Unique," *Sojourner*, no date, no pagination, found in Folder number 59, Women's Jazz Festival (KC314) SHSMO-KC.
35. Ibid.
36. Ibid.
37. Robert Trussell, "Varied Sounds Close Women's Jazz Event," *Kansas City Star*, March 25, 1985, 6B.
38. Ibid.
39. Tim O'Connor, "Women Vote to End Popular Jazz Festival," *Kansas City Times*, December 16, 1985.
40. Robert Trussell, "Women's Jazz Fest Simply Lacks Funds," *Kansas City Star*, December 16, 1985, 4C.
41. Ibid.
42. Press release, "Women's Jazz Festival for 1986 Is Cancelled," January 5, 1986, Folder number 59, Women's Jazz Festival (KC314) SHSMO-KC.
43. Ibid.
44. Mary Hodges letter to Julie Hanson, January 27, 1986, Folder number 15, Women's Jazz Festival (KC314) SHSMO-KC.
45. Robert Trussell, "Women's Jazz Fest Simply Lacks Funds."

Epilogue

1. Author attended the American Jazz Museum's Women in Jazz Month Kick-off Celebration, Gem Theater, Kansas City, Missouri, March 5, 2015.
2. Judy Chaikin, *The Girls in the Band*, An Artist Tribe/One Step Production, 2009.
3. Ibid.
4. Ibid.
5. Ibid.
6. Carol Comer interview with author, March 26, 2015.
7. Dianne Gregg interview with author, March 26, 2015.
8. Judy Chaikin, *The Girls in the Band*, An Artist Tribe/One Step Production, 2009.
9. American Jazz Museum's Women in Jazz Month Kick-off Celebration, Gem Theater, Kansas City, Missouri, March 5, 2015.
10. Judy Chaikin, *The Girls in the Band.*
11. American Jazz Museum's Women in Jazz Month Kick-off Celebration, Gem Theater, Kansas City, Missouri, March 5, 2015.
12. Ibid.
13. Lisa Hittle interview with author, April 11, 2015.
14. Ibid.
15. Ibid.
16. Night Life, "Blue Note Jazz Festival," *New Yorker*, July 1, 2013, 10.
17. Washington Women in Jazz Festival home page, *www.washingtonwomeninjazz.com* retrieved March 11, 2015.
18. Women's Jazz Festival at the Schomburg Center for Research in Black Culture, New York Public Library, *www.nypl.org/.../women's-jazz-festival-catherine-russell* retrieved March 11, 2015.
19. California Jazz Conservatory, "Seventh Annual JCMS Girls' Jazz and Blues Camp," Community Music School, *http://chic.edu/community-music-school.../girls-jazz-blues-camp/*
20. Deborah Steinberg, "Lady Got Chops," *Women Arts*, retrieved March 11, 2015, *http:// www.womenarts.org/2012/05/24/lady-got-chops/*
21. Adam Bernstein, "Mary Lou Williams Women in Jazz Festival Begins Final Year as Women-only Showcase," *Washington Post*, May 15, 2013, retrieved March 11, 2015, *http://www.washingtonpost.com/entertainment/music/mary-lou-williams*
22. Ibid.
23. American Jazz Museum's Women in Jazz Month Kick-Off Celebration, Gem Theater, Kansas City, Missouri, March 5, 2015.
24. Lisa Hittle interview with author, April 11, 2015.
25. Ibid.
26. Ibid.
27. American Jazz Museum's Women in Jazz Month Kick-off Celebration, Gem Theater, Kansas City, Missouri, March 5, 2015.

Bibliography

Books

Bolden, Tonya. *Take Off: American All-Girl Bands During World War II.* New York: Alfred A. Knopf, 2007.

Brooks, Tim, and Earle Marsh. *The Complete Directory to Prime Time Network and Cable TV Shows.* New York: Ballantine Books, 1999.

Bunker, Edward, and Flora Purim. *Freedom Song: The Story of Flora Purim.* New York: Berkley Books, 1982.

Carey, Joseph Kuhn. *Big Noise from Notre Dame.* Notre Dame, IN: University of Notre Dame Press, 1986.

Dahl, Linda. *Morning Glory: A Biography of Mary Lou Williams.* Berkeley: University of California Press, 1999.

———. *Stormy Weather: The Music and Lives of a Century of Jazzwomen.* New York: Limelight Editions, 1984.

De Barros, Paul. *Shall We Play That One Together? The Life and Art of Jazz Piano Legend Marian McPartland.* New York: St. Martin's Press, 2012.

Driggs, Frank, and Chuck Haddix. *Kansas City Jazz, From Ragtime to Bebop: A History.* New York: Oxford University Press, 2005.

Duncan, Amy. *Getting Down to Brass Tacks: My Adventures in the World of Jazz, Rio, and Beyond.* U.S.A.: Self-published, 2012.

Enstice, Wayne, and Janis Stockhouse. *Jazzwomen: Conversations with Twenty-One Musicians.* Bloomington: Indiana University Press, 2004.

Gordan, Lorraine, as told to Barry Singer. *Alive at the Vanguard: My Life In and Out of Jazz Time.* New York: Hal Leonard, 2006.

Gourse, Leslie. *Madame Jazz: Contemporary Women Instrumentalists.* New York: Oxford University Press, 1995.

Handy, D. Antoinette. *The International Sweethearts of Rhythm: The Ladies Jazz Band from Piney Woods Country Life School.* Lanham, MD: Scarecrow Press 1998.

Herzig, Monika. *David Baker: A Legacy in Music.* Bloomington: Indiana University Press, 2011.

Johnson, Ellen. *Jazz Child: A Portrait of Sheila Jordan.* Lanham, MD: Rowman and Littlefield, 2014.

Jones, Quincy. *Q: The Autobiography of Quincy Jones*. New York: Doubleday, 2001.

Kenton, Leslie. *Love Affair*. New York: St. Martin's Press, 2010.

Kernfeld, Barry, ed. *The New Grove Dictionary of Jazz*. New York: St. Martin's Press, 1988.

Leder, Jan. *Women in Jazz: A Discography of Instrumentalists, 1913-1968*. Westport, CT: Greenwood Press, 1985.

Maggin, Donald L. *Dizzy: The Life and Times of John Birks Gillespie*. New York: Harper Entertainment, 2004.

McGee, Kristin A. *Some Like It Hot: Jazz Women in Film and Television 1928—1959*. Middletown, CT: Wesleyan University Press, 2009.

McPartland, Marian. *All In Good Time*. New York: Oxford University Press, 1987.

O'Day, Anita, with George Eells. *High Times Hard Times*. New York: Limelight, 1981.

Placksin, Sally. *American Women in Jazz: 1900 to the Present*. USA: Wideview Books, 1982.

Pool, Jeannie Gayle. *Peggy Gilbert and Her All-Girl Band*. Lanham, MD: Scarecrow Press, 2008.

Prial, Dunstan. *The Producer: John Hammond and the Soul of American Music*. New York: Farrar, Straus and Giroux, 2006.

Rustin, Nichole T., and Sherrie Tucker, eds. *Big Ears: Listening for Gender in Jazz Studies*. Durham: Duke University Press, 2008.

Scott, Allen. *Jazz Educated, Man: A Sound Foundation*. Washington D.C.: American International Publishers, 1973.

Smith, Chris. *The View from the Back of the Band: The Life and Music of Mel Lewis*. Denton: University of North Texas Press, 2014.

Stokes, W. Royal. *The Jazz Scene: An Informal History from New Orleans to 1990*. New York: Oxford University Press, 1991.

Terry, Clark. *Clark: The Autobiography of Clark Terry*. Berkeley: University of California Press, 2011.

Torff, Brian Q. *In Love with Voices: A Jazz Memoir*. New York: iUniverse, Inc., 2008.

Von Eschen, Penny M. *Satchmo Blows Up the World: Jazz Ambassadors Play the Cold War*. London: Harvard University Press, 2004.

Walker-Hill, Helen. *From Spirituals to Symphonies: African-American Women Composers and Their Music*. Chicago: University of Illinois Press, 2007

Wein, George, with Nate Chinen. *Myself Among Others: A Life in Music*. Cambridge, MA: Da Capo Press, 2003.

Wilmer, Valerie. *As Serious as Your Life: John Coltrane and Beyond*. London: Allison & Busby Limited, 1977.

Yanow, Scott. *The Jazz Singers: The Ultimate Guide*. New York: Backbeat Books, 2008.

Magazines / Newspapers

"Advertisement for Kool Cigarettes." *Down Beat*, April 1983.

Avakian, George. "Music Educators Take a Long, Close Look at Jazz." *Down Beat*, June 13, 1956.

Ball, Nancy. "Winds of March Will be Blowing Jazz for Kansas City." *Kansas City Times*, February 29, 1980.

Balliett, Whitney. "Profile: The Key of D Is Daffodil Yellow." *New Yorker*, January 20, 1973.

Balliett, Whitney. "Profile: Out Here Again." *New Yorker*, May 2, 1964.

Berg, Chuck. "Caught! International Premiere Women's Jazz Festival." *Down Beat*, August 10, 1978.

———. "Charlie Parker 'Connection' Thrills Crowd." *Kansas City Star*, June 3, 1979.

———. "Olympics Musician's Dream." *Kansas City Star*, June 3, 1979.

———. "Review." *Down Beat*, August 10, 1978.

———. "Women's Jazz Festival Returns after Hiatus," *Lawrence Journal-World*, March 17, 1985.

"Blue Note Jazz Festival." *New Yorker*, July 1, 2013.

Bouchard, Fred. "Profile: Jane Ira Bloom." *Down Beat*, December 1981.

Carlton, Jim. "Mary Osborne: Charlie's Angel." *Vintage Guitar Magazine*, December 5, 2012.

Church, Emmanuel. "Sheila Jordan/Harvie Swartz." *Down Beat*, April 1982.

D.O.M. "Heard in Person: Blossom Dearie—Stella Brooks." *Down Beat*, June 13, 1957.

DeMichael, Don. "Record Reviews: Sheila Jordan, *Portrait of Sheila*." *Down Beat*, March 14, 1963.

"Down Beat in Review." *Down Beat*, July 15, 1976.

Duncan, Amy. "ALIVE!—Five Women with a Special Brand of Music." *Christian Science Monitor*, November 9, 1981.

———. "Anita O'Day Can Still Command a Band—and an Audience." *Christian Science Monitor*, June 20, 1989.

———. "Better-Than-Ever Comeback for Anita O'Day." *Christian Science Monitor*, July 3, 1989.

———. "Big Names Needed—But Where Do You Find Them?" *Christian Science Monitor*, April 18, 1983.

———. "Groundbreaker for Vocal Jazz." *Christian Science Monitor*, August 12, 1982.

"Emotional Brass." *Time*, August 4, 1958.

Farrell, Kirby. "Classy Duo Makes Real Music." *Daily Hampshire Gazette*, June 22, 1982.

Feather, Leonard. "Everything's Up to Date in Kansas City." *Los Angeles Times*, March 21, 1978.

———. *International Musician*, 1961.

———. "Ladies Invitation." *Melody Maker,* April 15, 1978.

———. "The Organ In Jazz." *Down Beat*. October 24, 1963.

———. "Second Annual Women's Jazz Festival." *Down Beat*, June 7, 1979.

———. "Stop and Bop with Tommy Flanagan." *Los Angeles Times*, January 26, 1992.

———. "Toshiko Akiyoshi: The Leader of the Band." *Ms.*, November 1978.

———. "Women's Jazz Festival." *Down Beat,* July 1980.

Fox, Jeanne. "Musicians Finish on Low Note in Benefit Basketball Game." *Kansas City Times*, November 21, 1977.

Garrity, John. "Jazz Veterans Project Joyous Chemistry." *Kansas City Star*, June 3, 1979.

George, Nelson. "Pianist for a New Era." *Down Beat,* July 1980.

Gerber, Leslie. "Dave Holland Benefit." *Woodstock Times*, May 6, 1982.

Gillespie, Dizzy, with Ralph Ginzburg. "Jazz Is Too Good for Americans." *Esquire*, June 1957.

"Girls' Band Flees Dixie after Tiff with School." *Afro American*, April 26, 1941.

G.O.T. "Swing in Schooltime Pays Off, Klever Kids Kill Kats With Kapable Kombo." *Down Beat*, July 1, 1946, 13.

Hinely, W. Patrick. "Sheila's Songs of Joy." *Jazz Forum,* March 1982.

Hohl, Paul. "Women Blow in Kansas City." *Billboard*, April 5, 1980.

Hollan, William. "Women's Jazz Event to Resurface in '85: Money Being Raised." *Kansas City Times*, September 22, 1984.

———. "Kenton Withdraws from Stage Band Camps." *Down Beat*, October 24, 1963.

"Jazz Memorial." *Kansas City Times*, August 18, 1979.

Jeske, Lee. "Duets." *Jazz Journal International*, July 1981.

Jordon, Gerald. "A Spiritual Message." *Kansas City Star*, March 20, 1978.

Kart, Larry. "After Hours, This Secretary Sings with Pure Genius." *Chicago Tribune,* May 2, 1982.

Kenton, Stan. *International Musician*, 1961.

L.E.N. "Cuter Carroll Culling Classier Customers; Capitol Contract?" *Down Beat*, July 2, 1952. 8.

Laurence, Robert P. "Mixed Notes in Women's Jazz." *San Diego Union*, April 1, 1979.

Lee, Cathy. "Jazzing It up in KC." *Sojourner*, May 1983.

———. "K.C. Women's Jazz Festival 1985: Unique," *Sojourner,* no date, no pagination.

Lewis, Diane. "Jazzing It Up." *Wichita Eagle and Beacon,* April 1, 1979.

Liska, James. "Profile: Maiden Voyage." *Down Beat,* November 1981.

Marterie, Ralph. "Tomorrow's Bands In Schools Of Today." *Down Beat,* October 5, 1955.

McDermott, Tom. "Women's Fest Turns Six." *Down Beat,* June 1983.

McHenry, Susan, and Jill McManus. "A Woman's Place Is in the Groove." *Ms.,* November 1978.

McPartland, Marian. "Mary Lou Williams: Into the Sun." *Down Beat,* August 27, 1964.

———. "The Untold Story of The International Sweethearts of Rhythm," 1980. In Mike Ning collection.

Morgan, Ray. "Jazz Award to Kansas City Women." *Kansas City Times,* August 18, 1979.

"Mrs. Cugat Can't See Gals as Tooters; Kills Glamour." *Down Beat,* May 4, 1951.

O'Connor, Tim. "Women Vote to End Popular Jazz Festival." *Kansas City Times,* December 16, 1985.

Oestreich, James R. "Berlin in Lights: The Woman Question." *Arts Beat Magazine,* November 16, 2007.

Palmer, Robert. "Sheila Jordan: The Music Stays Pure." *Rolling Stone,* July 23, 1981.

"The Parks Will Resound." *Kansas City Times,* June 17, 1973.

Paton, Maureen. "Bley Time." *Melody Maker,* September 10, 1977.

Paul, Steve. "Innovation, Energy Guide Jazz Performers." *Kansas City Star,* March 20, 1978.

———. "Music: The Bond That Counts." *Kansas City Star,* March 19, 1978.

———. "Women's Jazz Festival a Major Event." *Kansas City Star,* July 17, 1977.

Pogrebin, Letty Cottin. "Reagan Accused of Being 'Anti-woman'." *Kansas City Times,* March 27, 1981.

Poses, Jonathan. "KOOL Jazz Festival to Skip Kansas City." *Kansas City Times,* no date.

"In Review: In Memory of Billie." *Down Beat,* July 21, 1960.

Rothbart, Peter. "Toshiko Akiyoshi: Arranging on a Steady Ascent." *Down Beat,* August 1980.

Salaam, Yusef. "Profile: Janice Robinson." *Down Beat,* April 1981.

"School Jazz." *Down Beat,* July 20, 1961.

"Singers: The Greatest Pretender." *Time,* July 17, 1964.

Sloane, Carol. "A Drum Is a Woman: The Swinging Dottie Dodgion." *Down Beat,* March 20, 1969.

Sokol, David. "Sheila Jordan/Harvie Swartz." *Valley Advocate*, June 16, 1982.

"Spotlight on School Jazz, University of Denver Stage Band." *Down Beat*, July 4, 1963.

Stein, Shifra. "Aerial Sounds Fly to Tempo of Its Choice." *Kansas City Star*, March 22, 1979.

———. "Cohn Group Gets Sessions Cooking." *Kansas City Times*, June 2, 1979.

———. "Drummer to Provide K.C. Beat to Jazz Olympics." *Kansas City Times*, June 1, 1979.

———. "Festival Proves Jazz Prowess of Women." *Kansas City Times*, March 17, 1978.

———. "First Festival for Women Jazz Artists a Big-Time Event." *Kansas City Star*, March 23, 1978.

———. "Jazz Greats Open Olympics." *Kansas City Times*, June 2, 1979.

———. "Jazz Olympics to Bring Back Music That Blew Kansas City Wide Open." *Kansas City Times*, May 18, 1979.

———. "KC Jazz: Is It All Past Glory?" *Kansas City Star*, March 4, 1979.

———. "Musicians Pick Up Basketballs for Good Cause." *Kansas City Star*, November 17, 1977.

———. "Promoter of Jazz Olympics Paid for Missing the Beat." *Kansas City Times*, June 8, 1979.

———. "Women Dispel Jazz Myth." *Kansas City Star*, March 26, 1979.

———. "Women's Festival a Labor of Love." *Kansas City Star*, March 20, 1978.

———. "Women Jazz It Up at Clinics." *Kansas City Star*, March 25, 1979.

Stokes, Royal W. "Jordan/Swartz." *The Washington Post*, March 15, 1982.

Sudhalter, Richard M. "Jordan: The Thrill Is Here." *New York Post*, May 19, 1981.

Tracy, Jack. "The First Chorus." *Down Beat*, June 13, 1957.

———. "Jazz Festival Roundup." *Down Beat*, June 13, 1957.

———. "College Jazz." *Down Beat*, June 13, 1957.

Teachout, Terry. (untitled) *Kansas City Star*, March 29, 1982.

———. "All That Jazz Simply Amazing." *Kansas City Star*, March 24, 1980.

———. "The Beat Goes on for Women in Tune at Jazz Festival." *Kansas City Star*, March 23, 1982.

———. "Jazz Singer Anita O'Day Is in a Class by Herself." *Kansas City Star*, March 28, 1983.

———. "McPartland-Flanagan Start Jazz Festival Swingin'." *Kansas City Star*, March 24, 1983.

———. "A More than Worthy Successor." *Kansas City Star*, March 30, 1981.

———. "New Groups Get a Chance to Shine." *Kansas City Star*, March 30, 1981.

———. "Perfection Personified." *Kansas City Star*, March 25, 1982.

———. "Women Came Long Way from All-Girl Orchestra." *Kansas City Star*, March 25, 1979.

———. "Women's Jazz Festival First-Rate." *Kansas City Star,* March 27, 1983.

———. "Women's TNT Jazz Show Is Dynamite." *Kansas City Star*, March 23, 1980.

Trussell, Robert. "TNT Blows up a Storm in Women's Jazz Event." *Kansas City Star*, March 24, 1985.

———. "Varied Sounds Close Women's Jazz Event." *Kansas City Star*, March 25, 1985.

———. "Women's Jazz Festival Is Cancelled for 1984." *Kansas City Star*, December 15, 1983.

———. "Women's Jazz Fest Simply Lacks Funds." *Kansas City Star*, December 16, 1985.

Twardy, Chuck. "Jazz Fest Offers Look into Promising Future." *Lawrence Journal-World*, March 31, 1985.

Ullman, Michael. "Sheila Jordan: The Jazz Life." *Mother Jones*, February/March 1981.

Vollers, Maryanne. "Women's Jazz Festival Makes a Joyful Noise." *Rolling Stone*, May 18, 1978.

Walls, Seth Colter. "Jazz Is Dead (Commercially), Long Live Jazz Creatively." *Newsweek*, December 9, 2009.

Waz, Joe. "Annual Women's Jazz Festival—Kansas City." *International Jazz Federation*, April 1978.

"Whatever Happened to Melba Liston." *Ebony*, June 1977.

Williams, Mary Lou. "Teaching Music in Public Schools." *People's Voice*, 1946.

Wilson, John C. "Concert Ends Women's Jazz Festival." *New York Times*, March 21, 1978.

———. "Review." *The New York Times*, March 21, 1978.

———. "Stan Kenton, Band Leader, Dies; Was Center of Jazz Controversies." *New York Times on the Web*, August 27, 1979.

Wiskirchen, George. "Jazz on Campus." *Down Beat,* May 23, 1963.

Audio Recordings

Akiyoshi, Toshiko. *From Toshiko with Love*, BMG Funhouse, Inc. Tokyo, BVCJ-37328, 1981.

Anderson, Ernestine. *Hot Cargo*, CD, Fresh Sound Records, Spain, FSR-CD-482 (originally 1956), 2008.

———. *Never Make Your Move Too Soon*, CD, Concord Jazz, Inc., Concord, California, CCD-4147, 1981.

Audio recording of 1979 concerts, loaned to author by Carol Comer and Dianne Gregg, April 22, 2010.

Audio recording of 1980 WJF Tribute to the International Sweethearts of Rhythm, loaned to author by Carol Comer and Dianne Gregg, April 22, 2010.

Bley, Carla. *Big Band Theory*, WATT/25, New York, LC4438, 1993.

———. *Social Studies*, WATT, New York, 831-831-2, 1981.

Bloom, Jane Ira. *The Red Quartets*, Arabesque Jazz, New York, AJ0144, 1999.

———. *Wingwalker*, Outline, New York, OTL140, 2010.

Brackeen, Joanne. *Popsicle Illusion*, Arkadia Jazz, New York, 70372, 2000.

———. *Tring-A-Ling*, ChoiCe, CHCD 71016, 1978.

Brown, Deborah. *Songbird*, Jazz'N Pulz, The Netherlands, BMCD 397, 2002.

Cheatham, Doc. *You're a Sweetheart with Rosemary Galloway's Swing Sisters,* CD Sackville Recordings, Toronto, SKCD2-2038, 1992

Corea, Chick. *Return to the 7th Galaxy*, CD, Verve, New York (originally 1971) 314533108-2, 1996.

Cutler, Jim, Jazz Orchestra. *In Progress*, CD, Pony Boy Records, Redmond, Washington, PB50152-2, 2006.

DeGreg, Phil. *The Green Gate*, J Seven Records, Cincinnati, Ohio, J7998, 1998.

Dudziak, Urszula. *Future Talk*. CD, Inner City Records, Elmsford, New York, IC 1066, 1979.

Fettig, Mary. *Brazilian Footprints,* F major Records, FM5808, 2008.

———. *Relativity*. Lau Lau Records, Pleasant Hill, California, LLR 365225, 2004.

Grauer, Joanne. *Joanne Grauer Trio*. CD, Mode Records, San Diego, California, Mode #113, (recorded 1957) 2003.

Griffith, Joan. *Sambanova*, Pleasing Dog Music, 001, 2008.

Hutton, Ina Ray. *Ina Ray Hutton and Her Melodears (1934–1944)*, Vintage Music, Hollis, New Hampshire, VMP 0081, 2001.

Jazz Composer's Orchestra. *Jazz Composer's Orchestra*, CD, JCOA Records, New York, JCOA 1001/2 1968.

Jones, Quincy. *Around the World, I Dig Dancers*, Fresh Sound Records, FSR-CD 689, 2012.

Jordan, Sheila, and S. Harvie. *Yesterdays*, CD, HighNote Records, New York, HCD 7234, 2012.

Kenton, Stan. *7.5 on the Richter Scale*, CD, Creative World Records, Los Angeles, STD 1070, (recorded August 17, 18, 1973) 1991.

Liston, Melba. *Melba Liston and Her Bones*, Fresh Sound Records, FSR-CD 408, 2006.

Maricle, Sherrie. *Diva Jazz Orchestra, Live in Concert*. CD, Lightyear Entertainment, 54698-2, 2005.

McClure, Kit. *The Sweethearts Project*. Redhot Records, New York, RH 9004, 2004.

McPartland, Marian. *85 Candles—Live in New York*. Concord Jazz, Beverly Hills, CCD2-2218-2, 2005.

———. *At the Festival*. Concord Jazz, Concord, California, CCD-4118, 1980.

———. *Now's the Time*, LP, Halcyon Records, Merrick, New York, Hal 115 Stereo, 1977.

———. *Piano Jazz: Barbara Carroll*, CD, The Jazz Alliance, Concord, Ca., TJA-12008, 1990.

———. *Piano Jazz: Mary Lou Williams*, CD, The Jazz Alliance, Beverly Hills, TJA-12045-2, 1995.

———. *Timeless*, Savoy Jazz, Santa Monica, California, SVY 17117, 2002.

Montclair Women's Big Band. *Montclair Women's Big Band*, Pivotal Records, Marin County, California, 83707 08130, 2005.

Moses, Kathryn. *Music in My Heart*, Celeste, New York, CMYK-6172, 1978.

Purim, Flora. *Butterfly Dreams*. CD, Milestone Records, Berkeley, California, (originally 1973) MCD-30184, 2007.

———. *Stories to Tell*, CD, Fantasy Studios, Berkeley, California, (originally 1974) M-90581991.

Purim, Flora, and Airto Moreira. *Live in Berkeley*. CD, Airflow Productions, Berkeley, California, 801097003840, (recorded 1990) 2012.

———. *The Magicians*. CD, Crossover, Concord, California, CCD-15001, 1986.

The Real Kansas City of the '20s, '30s, and '40s, Columbia/Legacy, New York, CK 64855,1996.

Reeves, Dianne. *Live at Women's Jazz Festival,* March 21, 1980, personal recording loaned to author by Paul Smith.

Remler, Emily, *East to Wes*, Concord Records, Concord, California, CCD-4356, 1988.

Rich, Buddy. *Speak No Evil*, BGO Records, Suffolk, England, BGOCD962, 2010, (originally RCA Studios, New York, 1977)

Robinson, Janice. *I'll Stand By You*, CD, Ejani.

Rowe, Ellen. *Wishing Well*, CD, PKO Records, University of Michigan, Ann Arbor, Michigan, PKO # 054, 2009.

Rowles, Jimmy, and Stacy Rowles. *Looking Back*, Delos International, Inc., Hollywood, California, DE 4009, 1989.

Scott, Shirley. *Acid Jazz*, CD, Prestige Records, Berkeley, California, ISBN 25218-5200-2, 1998.

———. *Shirley Scott Memorial Album*, CD, Prestige Records, Berkeley, California, PRCD-11027-2, 2003.

Seattle Women's Jazz Orchestra. *Meeting of the Waters*, CD, OA2Records, Seattle, OA2-22033, 2007.

Sheldon, Nina. *Harvest*, Jazzed Media, Littleton, Colorado, JM 1041, 2009.

Sudler, Monnette. *Live in Europe*, SteepleChase, Denmark, SCCD 31102, 1996.

Swartz, Harvie. *In a Different Light*. CD, Bluemoon Recording, New York, R279153, 1990.

Terry Clark. *Big-B-a-d-Band Live at the Wichita Jazz Festival 1974*. Vanguard, Santa Monica, 1975, VMD 79355.

Terry Clark and his Septet/Terry Pollard and her Septet. *Cats vs. Chicks*, CD, Membran Music, Hamburg, 222976-203, 2005 (originally recorded June 2, 1954, MGM 2084)

Tintomara. *Lek*, LP, Amigo Musik AB, Stockholm, Sweden, 1981.

Watkins, Mary. *Something Moving*, LP, Olivia Records, Oakland, California, 1978.

Weston, Randy, and Melba Liston. *Volcano Blues*, Gitanes Jazz Productions, New York, 314 519 269-2, 1993.

Williams, Mary Lou. *Mary Lou's Mass*, Smithsonian Folkways Recordings, Washington D.C., SFW CD 40815, 2005.

———. *My Mama Pinned a Rose on Me*, Pablo Records, Beverly Hill, California, OJCCD-1108-2, 2005 (remastered from 1977 recording at RCA Studios, New York City)

———. *At Rick's Café American*, Storyville Records, made in the EU, recorded live at Chicago's Rick Café American, November 14, 1979, 1038420, 2011.

———. *Roll 'Em*, CD, Solo Art, New Orleans, SACD-43, 1988.

———. *Zodiac Suite*, Smithsonian Folkways Recordings, Washington D.C., SF CD 40810, 1995.

Zumbrunn, Karen, *Twilight World*, North County Distributors, Princeton, New Jersey, 86497 52362, 2002.

———. *Snowfall*, No Comment Studios, New Jersey, 1999, 24075 30382.

Films and Videos

Akiyoshi, Toshiko. *Strive for Jive*. View Video, 2336, 2009.

Bach, Jean. *A Great Day in Harlem*. Home Vision Entertainment, HV3035DVD, 1994.

Burns, Ken. *Jazz, Swing: Pure Pleasure Episode 5*. Warner Brothers, Florentine Films, PBS, B8267D, 2000.

Carter, Graham. *Stan Kenton, Artistry in Rhythm*. Jazzed Media, JM9004, 2011.

Cavolina, Robbie, and Ian McCrudden. *Anita O'Day: The Life of a Jazz Singer*, Elan Entertainment, 101819, 2012.

Chaikin, Judy, writer, director, producer, *The Girls in the Band*, Artist Tribe and One Step Productions.

Dudziak, Urszula. *For You*, Alpha Centauri Entertainment, ACE 11082 C, 2004.

Foremothers, Volume 1. *Jazz Women on Video 1932-1952*, Rosetta Records, RRV 1320, 1990.

Huey. *In Good Time: The Piano Jazz of Marian McPartland*, Huey, ISBN 0-9729294-5-2, 2011.

Hutton, Ina Ray. *Ina Ray Hutton and Her Melodears Orchestra*, Swingtime Video, ISBN 0-87176-557-8, 1984.

International Sweethearts of Rhythm. *International Sweethearts of Rhythm*, A Jezebel Production, ISBN 3701 32798, 2007.

Moreira, Airto, and Flora Purim. *Airto & Flora Purim*, View Video, 2311, 2006.

Williams, Mary Lou. *Mary Lou Williams '78*, Norman Granz Jazz in Montreux, Laser Swing Productions, EE 39053-9, 2004.

Interviews

Aiken, Gene: August 27, 2015 (email).

Bell, Sylvia: July 26, 2013 (phone and email).

Bloom, Jane Ira: September 9, 2012 (email).

Brackeen, Joanne: June 16, 2013 (email); June 26, 2013 (email).

Comer, Carol: April 22, 2010; April 11, 2011; March 3, 2012; July 30, 2012; July 30, 2013; March 26, 2015 (all in person).

Cusick, John: July 30, 2015 (in person).

DeGreg, Phil: December 10, 2012 (phone); July 26, 2013 (email).

Dodgion, Dottie: August 19, 2013 (phone).

Duncan, Amy: September 12, 2012 (email).

Embrey, Danny: October 6, 2014 (in person).

Fettig Mary (Park): November 17, 2012 (email); November 25, 2012 (phone); August 31, 2015 (email).

Fineberg, Jean: December 8, 2012 (email).

Fleeman, Rod: July 5, 2013 (in person).

Glenn, David: July 11, 2015 (phone).

Griffith, Joan: September 29, 2012 (phone).

Gregg, Dianne: April 22, 2010; April 11, 2011; March 3, 2012; July 30, 2012; July 30, 2013; March 26, 2015 (all in person).

Hittle, Lisa: April 11, 2015 (phone).

Kaye, Carol: February 2, (email); February 4, 2014 (email); September 8, 2015 (email).

Leisenring, John: August 25, 2014 (email).

Marquette, Helen: September 21, 2013 (in person).

Metheny, Mike: June 27, 2013 (email).

Ning, Mike: July 26, 2012 (in person).

Riley, Lynn: November 9, 2012 (phone).

Robinson, Janice: August 25, 2014 (email); September 2, 2015 (email).

Rowe, Ellen: December 4, 2012 (email); January 7, 2013 (phone).

Ruskin, Julie Turner: June 25, 2013 (email).

Ruskin, Tommy: June 25, 2013 (email).

S. Harvie: February 7, 2013 (phone).

Sheldon, Nina: February 9, 2013 (phone); September 4, 2014 (email).

Smith, Paul: June 26, 2013 (in person); July 1, 2013 (phone); August 17, 2014 (email); July 16, 2015 (email).

Sudler, Monnette: January 28, 2014 (phone); August 29, 2015 (email).

White, Mike: July 22, 2013 (phone).

Whitfield, Greg: June 11, 2013 (phone).

Wright, Brooks: June 26, 2013 (phone).

Websites

"Berklee College of Music, A Brief History." *http://www.berklee.edu/about/brief-history* (accessed July 6, 2015).

Bernstein, Adam. "Mary Lou Williams Women in Jazz Festival." *http://www.washingtonpost.com/entertainment/music/mary-lou-williams* (accessed March 11, 2015).

Blecha, Peter. "Ernestine Anderson, Jazz Singer." HistoryLink.org.HistoryLink Essay8520 (accessed October 10, 2014).

Cloud, Suzanne. "Monnette Sudler: Daring to Dream." *http://www.allaboutjazz.com/php/article.php?id=45585* (accessed January 23, 2014).

"The Columbus Senior Musicians Hall of Fame: Karen Fanta Zumbrunn." *http://seniormusicians.homestead.com/Zumbrunn.html* (accessed January 25, 2014).

"The Creative World of Stan Kenton." *http://www.stankenton.org* (accessed July 6, 2015).

Eastwood, Clint. "World Renowned Pianist Joanne Grauer." *www.neweb4u.com/grauer/index.html* (accessed May 8, 2015).

"Ellen Rowe: Biography." www.ellenrowe.com (accessed July 15, 2015).

Feather, Leonard. "Pianist Grauer's Intimate Style." *articles.latimes.com>collections* (accessed May 8, 2015)

Fleet, Susan. "Women Who Dared: Melba Liston." *http://archives.susanfleet.com/documents/melba_listonhtml* (accessed January 9, 2014).

Ferguson and Marsalis. "KOOL Jazz Festival History." *http://www.boogie/com/Newport.Jazz16.html* (accessed June 29, 2015).

Giddins, Gary. "Leonard Feather: The Last Post." *http://www.jazzhouse.org/gone/lastpost2.php3?edit=920654712* (accessed June 21, 2013).

Gilbert, Andrew. "Ernestine Anderson: A Strong Second Act." *jazztimes.com/articles/24596-ernestine-anderson-a-strong-second-act* (accessed May 16, 2015).

Gluckin, Tzvi. "Forgotten Heroes: Emily Remler." *http://www.premierguitar.com/articles/21113-forgotten-heros-emily* (accessed July 13, 2015).

Goodwin, Gordon. "About the Big Phat Band: Rick Shaw." *www.bigphatband.com/rck-shaw* (accessed July 15, 2015).

Hevesi, Dennis. "Elaine Lorillard, 93, A Founder of the Newport Jazz Festival Is Dead." *http://www.nytimes.com/2007/11/28/arts/music/28lorillard.html?_r=1&* (accessed July, 6, 2015).

Hill, Constance Valis. "Cobi Narita." *www.cobinarita.com/aboutcobi.html* (accessed June 8, 2014).

"History of Newport Cigarettes." *http://www.lemengb4.blog.com/Newport-cigarette-of-history*

Holden, Stephen. "Blossom Dearie." *http://www.nytimes.com/2009/02/09/arts/music/09dear.html?_r=0* (accessed June 10, 2015).

"International Women's Brass Conference, IWBC Pioneer: Nadine Jansen." *http://www.myiwbc.org/nadine-jansen* (accessed July 13, 2015).

Jack, Adrian. "Blossom Dearie." *http://www.theguardian.com/music/2009/feb/09/obituary-blossom-dearie* (accessed June 11, 2015).

Joyner, David and John Murphy. "The History of Jazz at North Texas." *http://www.jazz.unt.edu/history* (accessed July 6, 2015).

Kohlhasse, Bill. "Patterson Blows the Horn of Women Musicians." *articles.latimes.com>collections* (accessed March 20, 2015).

"Leonard Feather Collection." *www.ijc.uidaho.edu/feather_leonard/author.html* (accessed August 9, 2015).

Lester, Charles Richard. "Don Leslie, The Story of the Leslie Speaker." *www.1377731.com>hammond>leslie* (accessed June 2, 2015).

"Mary Osborne." *http://classicjazzguitar.com/artist/astists_page.jsp?artist=21* (accessed February 8, 2013).

"Melba Liston: Bones of an Arranger." *http://www.npr.org/2008/07/09/92349036/melba-liston-bones-of-an-arranger* (accessed July 17, 2014).

"Melba Liston-Randy Weston, African Rhythms." *www.randyweston.infor/randy-weston-sidemen-pages/melba=liston.html* (accessed January 9, 2014).

Minderovic, Christine. "Contemporary Black Biography." *www.encyclopedia.com/topic/Diane_Reeves.aspx* (accessed March 27, 2014).

"Nancy Wilson." *http://musicians.allaboutjazz.com/nancywilson* (accessed June 24, 2015).

"A Portrait of Five Women: Ruth Kissane." *http://animatorionguildblog.blogspot.com/2006/09/portrait-of-five-women* (accessed August 1, 2013).

Ratliff, Ben. "Stacy Rowles, Jazz Musician, Is Dead at 54." *http://www.nytimes.com/2009/11/07/arts/music/07rowles.htm* (accessed April 21, 2014).

Ratliff, Ben. "Tommy Flanagan, Elegant Jazz Pianist, Is Dead at 71." *http://www.nytimes.com/2001/11/29/arts/tommy-flanagan-elegant-jazz* (accessed July 2, 2015).

Smith, Arnold Jay. "OctoJAZZarian Profile: Barbara Carroll." *http://www.jazz.com/features-and-interviews/2009/2/15/the-octojazz* (accessed June 22, 2015).

Steinberg, Deborah. "Lady Got Chops." *http://www.womenarts.org/2012/05/24/lady-got-chops/* (accessed March 11, 2015).

"Teri Koide: Profile." *http://www.terikoide.com* (accessed July 15, 2015).

Thursby, Keith. "Stacy Rowles Dies at 54; Jazz Trumpet and Flugelhorn Player." *http://www.latimes.com/local/obituaries/as-me-stacy-rowles-2009n* (accessed April 21, 2014).

"Tommy Flanagan: Poet of Piano." *www.npr.prg/2008/07/16/92568276/tommy-flanagan-poet-of-piano* (accessed July 2, 2015).

Vosbein, Terry. "Artistry in Jazz Education: Jazz Camps." *http://www.vosbein.com/lagniappe/wprds/jazz_education_article/* (accessed July 6, 2015).

Wall, Seth Colter. "Jazz Is Dead (Commercially), Long Live Jazz Creatively." *www.newsweek.com/jazz-dead-commercially-long-live-jazz-creatively-756* (accessed June 10, 2013).

"Washington Women in Jazz Festival." *www.washingtonwomeninjazz.com* (accessed March 11, 2015).

"What's My Line Episode Guide." *www.tv.com/shows/what's-my-line* (retrieved March 13, 2015).

Wikipedia, "Equal Rights Amendment" (accessed May 30, 2014); "Hammond Organ" (accessed June 2, 2015); "History of Newport Cigarettes" (accessed June 29, 2015); "Jimmie Lunceford" (accessed July 6, 2015); "KOOL (cigarette)" (accessed June 29, 2015); "List of Hammond organ players" (accessed June 2, 2015); "Nancy Wilson" (accessed June 24, 2015); "Newport Jazz Festival" (accessed June 28, 2015); "Novachord" (accessed June 2, 2015); "Olivia Records" (accessed June 12, 2013); "Roberts Wesleyan College: Dina Alexander" (accessed July 15, 2015); "Stan Kenton Band Clinics" (accessed July 6, 2015); "Timeline of Jazz Education" (accessed July 3, 2015).

Wilson, John S. "Stan Kenton, Band Leader, Dies: Was Center of Jazz Controversies." *http://www.nytimes.com/learning/general/onthisday/bday/0219.html* (accessed July 6, 2015).

"Women and Jazz: International Sweethearts of Rhythm, You Tube." *www.youtube.com/watch?v=_Cjmg8Jepvw* (accessed July 15, 2013).

"Women's Jazz Festival at the Schomburg Center for Research in Black Culture." *http://www.nypl.org/.../women's-jazz-festival-catherine-russell* . . . (accessed March 11, 2015).

Index

B

C

E

H

I

J

O

P

S